FREEDOM OF EXPRESSION AND THE CRITICISM OF JUDGES

Freedom of Expression and the Criticism of Judges

A comparative study of European legal standards

Edited by

MICHAEL K. ADDO
School of Law, University of Exeter

Ashgate

DARTMOUTH

Aldershot • Burlington USA • Singapore • Sydney

© Michael K. Addo 2000

Published by
Dartmouth Publishing Company Limited
Ashgate Publishing Limited
Gower House
Croft Road
Aldershot
Hants GU11 3HR
England

Ashgate Publishing Company
131 Main Street
Burlington
Vermont 05401
USA

Ashgate website: http://www.ashgate.com

British Library Cataloguing in Publication Data
Freedom of expression and the criticism of judges : a
    comparative study of European legal standards
    1. Judges – Europe 2. Freedom of speech – Europe 3. Justice,
    Administration of – Europe
    I. Addo, Michael K.
    347.4'014

Library of Congress Cataloging-in-Publication Data
Freedom of expression and the criticism of judges : a comparative study of european
legal standards / edited by Michael K. Addo.
        p. cm.
    Includes index.
    ISBN 0-7546-2129-4 (hb)
    1. Judges–Europe–Public opinion. 2. Justice, Administration of—Europe—Public
opinion. 3. Freedom of speech—Europe. 4. Judicial power—Europe. I. Addo, Michael K.

KJC3716 .F74 2000
342.4'0853—dc21   00-030625

ISBN 0 7546 2129 4

Printed in Great Britain by
Antony Rowe Ltd, Chippenham, Wiltshire

Contents

Foreword

It was relatively easy for Lord Atkin to remark in 1936 that justice was not a cloistered virtue and must be prepared to suffer the respectful, even though outspoken, comments of ordinary men. It was, after all, in the same year that Lord Hewart CJ felt able unblushingly to tell a City audience that His Majesty's judges were satisfied with the almost universal admiration in which they were held. ('Almost' seems an excess of modesty in the circumstances.) Any criticism – and Hewart himself was a worthy candidate for a fair amount of it – tended to be muted and to circulate away from the front pages.

Everybody in the United Kingdom now accepts that judges, as Lord Widgery CJ told the Phillimore Committee on contempt of court, must have broad backs. The same is true, as this pioneering volume shows, throughout the countries which make up the Council of Europe. Olowofoyeku's *Suing Judges* has shown, in parallel, how in most of the common law world criticism of judges can extend to litigation against them.

In Britain today there is effectively no limit not only to the extent but to the degree of comment to which parts of the press are prepared to subject judges. Within the last few years, to take a single example, a conscientious and able High Court judge was described by a tabloid journalist – not some hack but a leading political commentator – as a weevil in the body politic because he had given a decision against the Home Secretary in relation to the conditions of imprisonment of IRA prisoners. It's difficult, by contrast, to remember when one last read an editorial commending a judge for taking an unpopular but principled decision. Ministers for their part have in the not too distant past been prepared to use the lobby system of unattributable briefings, dependant as it is on compliant journalists, to launch attacks on judges whose decisions they have found it easier to criticise than to appeal. This is a world which neither Hewart nor Widgery dreamed of.

With the coming into our municipal law of the European Convention on Human Rights even more regard than hitherto will have to be paid to the right of the media to report and comment as they think fit. There is no corresponding Convention right in the public to be told the truth. Readers, viewers and listeners will continue to get bite–sized pieces of information about judicial decisions of considerable sensitivity and complexity, produced sometimes by journalists who have worked hard to distil the essential point but as often by journalists who have not even bothered to grasp the issues. They will continue to be given a false picture of the incidence of violent crime and of how sentencing judges deal with it – a process which is not a matter of impression but of quantified proof[1], none of which shows any sign of modifying press behaviour.

Judges for their part have to rely on the quality of their decisions. In the years since Lord Mackay's sensible abrogation of the Kilmuir Rules which prevented judges from taking part in public discourse, judges have begun to speak much more freely in public about the business of adjudication and its social ramifications. But they do not as a rule discuss or defend their own decisions: for plain reasons these have to speak for themselves. This has two outcomes, one much less obvious than the other.

The obvious one is that attacks in the media tend to go unanswered. The less obvious one is that however resolutely they set their minds against it, judges may be affected in giving their decisions by concern at what the media reaction will be. Those whose response is that, for an unelected judiciary, this would be no bad thing should pause. Unelected judges who hear both sides in full and whose reasoning is public and open to appeal are one thing. Unelected editors and columnists with political and sometimes personal agendas of their own are another.

The jurisdiction to punish for contempt of court inexorably makes the bench judge in its own cause, and courts are for that reason among others chary of exercising it. Even so, it is a power which Article 10(2) of the Convention expressly preserves; and it remains to be seen how far section 12(4) of the Human Rights Act, seemingly prioritising the right of free expression over other rights, is itself Convention–compliant.

This brief introductory note is not, however, a call for a return to a culture of deference reinforced by the big stick of contempt. My own belief is that judges need more, not less, feedback on how well they are performing. What I think this book will encourage its readers to reflect usefully on is the difference between judge–bashing, an easy but foolish activity, and a public critique which values the integrity of adjudication and seeks to improve its quality. Those who neglect the difference create the risk that the rule of law will be the real casualty.

Stephen Sedley
Royal Courts of Justice
April 2000

---

1   M. Hough and J. Roberts, *Attitudes to Punishment: findings from the British Crime Survey* (Home Office Research Study #179, 1998. See also the *Crown Court Study*, #19, for the Royal Commission on Criminal Justice, 1993.

Acknowledgements

A book of this nature would be extremely difficult for one person to write. The success of this project must therefore be attributed to the truly collaborative effort of all the contributors who so generously gave of their time and expertise. In addition, a long list of non-contributors have assisted in different ways towards the preparation of the essays in this book. Special mention should be made of Natalia Schiffrin, Anne Bonnie, Carola Thielecke, David Pugsley and Dario Castioglione who so kindly undertook to review different essays in the book.

Gratitude is also due to John Irwin and his team at Ashgate for their support and professionalism.

Michael K. Addo
November 1999

Notes on Contributors

Michael K. Addo teaches constitutional law and human rights at the University of Exeter. He is the editor of *Human Rights Standards and the Responsibility of Transnational Corporations* (Kluwer, 1999).

Michael Bohlander is a judge (*Richter am Landgericht*) currently on leave from his judicial duties; he is the Senior Legal Officer of Trial Chamber II of the International Criminal Tribunal for the former Yugoslavia (ICTY). He holds a doctorate in law from the University of the Saarland and is an Honorary University Fellow at the School of Law of Exeter University. He has also been a Visiting Scholar at the Northwestern University School of Law in Chicago. He has published three books and over 50 articles, mostly in the fields of criminal and comparative law, including a book on duty solicitor schemes, *Verteidigernotdienst im strafprozessualen Ermittlungsverfahren* (Peter Lang Verlag, 1992) and another with Christian Latour, entitled *The German Judiciary in the Nineties* (Shaker Verlag, 1998).

Bill Bowring is Reader in Law at the University of Essex where he specializes in human rights in the former Soviet Union and Eastern Europe. He is Consultant on human rights and law reform in Russia to the Department for International Development's Know How Fund, and is a legal expert on a number of European Union and other projects. As Director of the University's Pan-European Institute, he coordinates interdisciplinary teaching, research and consultancy in relation to the European Union, Central and Eastern Europe, and the former Soviet Union.

Marianne Holdgaard is Associate Professor at the Department of Jurisprudence at the University of Aarhus, Denmark. She teaches human rights at the university where she previously graduated with a Master of Laws degree. She has been Guest Researcher at the Norwegian Institute of Human Rights and has published widely on the subject of freedom of expression and fair trial. She holds a PhD in Human Rights from the University of Aarhus.

Leny E. de Groot-van Leeuwen is Assistant Professor at the Law Faculty of the University of Nijmegen, the Netherlands. She holds an MA and PhD from Leiden University. She has written extensively on the Dutch judiciary and co-authored (with N. Doornbos) *Klachten op Orde* (Complaints about Lawyers) (Deventer, Kluwer, 1997).

Annamaria di Ioia is a researcher at the European Public Law Center in Athens. She also works with Article 18, a UK-based non-governmental organization and collaborates at the European Review of Public Law.

Ga'bor Halmai is Professor of Law and Director of the Hungarian Human Rights Information and Documentation Centre from where he continues to act as country reporter for the East European Case Reporter on Constitutional Law. From 1990 he was Chief Counsellor to the President of the Hungarian Constitutional Court. He has published books on *Freedom of Association* (1990), and *The Limits of Free Speech* (1994).

Jørgen Albaek Jensen is Associate Professor and Director of Studies at the University of Aarhus, Denmark, where he teaches constitutional and administrative law. He is the author of *Parlamentarismens statsretlige betydning* (The Constitutional Impact of Parliamentarism) (1997).

Agust Karlsson is a practising attorney in Reykjavik and a member of the Icelandic Bar Association. He has a special interest in human rights law and regularly conducts cases on human rights principles. He holds an LL.M in International Business Legal Studies from the University of Exeter, UK.

Mary Kotsonouris served as a judge of the Dublin Metropolitan District for nine years. She is the author of *Talking to Your Solicitor* and *Retreat from Revolution: The Dáil Courts 1920–1924* and is currently writing a book on the Judicial Winding-up Commission for the Irish Legal History Society.

Lefteris Ktistakis practices law at the Thebes Bar, specializes in business law and he holds degrees from the Universities of Thrace, East Anglia and Exeter.

Hélène Lambert teaches European and international law at the University of Exeter. She is the author of *Seeking Asylum: Comparative Law and Practice in Selected European Countries* (Martinus Nijhoff/Kluwer Law International, 1995). She has also written numerous articles on refugee law.

Rasmus M. Madsen is Master of Laws from the University of Aarhus, Denmark, and holds an LLM in European Legal Studies from the University of Exeter, UK. He is now employed at the Danish Ministry of Justice.

J. Michael Rainer is Jean Monet Professor of European Private Law at the University of Salzburg where he has been Professor of Law since 1995. He is an expert in comparative law and has published widely in various international journals. He has also held visiting appointments at other universities including the University of Trieste and Munich.

Thomas Tschaler is a qualified lawyer in Austria. Until June 1999 he worked as a teaching and research assistant to Professor J. Michael Rainer at the Department of Austrian and European Civil Law in the University of Salzburg. He gained an MA and a PhD from the University of Salzburg.

Dirk Voorhoof is Professor at the University of Ghent where he teaches and researches in media law and copyright law. He has published widely on media-related issues in English, French and Dutch, including *On Freedom of the Press, Broadcasting Law and the New Media* (Kluwer, 1987), *Access to Government Information* (Kluwer, 1991), *Freedom of Expression, Racism and Revisionism* (Ghent Academia Press, 1995) and *Critical Perspectives on the Scope and Interpretation of Article 10 of the ECHR* (Council of Europe Press, 1995).

PART I
GENERAL INTRODUCTION

1   Can the Independence of the Judiciary Withstand Criticism? An Introduction to the Criticism of Judges in Europe

Michael K. Addo

Introduction

As the key players of the judicial arm of government, judges' role in liberal democratic society is not in doubt. With primary responsibility to uphold the rule of law and to defend the constitution, the judiciary is a uniquely different organ of government whose effective functioning depends critically on its independence. In the allocation of constitutional tasks, the judicial arm of government, unlike its legislative or executive counterparts, is not expected to participate directly in the day-to-day political governance of the country. Theirs is the isolated task of adjudicating on disputes and often overseeing the compliance of the other two branches with the law and the constitution. In practice, judges have been perceived as specialist professionals whose authority must be secured at all costs against public interference. The isolated stage for the performance of judicial tasks is deliberately made unsuitable for public scrutiny and, consequently, judges are today the least understood of the three branches of government. Nevertheless, fundamentally, judges are also public officials, even if they are no more than a special category of bureaucrats who undertake their responsibilities on behalf of the people. They carry out tasks for which democratic doctrine requires that they be held to account.[1] Generally, it is true that judges cannot be held to account on exactly the same terms as politicians – that is, through periodic elections – without undermining their independence and authority.[2] Furthermore, the law invests judges with full authority to be masters within their court and, in addition, unquestionably imposes respect for judicial authority regardless of how well judges undertake their tasks. Because such respect for judicial authority is presumed to facilitate the independence with which judges are expected to undertake their duties, the very idea of challenging what judges do risks undermining their independence. This therefore makes the courtroom particularly unsuitable for any meaningful debate about the work of the judiciary. However, respect for judicial authority is neither an overriding principle of European liberal democracy for which all other principles (such as freedom of expression, accountability and transparency) must always be relinquished, nor is it incompatible with other principles. Ideally, all liberal democratic principles must complement each other in the long run and thus effective constitutional democracy would endorse forms of accountability which do not undermine judicial independence.[3]

Open discussion, including the criticism of judges and their work which is mindful of its impact on the independence of the judiciary, may provide an acceptable forum for maintaining the accountability of the judicial branch of government.[4] The publicity generated by open discussion and the criticism of judges can contribute to a better understanding of the judiciary. Lord Macnaghten is said to have argued that 'Publicity is the very soul of justice. It is the keenest spur to exertion and the surest of all guards against improbity. It keeps the judge himself while trying on trial.'[5] In fact, the value of open discussion in democratic society is more than just the opportunity it provides for judicial accountability. As a component of freedom of expression it is a core value for liberal democratic society because it offers one of the few opportunities for the public to participate in the work of the judicial arm of government. As participation is an indispensable ideal in such a society, there is therefore merit in the proposition that it is improper to curb open debate, especially in matters which are of public interest.[6] It therefore follows that, in so far as the work of the judiciary in general, and of judges in particular, are in the public domain and so of public interest, the value of freedom of expression applies, in principle, with equal force to their work.

However, democratic entitlement to participate in public affairs is not absolute; its scope, in practice, is affected by other equally compelling liberal constitutional values such as the independence of the judiciary.[7] Liberal democratic discourse is full of these competing values which are reconciled through compromises defined by the circumstances of each case, and taking into account the necessary legal, political, cultural and historical factors.[8] Inevitably, the dynamic nature of constitutional democracy itself makes the management of competing values such as freedom of expression, the accountability of public officials and the independence of the judiciary difficult to prescribe. Conventional wisdom for the determination of priorities may change from place to place and from time to time. Indeed, it is quite possible that the choices which underlie today's conventional wisdom for determining compromises may themselves be overtaken by different circumstances. Consequently, the bias in favour of one constitutional value may often change in favour of another competing value as a result of reappraisal and re-evaluation as and when the doctrines are put into practice.

Within the contexts of a group of countries in, say, Europe, Asia or North America, minimum basic standards of compromise, which can be used as guidelines for the assessment of the acceptability of individual compromises, may be discerned. These guidelines are often the result of decades and, in some cases, centuries of trial and error in the effort to define the most appropriate compromise applicable to the group. Rather predictably, these guidelines for the management of conflicting liberal or constitutional values cover a wide spectrum in which some countries operate at the lowest level while others operate at the highest. The important question in these circumstances is often not whether there has been any doctrinal recommendation or practical implementation of guidelines for the management of conflicting values such as freedom of expression, the accountability of public officials and independence of the judiciary: all over the world, there is evidence of some kind of doctrinal explanation or practical treatment of freedom of expression as it affects the judiciary. The difficulty is rather one of defining and explaining the trend of change in the acceptable compromise used for the management of conflicting values. This difficulty exists in the context of modern Europe as it does in other contexts. This book contains a collection of essays written around the common theme of managing the conflicting claims to freedom of expression, the accountability of judges as public officials and the independence of the judiciary in a European context. The essays collectively explore the factors which affect the determination of the appropriate balance between these liberal democratic ideals.

For a variety of reasons, the assessment of the narrow European focus of subject is of considerable importance to any wider debate. First, since Europe, as the undisputed cradle of modern liberal democracy, moulded the doctrines and defined any compromises on the management of conflicting values, any new and emerging European directions in this field will be of interest to other democracies across the globe. However, European countries – as does the rest of the world – differ widely in law, culture and history; this affects the practical implementation of compromise and, often, different countries have been, and perhaps continue to be, guided by the different levels available across a wide spectrum. Some countries attach more importance to freedom of expression, others may emphasize the importance of judicial independence, but none will dispute the importance of the accountability of public officials. Some, especially the mature democracies, are likely to achieve accountability and transparency more easily than the recently emerging democracies. It is, however, arguable that developments such as the system for the protection of human rights in Europe,[9] the ending of the Cold War and the growing influence of non-European legal thought[10] may well foster the emergence of common European standards in this field. The importance of identifying any common European standards in the management of the conflict between freedom of expression and the independence of the judiciary is driven by the increasing integration among the countries of Europe. In the most successful integration processes under the Council of Europe and the European Union, where there is an underlying theme of harmonization of legal policy and practice, the management of conflicting democratic values is an invaluable undertaking.

The Focus of This Book

The main body of this book is set out in five broad parts containing essays which have been contributed mainly by natives of the countries concerned in the hope of ensuring that the most important perceptions have been appreciated. In the only instance where it has not been possible to secure the expertise of a native Russian, the essay has been written by an acknowledged 'foreign' expert on Russian affairs.

In this book the criticism of judges is considered significant because of its connection with their accountability. In this wider context, it must be acknowledged that there are other processes through which judicial accountability may be secured. There are, for example, informal processes in judges' daily contacts with the wider community by which some form of accountability may be secured. There are also formal processes of accountability through disciplinary procedures and the legal process. The criticism of judges, however, falls into the category best referred to as participatory accountability – in other words, processes by which public involvement in the work of judges may enhance judges' accountability. This approach to accountability involves the intriguing interaction of liberal values such as transparency, freedom of expression and judicial independence.

This introductory chapter attempts to highlight some of the broad issues raised when public freedom of expression is asserted by criticizing judges. In the European context, these, often conflicting, values are generally managed by means of the conventional compromise developed in favour of securing judicial independence at all costs. This compromise is defined in the law – by statutes, judicial practice and popular culture – and justified by the portrayal of the judge as a vulnerable and delicate public official in need of protection from public scrutiny, and it is the current validity of this conventional wisdom that is assessed throughout the essays in this collection. Although the book focuses on European practice, it also assesses the impact of external factors such as international human rights law and the domestic practice of non-European jurisdictions such as the United States. The broad highlights of this introductory chapter, which draws on conclusions reached in the contributed essays, include the following propositions:

- The process of reconciling conflicting liberal democratic values, such as freedom of expression and the independence of the judiciary, is itself a moving target. It continues to change with time and circumstances.
- Traditional conventional biases in favour of judicial independence are losing credibility because constitutional maturity has now secured judges' place in society. According special protection to judges is viewed as patronizing to a highly professional and well trained group of public officials.
- There is a global convergence of human rights policy and practice (at both the national and international levels) which follows the pioneering jurisprudence of the US Supreme Court and the European Court of Human Rights in prioritizing freedom of expression over the independence of the judiciary as an acceptable approach to judicial accountability.
- In most European jurisdictions the priority of freedom of expression would seem to be confirmed by the emerging trend to refrain from bringing prosecutions for criticizing judges. Statutes to protect judges from criticism are rapidly becoming *passé*.

The very nature of the subject precludes immutable answers on how best to reconcile freedom of expression, public accountability and judicial independence. Today's solutions may well be overtaken by tomorrow's events. The greatest value of this introduction lies in its emphasis on the dynamic nature of the subject as a confirmation of the changing practices identified in the rest of the book.

In Parts II to VI, the essays are gathered together on the basis of connecting strands in their legal character. For example, the essay on England and Wales, as well as the one on Ireland, are placed together because of their common law strand. Both countries have, in the past, relied heavily on the conventional wisdom that judges must be protected from public scrutiny at all costs. Both jurisdictions have fused the public and private lives of judges and it would therefore be uncharacteristic for judges to publicly pursue defamation proceedings for criticism of their private lives. However, there are differences in how and why the conventional wisdom for the management of conflicting values has evolved over time. Nowadays, neither jurisdiction subscribes to the rigid view that judges should be protected from public scrutiny. In England and Wales the revised approach to judicial independence is largely a consequence of constitutional maturity, whereas in Ireland the process is inextricably linked to its history. According to Judge Kotsonouris (Chapter 3) Irish judges were subjected to public criticism long before independence in 1922 because of their unavoidable involvement in the controversial political cases associated with the independence movement. In her words:

> ... it is not surprising, then, that contempt of court issues were particularly sensitive in Ireland, allied as they so often were to questions of territorial claims and the near irresistible temptation to ripe and righteous rhetoric.

It is important to note that both authors of the essays on Ireland and England and Wales agree that the acceptable standard for the management of the conflicting values associated with the criticism of judges is that defined by the European Court of Human Rights.

The influence of the standards set by the European Court of Human Rights is also evident in the essays from continental Europe which have been grouped together in Part III because they resolved the value conflicts through the ordinary law.[11] The contributors from Belgium, Denmark and Iceland specifically devote space to this subject, although the influence of the European Court of Human Rights is not discounted in the other contributions. In Germany, for example, Michael Bohlander (Chapter 4) concludes that the emerging bias in the jurisprudence of the *Bundesverfassungsgericht* in favour of freedom of expression is unlikely to be altered in cases involving the criticism of judges. An important fact which runs through the essays in this Part, and through other Parts is the paucity of litigation for the criticism of judges, more credibly explained by judges' ability to withstand the criticism. Michael Rainer and Thomas Tschler in Chapter 5 on Austria choose to focus on the narrow aspect of recusing a judge as part of the process of participatory accountability. This focus is based on the premise that 'All human beings are fallible in their actions, and so is the judge'. Apart from addressing the issue of when a judge may be called upon to recuse himself from a case, it also discusses the consequences of such a decision on judicial independence, and on judgments made before and after recusion. It provides a clear profile of diverse forms of accountability through the opportunity to recuse a judge.

Essays on countries such as the Netherlands, Italy and Greece also draw on the ordinary law but, in addition, they also demonstrate a distinguishing character of their own: the heavy influence of cultural and historical factors in the development of the law. In Chapter 10 de Groot-van Leeuwen emphasizes the importance of consensus culture in the management of social conflict in the Netherlands. Here, although public criticism of judges certainly occurs, it is often the exception rather than the rule; there is no polemical approach to the criticism of judges. When criticism does occur attention tends to focus more on the solutions rather than on the judges contesting, counter-arguing or belittling their adversaries.

A completely different sort of culture underlies the approach to value management in Italy where private institutions heavily influence the public domain. A strong and vociferous media has emerged to expose corruption and injustices in public life. In the 1960s the *Magistratura Democratic*, an association of critical judges, was prepared to object to convictions for what became known as 'opinion crimes' then listed in the criminal code. More recently, the concern has been about the role of judges in trials against corruption. Although prosecutions may still be brought for criticizing judges, primacy in practice has, according to di Ioia (Chapter 11) been accorded to freedom of expression. In Greece today, public policy continues to labour heavily under the influence of the country's unstable past. Here, evident preference in both doctrine and practice to uphold human rights has caused the notion of supremacy of judicial decisions to be abandoned. The criticism of judges and their decisions is no longer an offence in Greece.

Russia and Hungary clearly deserve to be placed together as both have recently emerged from the yoke of a completely different political ideology – communism. Since the end of the Cold War, these countries have joined with other Western liberal democracies under the umbrella of the Council of Europe and have, in the process, pledged to pursue liberal democratic ideals. Their approach to reconciling freedom of expression and judicial independence in this period of transition is of considerable academic and practical interest. Bill Bowring's chapter on Russia reviews the development of the place of the Russian judge from the period before the 1917 Revolution to today. Until recently, the conventional standard was one set by the Revolution: judges were not independent, they were members of the Party and, as such, not separated from the state apparatus. Criticism was therefore clearly out of place. The Yeltsin administration has sought, through the enactment of a new constitution and new laws, to implant a Western-style independent judiciary with security of tenure and salaries (albeit rather low ones). There are also laws to protect judges against unnecessary interference. At the same time other human rights, such as freedom of expression, take pride of place. The work of the independent media has led to lawsuits brought by some judges to defend their honour and reputations. Russia is still in transition in this context and will no doubt continue to be influenced by external standards.

There was no revolution to usher in the Hungarian transition from communism to liberal democracy. The majority of judges after the transition are the same as in the old system, and the new law to vet the background of public officials was applied only to judges of the Supreme Court and the

Constitutional Court. This may well be a significant factor in the development of rule of law in that country. The Constitutional Court has undertaken a pioneering role in assessing the relationship between conflicting liberal values. In 1992 the Court confirmed the privileged nature of freedom of expression among other human rights and, in 1994, held Article 232 of the Penal Code to be incompatible with Article 61 of the Constitution which guaranteed freedom of expression. The annulled provision in the Penal Code sought to create an offence of criticizing 'an official person', defined to include judges, members of parliament and so on. Unlike Russia, Hungary has been more successful in its effort to adopt credible practices in the management of liberal values during its transition. This may be attributed partly to the government's political commitment to achieve a successful political transition and also, according to Professor Halmai's analysis in Chapter 13, partly to the close attention paid by the Constitutional Court to the case law developed by the European Court of Human Rights.

Finally, Part VI contains two essays on the influence of the European Convention on Human Rights. These essays are particularly significant because most European countries are either party to this treaty or are aspiring to accede to it. Furthermore, the Convention is well placed to act as a good barometer of the appropriate level of reconciliation between freedom of expression and judicial independence, as both values are expressly recognized in the Convention. Above all else, the Convention provides decisions which are genuinely detached from the narrow biases of individual countries. The European Convention on Human Rights standards are more likely than any other in Europe today to define common European standards on the subject.

Democratic Society

Today's European democratic society is totally different from that of three centuries ago. Whereas, during the period when democratic political ideology was being formulated the influence of philosophers' abstract and ideal thought bore heavily upon public policy, we now have the benefit of centuries of practice in the definition of the limits of the democratic ideals. The primary task in most European societies in the golden age of democratic ideals was to devise and invent the ideology. Processes were rudimentary, primitive and partisan. Policy was inevitably uncertain and influenced largely by abstract thought. Today, with the emphasis on constitutionalism, things are different: there is sufficient doctrinal basis upon which to build a firm practical constitutional democracy. Of course, modern constitutional democracy continues to be guided by the doctrinal ideals of democracy but, in practice, democracy is heavily dependent on the practicability of the relevant aspects of such ideals.[12] The importance of practicability is driven by the acknowledgement of the ad hoc and partisan nature of philosophical writings about the principles of democracy. For example, a consequence of the Western liberal democratic attachment to constitutionalism is the central importance of ideas such as the separation of powers, rule of law, transparency and accountability. In practice, the inherent conflicts between these doctrines require practical compromises based on historical events, cultural circumstances and other similar dynamic factors. European liberal democracy may therefore take different emphasis from society to society. Despite the differences which may exist between jurisdictions in the practice of democracy, each society always aims to derive maximum possible benefit for the community. This utilitarian approach to community provides one of the credible strings for drawing together otherwise disparate principles of liberal democratic doctrine. Utilitarianism alone is, however, insufficient because the so-called maximum possible benefit has to be workable in and acceptable to the individual community.

Accountability through Criticism

For the criticism of public officials to contribute towards their accountability, it has to be purposive, either in terms of contributing factual knowledge to the society's understanding of itself or contributing to a better appreciation of the work of the particular public official or institution which is being criticized. In relation to the criticism of judges it is important to ensure that the call to account does not overwhelm judicial independence or the process of accountability itself will be unworkable and therefore unacceptable. Whether criticism is purposive and how to assess criticism as purposive will depend on the facts and circumstances of each event. For example, the nature of the criticism itself may have to be assessed. Criticism can take various forms, the effect of each of which may vary depending on the content, the target, the forum and the possible consequences of the criticism itself. It may take the form of an expression of disagreement, or of disapproval or even as an indication of disrepect for the target of the criticism. It could also take the form of open and public criticism or closed and limited criticism. There could be a further difference in terms of criticism as part of performing a professional responsibility or as a private undertaking.

The requirements for justification, for instance, may be higher in an open and public criticism than in the case of private and limited criticism. Often, judges criticize their colleagues on a professional level, particularly via the avenue of dissenting opinions.[13] These are legitimate not only for the purpose of contributing to a better understanding of the issues in the relevant cases but also because such criticisms are normally undertaken within the strictly defined rules of the judicial profession. The room for abuse in such a context is rather minimal.[14] In a similar vein, the value of criticism as a direct part of the democratic process, such as in the proceedings in a parliament or similar legislative body, may be more easily appreciated as criticism which is spontaneous, unstructured and subject to little or no professional discipline.

On the other hand, that judges should be free from all forms of unnecessary interference in the performance of their judicial duties not only makes common sense but is central to the survival of the rule of law. It is the independence of the judiciary that enables the judicial arm to act as a check on the other two arms of government in fulfilment of judges' duty to uphold the law. There are also other dimensions of the rule of law which are relevant, such as the human right of all to a fair trial by an independent and impartial tribunal.[15] The confidence in any legal system can often be assessed by the independence enjoyed by its judiciary. In most liberal democratic societies judges have security of tenure and their salaries are similarly safeguarded. In addition there are widespread legal mechanisms to protect them from interference and a general recommendation to avoid courting the sort of controversy which will undermine their independence. There can be no objection to the unqualified legal protection of the formal aspects of judges' independence relating to their tenure, salaries and so on and, in any case, the criticism of these formal aspects of judicial independence is unlikely to undermine judges' authority. However, protection against public criticism may not be extended so justifiably to the substantive aspects of judges' duties. From the little that is known about the judiciary, internal quality control alone of judges' work has so far proved insufficient. Internal quality control is often slow and, in any case, structural errors may best be reviewed externally. In the context of today's advanced appreciation of the limits of liberal democracy most people will find the restriction of judicial accountability to internal procedures alone totally unacceptable. The relative mystery in which judges' work is shrouded is clearly at odds with the practical aspects of such a democratic system.

Nevertheless, the conventional wisdom which accords judges the status of vulnerable and untouchable professionals continues to exercise some influence on policy-making in some European countries in so far as the criticism of judges is concerned. Not only have countries such as Austria and Belgium enacted laws, much like most other European countries, against the criticism of judges, but these laws are often rigorously enforced. This rigid application of the law in favour of judicial independence is often justified by the argument that, by the nature of their tasks, judges cannot respond to criticism and, for that reason, need to be protected. Other similar arguments postulate the need to compel respect for, and confidence in, the administration of justice as a basis for the bias in favour of the independence of the judiciary.

In most European legal systems today, the image of the reserved and restrained judge is a myth in at least two respects. In jurisdictions where restraint is practised,[16] the absence of judicial response to criticism is not driven by any justifiable principle of liberal democracy nor compelled by law but is, rather, a self-imposed convention: it is judicial reticence. Unfortunately, this self-imposed restraint is not always for objective purposes but may be imposed to strengthen the enigma surrounding the judiciary and to forestall any criticism of any shortcomings in its work. According to a former UK Lord Chancellor, Lord Kilmuir, 'so long as a judge keeps silent his reputation for wisdom and impartiality remains unassailable'.[17] A similar view was expressed by the Australian Judge Sir Anthony Mason when he wrote:

> Putting to one side the exceptional case which requires an exceptional response, I favour a cautious approach. Judicial reticence has much to commend it. It preserves the neutrality of the judge; it shields him or her from controversy. And it deters the more loquacious members of the judiciary from exposing their colleagues to controversy.[18]

None of the virtues advanced for judicial silence to criticism, such as the reputation of wisdom, impartiality or shield from controversy, is corroborated in practice. The quality of judges' wisdom or their impartiality can be appreciated, or indeed advanced, through the discussion and scrutiny of their work.

In a related way judicial restraint in responding to criticism lacks an objective character because, in practice, the reticence is selective. Judges in most continental European countries have recourse to the ordinary law of tort to pursue claims of unjustifiable criticism. Similarly, in most European countries, court press officers whose primary responsibility is to help explain the complexities of judgments to the public can often use this process to defend judges and their conclusions. It is therefore neither true nor justifiable to argue, as one judge has done, that:

> No effective answer can be given by the courts themselves. The courts cannot be advocates to plead their own cause in justification of their judgements. If they were, they would be induced to temper their judgements to protect their own interests. Impartiality would be gone, traded for protection from attacks.[19]

It would indeed be a sad day for liberal constitutionalism if judges ever felt the need to 'temper their judgements to protect their own interest'. Surely, this would amount to failure in the delivery of their public service and rather unlikely to happen often enough to cause concern. In reality, when confronted with unfair interference in the performance of their tasks, some judges are guided by the advice attributed to Lord Chamberlain Polonius to his son that:

> Every judge worthy of the name recognises that he must take each man's censure; he knows full well that as a Judge, he is born to censure as the sparks fly upwards; but neither in preparing a judgement nor in retrospect may it weigh with him that the harvest he gleans is praise or blame, approval or scorn. He will reply to neither; he will defend himself not at all.[20]

For other judges, such as Judge H. Sarokin of the US Court of Appeals for the Third Circuit, the option of resignation is preferable to having to temper his judgments on account of public criticism. In his letter of resignation to the President of the United States Judge Sarokin pointed out that 'the first moment I considered whether or how an opinion I was preparing would be used was the moment I decided that I could no longer serve as a federal judge'.[21]

In common law jurisdictions where the restraint on judicial response or litigation is firmest, there is a growing trend of change. By convention, attorney-generals or other ministers of justice have acted as guardians of judges' reputations and have frequently defended them against criticism.[22] Similarly, chief justices have undertaken to speak for, and on behalf of, judges. That judges are able to defend themselves against criticism has ceased to be a novelty in Europe. Indeed the United Nations Basic Principles on the Independence of the Judiciary (1985) expressly recognize judges' freedom of expression.

Fortunately, the understanding of the principles of constitutional democracy are now far advanced and more understood. Policy is driven far less by the philosophical writings from the twilight age of democracy and more by the evidence drawn from what, in the European context, is now centuries of experience of liberal democratic practice. Most European countries have grown to appreciate the strengths of constitutional democracy and are gradually abandoning policies which are clearly unjustified by the practical aspects of democracy. It is now fairly common to argue that judges are human and, as such, tend to interact widely with the rest of society. Being human, judges are not infallible and there are numerous opportunities for errors to occur in their work.[23] Similarly, as in other areas of human endeavour, judges, too, can be incompetent, ill-tempered and prejudiced[24] – unfortunate human traits which can lead to error, and any errors (especially errors of public officials) should be open to discussion. Similarly, it is absurd to conceive of judges as representing objective thinkers since they are just as much the product of their partisan upbringing in any society as anyone else. Their views should therefore be open to challenge in the appropriate circumstances. In practice, although judges cannot be said to be at the forefront of the public domain (compared with, say, politicians), their work is neither isolated nor free from interference.[25] In a democratic society it is right for no public institution to be exempt from public scrutiny, and public comment on the work of judiciary serves as a perfect point of interface between the judges and changing society.

This will serve to enhance the democratic requirement that public institutions and public officials, such as judges, should be accountable and transparent. It is also commonplace to hear judges themselves confirm that they and their institutions are not as vulnerable as previously portrayed in legal doctrine.[28] In most European countries judges would not be entirely unhappy to be judged by the quality of their performance as public officials rather than be protected by special laws.

There are other compelling reasons for subjecting the work of the judicial arm of government to open discussion, including criticism. Judicial decision-making can often amount to nothing less than law-making. This may be due partly to the inevitable nature of having to interpret broadly drafted legislation[27] or having to clarify uncertainties in the law. According to the Canadian Judge Beverley McLachlin:

> The Lawmaking role of the judge in commonwealth countries has dramatically expanded. Judicial lawmaking is no longer always confined to small, incremental changes. Increasingly, it is invading the domain of social policy, formerly the exclusive right of Parliament and the legislature.[28]

She attributes this expanding role, first, to the trend towards constitutionalizing rights, which increasingly implicates the courts in a broader range of social issues, and, second, to the perceived inability or unwillingness of legislative bodies to deal with pressing social issues.[29] In any case, judges do not always defer to the legislature in politically sensitive or legally uncertain cases. It would not be unusual for legislation to be struck down as unconstitutional even though it arises from a political manifesto commitment. Such judicial activism can often generate widespread debate, some of it critical of judges. It is right that the opportunity to contribute to debate on important issues of interest to the community as a whole is not stifled.

The slow abandonment of conventional approaches to making judges accountable through the reconciliation of freedom of expression and the independence of the judiciary has emerged not only as a consequence of empirical observation but because of developments such as the global convergence in the scope of human rights law. The pioneering jurisprudence of the US Supreme Court in asserting the higher value of freedom of speech under the First Amendment of the US Constitution[30] has been, and continues to be, emulated, albeit to different and often lesser degrees by other national and international jurisdictions. Canada has followed the United States expressly in this regard. Other jurisdictions, especially in Europe, have followed the American presentation in their failure to bring prosecutions for the criticism of judges.

Similarly, international human rights law has endorsed the American approach and, in addition, has infused considerable objectivity into the determination of the right balance between competing democratic values. The emergence of internationl human rights treaties as a direct reaction to the widespread abuse of power by public bodies and officials which led to the Second World War have provided human rights with moral and legal force to aid the definition of modern principles of liberal democracy. The supervisory institutions under these treaties, such as the European Court of Human Rights, have made the choices between the competing claims much clearer. These treaties, whose primary objectives are the advancement of European democracy through the protection of human rights, have reasoned that freedom of expression is fundamental to the survival of democracy in Europe and must therefore be limited in exceptional circumstances only. In this framework of thought special place is given to the press as conveyors of information which the public are entitled to receive and as watchdogs against abuse by public bodies and officials. The bias between the competing claims has therefore now clearly shifted in favour of freedom of expression.

This shift in the balance in favour of freedom of expression is justified for a number of reasons. The judicial domain, very much like other branches of government, can benefit from a healthy exchange and interaction of opinions. The administration of justice is better served by well informed participants than by ignorance, and freedom of expression can contribute to a full and rigorous assessment of information in the judicial context. Similarly, in modern European society, all individuals, but especially legal journalists, lawyers and other officials of the legal establishment, contribute to the architecture of judicial policy through the expression of their opinions. Freedom of expression in this context can also prove to be an instrument of individual and professional self-fulfilment. This is considered crucial in any society which is dependent on the participation of the people in public affairs.

The balance in favour of freedom of expression is, however, not absolute, and policy and practice at both national and international levels have to be backed by reasoned argument. In reality, whether criticism of a particular judge or group of judges is justified continues to be dependent on such factors as the nature and form of the criticism.

Criticism as Disagreement

In all European countries, criticism which takes the form of expression of disagreement with an opinion or a particular course of action is tolerated. This is healthy in any democratic society for, after all, it is out of disagreement that a consensus is likely to emerge. Disagreeing with a public body or official is equally legitimate, and perhaps more so, because it is likely to achieve another purpose of the democratic process in calling on such an institution or official to be accountable. Disagreements are, however, only useful in a democratic society if they take place in an environment in which all concerned may be able to participate. If one or more of the interested parties are constrained for any reason, then criticism expressed as a form of disagreement is unlikely to achieve any useful purpose. Nevertheless, lack of immediate and direct purpose is no justification for the law to intervene in order to outlaw criticism. However, if, in addition to not serving any direct democratic purpose, it also positively undermines the democratic process then perhaps the intervention of the law may be necessary to safeguard the established democratic principles of that society. The criticism of government policy or of a politician is likely to elicit a response and, in most cases, such a response may be a part of a wider public debate on the issue under discussion. Because they are directly elected and representative of the people, if politicians refuse to respond, they will be considered to be failing in the performance of their public duties.

This standard of assessment may not hold for judges. Criticism of judges by way of disagreeing with them may either be in relation to their personal views or to their functional opinions delivered through their judgments. Most incidents of criticism relate to the latter form although there are a few instances where a judge's personal life may be the subject of criticism.[31] However, even then, the personal disagreement is generally inextricably linked to the official aspects of his or her role as a judicial public officer. In most modern democratic societies judges have imposed on themselves a duty of extreme discretion in matters relating to judgments which they have delivered. Conventional wisdom suggests that judges must not join or engage in public discussions about their official duties. This practice is not only justified by common sense but is said to be useful in upholding the independence of the judiciary and the credibility of the judicial process. As already indicated, this convention is today honoured in its breach rather than in its observance. One may, it would seem, freely disagree with the official decisions of a court and judges may respond to the disagreement without undermining the ideals of democratic society. This is true as long as the subjects are not *sub judice* and the criticism is not gratuitous and abusive. Criticism of judges in cases which are *sub judice* is likely to undermine the independence of the judiciary, while abusive criticism not only clouds the focus of argument but could undermine the credibility of the judicial process.

Of course, in far more advanced democracies where the status of the judicial process is well established, criticism is unlikely to be seen as capable of derailing public confidence in the work of the courts. Criticism of judges by way of disagreement is tolerated to a larger extent than in less mature democracies. The approach to the criticism of judges in the United States best illustrates this development, and this is captured by the view of Frankfurter J in the landmark *Communications Inc.* v. *Virginia*[32] case in which he pointed out that judges are not anointed priests entitled to special protection from the clamour of democratic society. The law gives judges and the institutional reputation of the courts 'no greater immunity from criticism than other persons or institutions'.[33] Canada has also moved closer to this higher level of maturity using its Charter of Rights and Freedoms.[34] Other countries may well be mature enough to tolerate criticism of judges but may have failed to formally take steps to incorporate this into policy and practice. The important fact may well be that European democracies might be unable to avoid the influence of the developments in comparable democracies such as the United States and Canada.

Criticism as Disapproval

Democracy entitles everyone to express disapproval as to how public office is conducted. This is inherent in the democratic principle of government for the people. Indeed, the whole process of periodic elections provides a forum for the electorate to criticize the government by expressing their disapproval if and when necessary. This form of disapproval is rather general and not targeted at an individual. In the case of specifically targeted criticism an important factor will be the contribution of the form of expression to the democratic process. This will depend on the subject matter of the disapproval, the context of the expression of disapproval and, perhaps more importantly, whether there have been other established avenues for expressing disapproval.

In relation to the work of judges, disapproval is best expressed as part of one's case and argument in court before the judge. If the disapproval relates to the case, and perhaps to the judgment, then an appeal may be the established course rather than a press conference. Professionals who are not party to the case, such as journalists in pursuit of the legitimate democratic aim of informing the public or academic writers in their reviews of judgments for teaching purposes or lawyers and legal representatives of litigants, may well be seen as an exception to the rule against disapproval to judicial opinion. The nature and aim of their tasks makes it possible for their professional disapproval to be seen as contributing towards enhancing democratic ideals, rather than undermining them.

Abusive Criticism

There is no simple way of identifying criticism which is abusive. The choice of language may provide no more than a guide. In other words, strong language alone may not be enough in determining whether a particular criticism is abusive. The language may be unimportant if the criticism represents a sufficiently legitimate concern either as an expression of disagreement or a disapproval of the acts of a public authority or person. Depending on the context, the form and the circumstances, it is not inconceivable for legitimate criticism to contain strong language. In certain cases, it may be the most appropriate. Any criticism must, however, satisfy the need to make a contribution to, or enhance, the democratic process. Unrestrained language, even as part of a structured democratic process, in a parliament or in a court of law tends to have the effect of clouding its central message.

The unhelpfulness of strong language is far more evident in relation to the criticism of judges, especially in the performance of their official functions. In the performance of their official responsibilities, judges are invariably confronted with competing claims which they are expected to settle without fear of intimidation. This is a central theme in the doctrine of an independent judiciary. Strong and abusive language could undermine this and thus lead to injustice. It is thus imperative that judges receive all the necessary assistance from all parties in the execution of their functions. Individual judges may react differently to different incidents and therefore it may be most appropriate for each judge to assess the nature and effect of abusive language in his court.

The prohibition of abusive language in the criticism of judges is one area in which the laws in all European legal systems are agreed. The consensus is that abusive criticism fails the general test of calling on public officials, especially judges, to be accountable and be transparent. This is, however, an area of the law in which the European Court of Human Rights may well hold the key to the appropriate standard. In its decision on the scope of freedom of expression the Court has made it clear that:

> Subject to paragraph 2 of Article 10, it [freedom of expression] is applicable not only to 'information' or 'ideas' that are favourably received or regarded as inoffensive or as a matter of indifference, but also to those that offend, shock or disturb the State or any sector of the population. Such are the demands of that pluralism, tolerance and broadmindedness without which there is no 'democratic society'.[35]

This opinion, no doubt, will tolerate exceptions depending on the circumstances of each case,[36] but it provides an excellent pointer to the direction in which European democracy is developing. It is in any case clear from the practice across European jurisdictions that the criticism of judges and their work, as such, is not prohibited and, as one English judge put it:

> The path of criticism is a public way: the wrong headed are permitted to err therein: provided that members of the public abstain from imputing improper motives to those taking part in the administration of justice, and are genuinely exercising a right of criticism, and are not acting in malice or attempting to impair the

administration of justice, they are immune. Justice is not a cloistered virtue: she must be allowed to suffer the scrutiny and respectful, even though outspoken, comments of ordinary men.[37]

Legitimate criticism must, however, be distinguished from 'personal, scurrilous abuse of a judge'.[38] In an attitude not entirely dissimilar to that adopted by the European Court of Human Rights in the *Prager and Oberschlick* case, the practice in most domestic courts is to accept temperate, reasoned and fair criticism.[39] Thus, according to Lord Justice Salmon in *R.* v. *Metropolitan Police Commissioner, ex parte Blackburn (No. 2)*, 'it follows that no criticism, however rigorous, can amount to contempt of court, provided it keeps within the limits of reasonable courtesy and good faith'.[40] In the *Prager and Oberschlick* case, for instance, the domestic Austrian courts and the European Court were persuaded by the immoderate nature of the language used. It was also felt that such language was unnecessary and rather disproportionate in view of the fact that there was no overwhelming evidence from the newspaper article that obvious injustices had occurred as a consequence of the judge's behaviour. In these circumstances, the criticisms seemed more like gratuitous value judgements than fair comments.

The Limits of Criticism of Judges

Only a few and extreme judges at worst, or (dare one assert) no judges, will argue that judges are not subject to democratic account. The controversy revolves around the manner in which they are called to account. Similarly, it is unlikely that anyone will argue that criticism is not an acceptable means for calling judges to account. After all, nowadays there is more than sufficient practical evidence to suggest that judges are not beyond criticism and that such criticism provides them with an opportunity to account for the services they undertake on behalf of the public. However, for criticism to be acceptable it has to serve some democratic value and, in that regard, may need to be constructive rather than destructive in effect. Whether criticism is constructive may often depend on its context, language and so on. These limits to criticism of judges are acceptable, *inter alia*, because they are applicable to all public officials with equal force.

The crucial question here is whether there can be further and special limitations on the criticism of judges. The Chief Justice of Australia, Sir Gerard Brennan, for example, argues strongly for special and broader limits on the criticism of judges. In his view, judges may be called to account for the exercise of their powers only through 'the reasons for judgement'[41] – a generic term that he uses to cover both judicial reasoning in cases as well as the judicial process. In the framework of his analysis, as judicial duties are owed to law, judges should be subject to no criticism other than for the performance of their official tasks.

That the criticism of judges must address the reasons offered for their decision, as well as the manner in which they conduct their judicial tasks, is in little doubt. There is, however, no basis for the suggestion that criticism can be limited to these alone. For one thing, as Sir Gerard Brennan rightly points out, reasons for judgments can often be technical and difficult to read and understand.[42] To restrict judicial criticism to the technical aspects of their tasks will amount to no more than exempting judges from a credible regime of democratic accountability.

Similarly, the distinction between the public and private sides of judges' lives may often prove difficult to draw precisely. It is possible that a judge's private outlook on life or his or her particular upbringing may underlie the reason for the judgment. Could one possibly separate his or her 'reasons for judgment' from his private life in such a case? Sir Gerard's insistence on such a separation underlies his objection to the criticism of judgments as such (perhaps because the public find them unacceptable) rather than the reasons for the judgment.[43] Such a restriction cannot be justified precisely because of some of the reasons he cites for public preference for wider criticism. The public's unfamiliarity with the technical aspects of the law directs their appreciation of judicial tasks. To insist on Chief Justice Brennan's recommendation for judicial criticism will limit the ability to participate in the work of the judiciary to the legally well informed alone. This cannot be acceptable in a democratic society, particularly because the logical extension of this argument would restrict judicial accountability to the hierarchical self-regulation within the legal system. Indeed, this extremely restricted view of judicial accountability has been canvassed within some judicial circles. Sir Robin Coke, for instance, has argued that:

> Judicial accountability has to be mainly a matter of self-policing; otherwise the very purpose of entrusting some decisions to the judges is jeopardised. The old question, *quis custodiet ipsos custodes*, remains unanswered as ever.[44]

Such a restricted view of accountability cannot be justified in practice because it presupposes that the hierarchical review extinguishes all possible human fallibilities and also that judges should be excluded from further scrutiny by external bodies. In fact, if the judiciary were to be accepted as a cloistered and insulated institution, judges would be unlikely to undertake their tasks effectively as public servants whose decisions are presented in a sufficiently transparent manner to enable the public – the ultimate constituency of the justice system – to appreciate their nature and effect. It is not impossible to prepare a socially unpalatable judgment without incurring the critical condemnation of the public.[45]

The Impartiality of the Tribunal

The current practice in Europe in relation to the accountability and transparency of judges is nothing like the doctrinal ideal. With regard to the criticism of judges, it exposes serious shortcomings. In all the countries about which the subject has been reviewed for this book, the investigation of the legitimacy of any criticism of judges is often undertaken by other judges. In protecting the judicial branch of government through the ordinary law or through the special mechanisms such as the law of contempt or other similar offences, courts are called upon to perform an impossible task of upholding the democratic process by, ironically, being judges in their own cause. The simple and perhaps unequivocal fact that, by the nature of their professional training, judges should be able to isolate most, if not all, of their prejudices does not necessarily address any external perceptions that the case is somehow tainted with some degree of partiality. Should the domestic and international courts, in recognition of this fact, be prepared to lend greater weight to the freedom of expression principle in this context? Although this issue is often not argued before the domestic and international courts, it deserves to be highlighted because of its potential impact on the quality of the judgments in such cases.

There is a specific requirement, for example, in Article 6(1) of the European Convention on Human Rights for an impartial tribunal in the determination of civil rights or criminal charge. This has been interpreted to involve two tests – a subjective test and an objective test. According to the Court of Human Rights:

> The existence of impartiality for the purpose of Article 6(1) must be determined according to a subjective test, that is on the bias of the personal conviction of a particular judge in a given case, and also according to an objective test, that is ascertaining whether the judge offered guarantees sufficient to exclude any legitimate doubt in this respect.[46]

It is the latter objective impartiality which is usually based on appearances,[47] rather than the subjective impartiality which is of interest in the present context. This notion of objective impartiality is the equivalent of the requirement, in most European law jurisdictions, that justice must not only be done but must also be seen to be done. The factor of inevitability – that is, only judges alone have the responsibility for adjudicating disputes of this nature – makes it impossible to remove the cases involving criticism of their colleagues from their jurisdiction. The issue of potential bias in the objective sense will have to remain unresolved, although it is possible to assess this same matter from a completely different angle – that of competing rights claims involving the freedom of expression on the one hand and maintaining confidence in the judicial process on the other.[48] On this score, the conflict has rightly been resolved in favour of judicial autonomy and independence. It is an unavoidable part of this process that judges alone have the moral and legal authority to investigate how best to strike a balance between these competing claims, even in cases involving the criticism of their colleagues.

Can the Independence of the Judiciary Withstand Criticism?

The question of whether the liberal constitutional requirement to maintain judicial independence can withstand criticism is easily answered: criticism is a central and unavoidable part of the democratic ideal. In relation to the judiciary, criticism is one clear way of ensuring public participation in, and scrutiny of, judges' work. Representative democracy, as practised across European jurisdictions, is based on the accountability of all public officials. This can often be achieved by a variety of ways including the open and often public criticism of these officials. There is no requirement, however, that the practice of criticism should be standardized across legal jurisdictions based on liberal democracy. The difference between the common law and the civil law countries, between the social cultures in European countries as well as the differences in the opportunity for litigation relating to the criticism of public officials, are all bound to affect the practice of the subject across Europe. Even within a particular legal system there are no standardized answers to questions relating to the criticism of public officials.

There is evidence that judges are seen as a special category of public official with special responsibilities which require that they are accorded protection if necessary. Every European legal system has had occasion to extend some form of protection to judges in their law. There are, however, considerable differences in the practice of the law in the various countries of Europe. In some European countries there has been the opportunity to contest the scope of the law in this field, while others remain unclear about the subject. Similarly, the differences in the levels of different countries' political maturity have had an impact on the importance of the special protection for judges. Countries such as the United Kingdom, the Netherlands, Germany and Greece may have progressed to the point where the law of special protection for judges will be applied in extreme cases only, and there is evidence that such an extreme event has not occurred in recent times. On the other hand, countries like Belgium, Austria and Denmark have had occasion in the last few years to punish for the criticism of judges.[49] The growing confidence of European judges in the performance of their duties may be a slow process in the emerging democracies of Eastern and Central Europe. These countries have yet to find their own balance in the struggle between the competing values of freedom of expression and the independence of the judiciary. However, they are fortunate enough to draw on the lessons and experiences of the mature constitutional democracies of Europe, in much the same way as they have all benefited from developments in the United States. Nonetheless, the role of the European Court of Human Rights in this matter must not be forgotten. Through its supervisory responsibilities under the European Convention on Human Rights, the Court has defined standards in this subject which, while they remain guidelines for application in domestic systems, deserve to be taken seriously for a number of reasons, including the benefit that the Court alone is able to draw from the contribution of judges from across the wide legal spectrum of Europe. At the moment, through its case law, the Court sees little impropriety in the criticism of judges in Europe[50] although in its earlier case law[51] it was a little less disposed to the idea. In the balancing of the competing interests between the freedom of expression and the independence of the judiciary it may well be that the Court of Human Rights leans heavily towards the former, confirming that modern democracy can withstand criticism.

Human rights law ultimately holds the balance in this matter. It is a regime which joins the competing claims posed by freedom of expression and judicial independence. As human rights are part of the democratic agenda, standards set under that regime are likely to be holistic and effective in practice. The consensus so far in human rights law is a convergence in favour of freedom of expression with due respect for judicial independence.

Notes

1   See, generally, A. Gutman and D. Thompson, *Democracy and Disagreement* (Cambridge, MA/London: Belknap, 1996) esp. ch. 4. See also, C. Pateman, *Participation and Democratic Theory* (Cambridge: Cambridge University Press, 1970) and D. Thompson, *Political Ethics and Public Office* (Cambridge, MA/London: Harvard University Press, 1987). On the subject of judicial accountability, see, Martin Friedland, *A Place Apart: Judicial Independence and Accountability* (Ottawa: Canadian Judicial Council, 1995). See also Antonio Lamer, 'The Rule of Law and Judicial Independence: Protecting Core Values in Times of Change', *University of New Brunswick Law Journal*, 45 (1996), p. 67.

2   On the impact of the process of election of judges on their independence in parts of the United States, see R.B. Bright, 'Political Attacks on the Judiciary: Can Justice be Done Amid Efforts to Intimidate and Remove Judges from Office for Unpopular Decisions?', *New York University Law Review*, 72 (1997), p. 308. See also Roger Handberg, 'Judicial Accountability and Independence: Balancing Incompatibles', *University of Miami Law Review*, 49 (1994), p. 127.

3 See, Antonio Lamer, 'The Rule of Law and Judicial Independence', *op. cit.*, p. 12.
4 Other ways of maintaining judicial accountability include informal censure by colleagues and the Bar, formal complaints systems, as well as public elections and procedures for the impeachment and removal of judges. For a review of the scope of these alternative methods see Vince Morabito, 'Are Australian Judges Accountable?', *Canberra Law Review*, 1 (1994), p. 73.
5 Quoted by Lord Shaw in *Scott* v. *Scott* [1913] AC 417 at 477.
6 For the place of these values in a democratic society see Barend van Niekerk, *The Cloistered Virtue. Freedom of Expression and the Administration of Justice in the Western World*, (London: Praeger, 1987), ch. 1. On the general principles relating to the value of freedom of expression see Eric Barendt, *Freedom of Speech* (Oxford: Clarendon Press, 1987) and Frederick Schauer, *Free Speech: A Philosophical Enquiry* (Cambridge: Cambridge University Press, 1982).
7 Robert B. Stevens, *The Independence of the Judiciary* (Oxford: Clarendon Press, 1993). See also Shimon Shetreet, *Judges on Trial* (Amsterdam/New York: North Holland, 1976). See also, Ken Marks, 'Judicial Independence', *Australian Law Journal*, 68 (1994), p. 173 and Pat Polden, 'Judicial Independence and Executive Responsibilities', *Anglo-American Law Review*, (1996), p. 1 (Pt. I) and p. 133 (Pt. II).
8 Human rights law provides the most excellent example of competing liberal democratic values. Apart from the competition which exists between rights such as freedom of expression, on the one hand, and privacy on the other, or freedom of expression and independence of the judiciary there are also other inherent conflicts between individual entitlements and wider community benefits. Most human rights instruments represent these conflicts by stating general entitlements to be followed by a list of permissible limitations.
9 Note, especially, the impact of the work of the Council of Europe human rights instruments on developments in the domestic jurisdiction of member states.
10 The most influential foreign legal jurisdictions have been those of the United States, Canada, Australia and India.
11 These include Germany, Austria, Belgium, France, Denmark and Iceland.
12 The democratic ideal behind the independence of the judiciary, for example, led the United Nations to appoint a Special Rapporteur on the Independence of Judges and Lawyers in 1994. The work of the Special Rapporteur is however undertaken in cooperation with relevant government and non-governmental institutions. His work involves consultations, discussions, visits to sites and promotional activities. See in this regard, UN Doc. E/CN.41997/32. Similarly, the International Commission of Jurists' Centre for the Independence of Judges and Lawyers is driven by the aim to preserve the democratic ideals behind independent judicial officers. In practice, their reports are based on investigated incidents on which governments are given ample opportunity to comment. See, for example, Mona Rishmawi and Lynn Hastings, *Attacks on Justice* (Geneva: ICJ, 1997).
13 This opportunity does not exist in countries where the practice of the courts is to write a single judgment to represent the decision of all judges.
14 See, for example, Lord Denning in *Candler* v. *Crane Christmas & Co.* [1951] 2 KB 164 and the Court of Appeal decision in *Goose* v. *Wilson Sandford & Co. and Another* (1998 unreported) in which the United Kingdom's Court of Appeal severely criticized the manner in which a High Court judge, Harman J performed his judicial duties.
15 This entitlement is embodied in most constitutions and in international human rights instruments such as Article 14 of the UN Covenant on Civil and Political Rights (1966) and Article 6 of the European Convention on Human Rights (1950).

16   Restraint on judicial response to criticism is not an issue in the United States where judges exercise their freedom of speech fully. They have been known to write books, grant press interviews and write letters to newspapers. Apparently, there is a similarly growing trend in Canada. On this subject see Stephen Bindman, 'Judicial Independence and Accountability', *University of New Brunswick Law Journal*, **45** (1996), p. 59.

17   A.W. Bradley, 'Judges and the Media – The Kilmuir Rules', *Public Law* (1988), p. 383, at p. 385.

18   Quoted in Sir Gerard Brennan, 'The State of the Judicature', *Australian Law Journal*, **72** (1998), p. 33 at p. 36.

19   Ibid., p. 41.

20   Quoted in Sir Frank Kitto, 'Why Write Judgements?', *Australian Law Journal*, **66** (1992), p. 787 at p. 790. See also Patricia Cumming, 'Governing Judicial Conduct', *University of New Brunswick Law Journal*, **45** (1996), p. 21 at p. 24 where she rightly argues that 'It is the duty of the judge both to recognise the mood of society and to resist being swept along by the flood of public outcry'.

21   Letter reproduced in Pollak, 'Criticising Judges', *Judicature*, **79** (1996), p. 229 and p. 302.

22   See Sir Gerard Brennan, 'The State of the Judicature', *op. cit.*, p. 33. See, however, the exception taken by the Australian Attorney-General who refused to see it as his task to defend judges against criticism arguing that 'In essence, I do not believe that the public perceives that the Attorney-General acts independently of political imperatives. An Attorney-General cannot be a wholly independent counsel who rushes to the defence of the judiciary when under attack. This is particularly the case when the attack comes from the executive arm of government.' Quoted in ibid., p. 41.

23   See examples given by Kitto, 'Why Write Judgements?', *op. cit.*

24   See Michael Kirby, 'Attacks on Judges – A Universal Phenomenon', *Australian Law Journal*, **72** (1998), p. 599 at p. 604.

25   Robert B. Stevens, 'The Independence of the Judiciary: The view from the Lord Chancellor's Department', *Oxford Journal of Legal Studies*, **8** (1988), p. 222. See also Pat Polden, 'Judicial Independence', *op. cit.*, p. 1 (Pt. I) and p. 133 (Pt. II).

26   See Cory JA in the Canadian case of *R.* v. *Kopyto*, 47 DLR (4th) 213 (1987) esp. at pp. 255–56. Lord Justice Salmon said in *R.* v. *Metropolitian Police Commissioner, ex parte Blackburn (No. 2)* [1968] 2 All ER 319 at p. 320 that 'The authority and reputation of our courts are not so frail that their judgements need to be shielded from criticism'.

27   A number of landmark cases from the US Supreme Court arose in this manner. See, for example, *Brown* v. *The Board of Education*, 347 US 483 (1954) where the Court struck down segregation, which neither Congress nor state legislatures were prepared to do. See also the abortion cases such as *Roe* v. *Wade*, 410 US 113 (1972) and *Planned Parenthood of South-Eastern Pennsylvania Act* v. *Casey* (1992). In Australia, see the cases relating to Native peoples' Land Rights such as *Mabo* v. *Queensland* (1992) 175 CLR and *Wik Peoples* v. *Queensland* (1996) 187 CLR 1.

28   See Beverley McLachlin, 'The Role of Judges in Modern Commonwealth Society', *Law Quarterly Review*, **110** (1994), p. 260 at p. 263. See also, Ken Marks, 'Judicial Independence', *op. cit.*, p. 182. For a contrary opinion see, Lord Devlin, 'Judges as Lawmakers', *Modern Law Review*, **39** (1976), p. 1.

29   Beverley McLachlin, 'The Role of Judges', *op. cit.*

30   See note 33 below.

31   A good illustration may be found in the criticism of Judge J of the Vienna Court of Criminal Appeals for, *inter alia*, laying a criminal complaint against a prostitute who took his money but refused to perform sexual services with him because he was too drunk: see *Prager and Oberschlick* v. *Austria*, Eur. Ct. HR, Series A No. 313 ; 21 (1991) EHRR, p. 1. In a similar

vein, the recent criticisms of the UK Lord Chancellor for his imprudent use of public
resources for decorating his official residence contained personal elements.

32 435 US 829, 838–839 (1978).
33 *Bridges* v. *California*, 314 US 252, 292 (1941). In that case, the consensus of the Supreme
Court was that:

> The assumption that respect for the judiciary can be won by shielding judges from
> published criticism wrongly appraises the character of American public opinion. For it
> is prized American privilege to speak one's mind, although not always with perfect
> good taste, on all public institutions. And an enforced silence, however limited, solely
> in the name of preserving the dignity of the bench, will probably engender resentment,
> suspicion and contempt much more than it would enhance respect (ibid., p. 270).

For further discussion of the subject in the United States, see *Pennekamp* v. *State of Florida*,
66 S.Ct. 1029 (1946); *Garrison* v. *State of Louisiana*, 379 US 64 (1964). See, further,
E. Barendt, *Freedom of Speech*, (Oxford: Clarendon Press, 1989); Monroe Freedman,
'The Threat to Judicial Independence by Criticism of Judges – A Proposed Solution to the
Real Problem', *Hofstra Law Review*, **25** (1997), p. 729; and Ronald Bacigal, 'The Theory
and Practice of Defending Judges Against Unjust Criticism' (1990), *Connecticut Law
Review*, p. 99.

34 See, for example, *R.* v. *Kopyto* 47 DLR (4th) 213 (1987).
35 *Handyside* v. *United Kingdom*, Eur. Ct. HR, Series A.24 (1976); 1 EHRR, p. 737; para.
49; see also *Sunday Times* v. *United Kingdom No. 2*, Eur. Ct. HR, Series A.217 (1992); 14
(1992) EHRR, p. 229; para. 50.
36 See, for example, *Prager and Oberschlick* v. *Austria*, Eur. Ct. HR, Series A.313 (1995);
21 (1996) EHRR, p. 1.
37 Per Lord Atkin in *Ambard* v. *Attorney-General of Trinidad and Tobago* [1936] AC 322,
335.
38 Per Lord Russell of Killowen CJ in *R.* v. *Gray* [1900] 2 QB 36, 40 in dealing with a
newspaper article which described a judge as an 'impudent little man in horse hair, a
microcosm of conceit and empty headedness'.
39 See *R.* v. *Western Printing and Publishing Limited* (1954), III CCC 122 – Newfoundland
Supreme Court, referred to in Borie and Lowe, *The Law of Contempt, op. cit.*, pp. 163–64;
R. v. *Wiseman* [1969] NZLR 55; *R.* v. *Gray, op. cit.* at p. 40 where Lord Russell pointed
out that 'judges and courts are alike open to criticism if reasonable argument or expostulation
is offered against any judicial act as contrary to law or the public good, no court could or
would treat that as contempt of court'. See also, *R.* v. *Fletcher, ex parte Kisch*, (1935) 52
CLR 248 and *Attorney-General* v. *Butler* [1953] NZLR 944.
40 [1968] 2 QB 150, 155.
41 Brennan, 'The State of the Judicature', *op. cit.*, p. 39.
42 Ibid., p. 39. A similar view has been expressed by Stephen Bindman, 'Judicial Independence
and Accountability', *University of New Brunswick Law Journal*, **45** (1996), p. 59, at p. 62.
43 Brennan, 'The State of the Judicature', *op. cit.*, pp. 40–41.
44 Sir Robin Coke, 'Empowerment and Accountability: A Quest for Administrative Justice',
Commonwealth Law Bulletin, **18** (1992), p. 1326 at p. 1331. Sir Robin's view has received
support from Justice Tompkins from New Zealand who, while conceding the judicial
decisions may be subject to academic, media and public criticism, nevertheless insists
that judges are accountable firstly because their courts sit in public and 'The second form
of accountability is, of course, obvious. Practically every decision a judge makes is subject
to appeal except the decisions of the ultimate Court of Appeal': see D.L. Tompkins, 'The
Independence of the Judiciary', *New Zealand Law Journal*, (1994), p. 285 at p. 289.

45   Sir Frank Kitto (a former justice of the High Court of Australia) provides excellent advice about how to write a good judgment in 'Why Write Judgements', *op. cit.*

46   *Hauschildt* v. *Denmark*, Eur. Ct. HR, Series A.154 (1989) para. 46; 12 (1990) EHRR, p. 266, para. 46.

47   *Sramek* v. *Austria*, Eur. Ct. HR, Series A.84 (1984) para. 42; 7 (1985) EHRR, p. 351, para. 42.

48   A similar sentiment was expressed by Mr Justice Black in the majority opinion in *Bridges* v. *California* 314 US 252, 260 where he indicated that 'free speech and fair trials are two of the most cherished policies of our civilisation, and it would be trying to choose between them'.

49   The authors of the Danish report however feel that the *Barfod* case was untypical and unlikely to be repeated.

50   See *De Haes and Gijsels* v. *Belgium* 25 (1997) EHRR 1 and also *Schopfer* v. *Switzerland* Judgement of the Eur. Ct HR, 20 May 1998.

51   See *Barfod* v. *Denmark*, Eur. Ct. HR, Series A.149 (1989); 13 (1991) EHRR, p. 493 and *Prager and Oberschlick* v. *Austria*, Eur. Ct. HR, Series A.313 (1995); 21 (1996) EHRR, p. 1.

PART II
THE COMMON LAW

2 Scandalizing the Court in England and Wales

Michael K. Addo

Introduction

The independence of the judiciary is central to the constitutional ideals on which the government of the United Kingdom[1] is based. As in most modern liberal democracies, judges' independence in England and Wales is maintained through a number of constitutional arrangements including security of tenure, guaranteed salaries, and defined procedures for their appointment, promotion and dismissal.[2] In addition, it is unconstitutional for anyone or any body to interfere, either directly or indirectly, in the work of judges – the administration of justice. Consequently, in England and Wales, as in most common law jurisdictions, the offence of contempt of court[3] exists to punish interferences with the due course of justice. The emphasis of this offence is on the facilitation of good administration of justice rather than the protection of the personal dignity of judges, save when the administration of justice and judges' personal dignity are inextricably linked. In England and Wales, judges may be subjected to criticism so long as this does not undermine public confidence in the rule of law and the administration of justice. The branch of contempt of court known as scandalizing the court[4] is the closest that the law may come to recognizing the relationship between judges' personal dignity and the administration of justice.

Attempting to draw distinct lines between the personal dignity of judges and their public roles can be a complicated exercise fraught with risks and so, in practice, the attitude of members of the legal profession and the general public, over the years, has been to desist from criticizing judges. According to David Pannick:

Laymen treat judges as a priestly caste to whom they are reluctant to apply the standards of criticism imposed on other public servants. Lawyers tend to be

31

conservative in their attitudes in this as in other respects. The iron of the doctrine of precedent has entered into their souls. If they do have suggestions for reform of the judiciary, or comments to make on judicial performance, they whisper them to each other over lunch in the Middle Temple or in professional journals remote from the public gaze. Such heresies are expressed cautiously, in deferential language . . .[5]

While the offence of contempt of court, especially the aspect known as scandalizing the court, continues to be a part of the common law in England and Wales, even though it does not impose a total prohibition on criticizing judges its nebulous scope will continue to act as a restraint on professional and public criticism of judges. This chapter will review the scope and relevance of the offence of scandalizing the court in England and Wales.

Respect for the Administration of Justice

In seeking to punish 'any act done or writing published calculated to bring a court or a judge of the court into contempt or to lower his authority, [as] a contempt of court'[6] the offence of scandalizing the court is a legal tool for insisting on, and maintaining respect for, the administration of justice. The offence is justified on account of the need 'to maintain the respect and dignity of the court and its officers, whose task it is to uphold and enforce the law, because without such respect, public faith in the administration of justice would be undermined and the law itself would fall into disrepute'.[7] Public confidence in the fair and effective administration of justice must be maintained through the regulation and, if necessary, the punishment of scurrilous and abusive criticism of the process and its officials. On the other hand, the administration of justice cannot be isolated from the normal requirements of democratic society. The judicial process is considered to be a sufficiently important public responsibility for any society on whose behalf it is undertaken to claim legitimate interests of participation and accountability. It is equally true that, despite its importance, the administration of justice is neither an objective nor a verifiable science. The quality of the process depends, *inter alia*, on opportunistic and subjective factors such as the available evidence, the arguments of counsel and the sagacity of the judges before whom each case is argued. In principle, therefore, the prohibition of strong public comment or criticism on the administration of justice in general, and on the inevitable errors or disagreements associated with the process in particular, will undermine the ideals of democratic society. Lord Atkin was right when he observed in *Ambard* v. *Attorney General of Trinidad and Tobago*[8] that:

The path of criticism is a public way: the wrong headed are permitted to err therein: provided that members of the public abstain from imputing improper motives to those taking part in the administration of justice, and are genuinely exercising a right of criticism, and are not acting in malice or attempting to impair the administration of justice, they are immune. Justice is not a cloistered virtue. She must be allowed to suffer the scrutiny and respectful, even though outspoken comments of ordinary men.[9]

This opinion has been endorsed by other judges, most notably by Lord Denning in *R. v. Commissioner of Police, ex parte Blackburn (No. 2)*[10] where he, too, conceded that:

It is the right of every man, in Parliament or out of it, in the press or over the broadcast, to make fair comment, even outspoken comment, on matters of public interest. Those who comment can deal faithfully with all that is done in a court of justice. They can say we are mistaken, and our decisions erroneous, whether they are subject to appeal or not.[11]

By its nature, therefore, the offence of scandalizing a court – which can take any manner of forms, including written or spoken words and deeds whether in or out of court – requires the establishment of a compromise between competing ideals, although the courts tend to insist on its use only in extreme cases of abuse.[12] Similarly, depending on the circumstances, the offence may be committed without reference to a specific litigation. The scurrilous abuse of a judge which falls foul of this offence involves words or deeds which are gratuitous in nature, serving no particularly useful purpose to the administration of justice and often set out in abusive and disdainful language.[13] Allegations of incompetence, unfairness and impartiality against a judge are taken to be potentially scurrilous unless they are based on proven fact and presented in measured language.[14] According to an Australian judge (and possibly summarizing the position in England and Wales):

I am not prepared to accede to the proposition that an imputation of want of impartiality to a judge is necessarily a contempt of court. On the contrary, I think that, if any judge of this court or of any other court were to make a public utterance of such a character as to be likely to impair the confidence of the public, or of suitors or any class of suitors in the impartiality of the court in any matter likely to be before it, any public comment of such utterance, if it were fair comment, would, so far from being a contempt of court, be for the public benefit.[15]

Criticizing judges for not being impartial is a sensitive subject, primarily because of the close relationship between allegations of bias on the one hand and the standing and public confidence in the administration of justice on the other.

It is reassuring, however, that the standard of proof normally required for the proof of this offence is high. In the majority of cases the law has insisted on the need to prove that the risk of undermining public confidence in the administration of justice arising from the criticism of a judge or judges is a real one.[16] In the Canadian case of *R.* v. *Kopyto*[17] the standard was said to be one requiring the demonstration of 'extreme imminence of those evil consequences, so that the apprehended danger to the administration of justice was shown to be real, substantial and immediate'[18] or that the criticism must be 'found to result in a clear, significant and imminent or present danger to the fair and effective administration of justice'.[19] In the event of any doubt, the consensus of opinion is to give the benefit of the doubt to the accused.[20]

In truth, judges in England and Wales have never been fully secured against all forms of criticism.[21] However, the legal rules for the determination of the extent to which judges are secured against criticism and of what kind of criticism have never been clear except for the broad and general rule relating to criticism which undermines confidence in the administration of justice. In practice, how any particular criticism of a judge or judges affects the administration of justice is, like most of the common law, made on an ad hoc and pragmatic basis, often on account of a mixture of various factors including the subject of the criticism, the social and professional reaction, if any, to the criticism, the standing of the author,[22] the range of the criticism and the forum through which it is disseminated.

Equally important is the standing of the judge who is the subject of the criticism and the language used in the process. In general, even harsh but constructive criticism of a judge or judges, in terms of its positive contribution to the administration of justice, and which in its context is considered to be delivered in measured language, will always be tolerated. Similarly, there cannot be a public redress through the offence of scandalizing a court for the criticism of a judge in his private capacity and which is clearly separable from his role in the administration of justice. Decisions as to whether any words or deeds amount to scandalizing the court will have to be taken within the context of established social mores including the restraint expected of judges in the pursuit of private litigation[23] or whether the subject and language of criticism are of the standard which the community has grown to tolerate. Decisions in this field must also take into account constitutional and political conventions such as the supremacy of parliament, the relationship between parliament and the judiciary (including the often crucial fact that some members of the judiciary are also members of the legislature – the House of Lords) and also the important principles of precedent and natural justice. Above all else, it has to be borne in mind that the remedy for scandalizing the court is a public remedy, and any decision in that field may have to be reserved for the extreme instances of abuse bearing in mind that there may be alternative and sometimes suitable private law remedies[24] or indeed, as a sign of a mature democracy, turning a blind eye to some forms of criticism. There is nothing particularly unusual about the complexities and uncertainties about the unpredictable nature of the offence of scandalizing the court in a common law jurisdiction: the decision-making processes are not entirely dissimilar in other common offences such as assault, nuisance or manslaughter.

Over the years, judges have been the subject of strong criticism in both their public and private roles by individuals and groups such as other judges, members of the media, the press and other pressure groups (non-governmental organizations) or sometimes by members of parliament, all of whom claim to make such criticism in the performance of their professional responsibilities. Judges have also been known to be criticized by private individuals and groups, especially litigants who are dissatisfied or who disagree with decisions rendered by judges. Every criticism has to be assessed fully and on its own to determine whether it undermines the administration of justice and, if so, what reaction should follow.

Professional and Lay Criticism

One normally accepts criticism by professionals during the performance of their duties to be detached and as objective as possible. In this regard, professional comments tend to be well argued, balanced and, as far as possible, presented in measured language. As independent personnel their focus should be on the subject matter of public concern rather than the person of judge. They are not entitled to the degree of offence which the potential or direct victim of the judge's act which they seek to criticize is, and hence should be able to moderate their language. In any case, they may pursue any grievance with a judge or his judgment in a professional manner through the appropriate channels of their own or the judge's profession, or through the courts. Also, as public representatives, they should avoid causing offence to other members of the public who may not necessarily agree with the specific issue as one for which judges may be subjected to criticism. The requirement of measured language may have relative and different applications in relation to different professional personnel. For example, language used by members of the legal profession or journalists who are subject to the discipline of their own professional practice may be looked upon differently from language used by other groups such as pressure groups (NGOs) who may not necessarily be subject to the same level of internal discipline.

The style of writing judgments in common law jurisdictions allows all members of the bench to express their opinions in their own words. This is so even if they end up repeating all that may already have been said by their colleagues in the same case. This means that judges who feel strongly about the opinions of their colleagues in the case in which they are sitting can express their dissent or disagreement. In the process judges have an opportunity to criticize other judges. In his famous dissenting opinion to the majority decision in *Candler v. Crane, Christmas & Co.*[25] Lord Denning accused his colleagues of being 'timorous souls'[26] which, in ordinary parlance, will imply cowardice and lack of imagination. Indeed Asquith, LJ felt sufficiently wounded to respond: 'If this [his refusal in joining Denning in extending the law] relegates me to the company of "timorous souls", I must face that consequence with such fortitude as I can command.'[27] Of course, arising as part of judges' performance of their judicial function, this form of criticism is, in any case, immune from punishment for scandalizing the court. The point of referring to it is, however, to indicate the importance of internal professional discipline among judges to be courteous even in the process of criticizing each other. However, criticisms made in their private capacity, such as those in judges' memoirs kept during their professional careers which may not always be immune from prosecution, often contain some of the plainest criticisms. One judge is quoted as describing another judge as 'a domineering, vulgar, unjust and decrepit old man, who is a blot on the administration of justice.'[28] In practice, criticism of judges by other judges couched in immoderate language, whether in or out of court, is more likely to provoke protests and reprimand from the Lord Chancellor's office.

Lawyers have responsibilities as officers of the court as well as duties to their clients. In their role as officers of the court they have a direct interest in maintaining respect for the administration of justice while being, at the same time, expected to argue the cases of their clients as vigorously as possible, and this may often bring them close to making comments and suggestions about judges or the judicial process which could be considered scurrilous. A lawyer can, for instance, in the interest of his client clash openly in court with the judge without being offensive or abusive. According to one author, lawyers are free:

> . . . to combat and contest strongly any adverse views of the judge or judges expressed on the case during its argument, to object and protest against any course which the judge may take and which the advocate thinks irregular or detrimental to the interest of his client, and to caution juries against any interference by a judge with their functions, or with the advocate addressing them, or against any strong view adverse to his client expressed by the presiding judge upon the facts of a case before the verdict of the jury thereon.[29]

The freedom of lawyers to be firm in their dealings with judges in court must be balanced with the equally important requirement to be disciplined and courteous. Lawyers should desist from being rude and insolent, although judges will normally be expected to be tolerant of lawyers in the manner in which they conduct their cases. Out of court their comments, writings and deeds should also conform to the appropriate professional standard, although lawyers have been known to use intemperate language in reference to judges and the administration of justice.

The prosecution of lawyers for scurrilous abuse of judges and the judicial system seems particularly rare in England and Wales these days. The unsuccessful prosecution of Mr Quintin Hogg QC, MP for his article in *Punch* is the most significant event and probably the turning-point in English law relating to the criticism of judges.[30] At least two reasons may be advanced in support of the clear and unequivocal departure from punishment for an act which, in the past, would have been considered as an offence of scandalizing the court.

It is possible to argue that professional discipline has matured amongst members of the legal profession especially among members of the bar from whom most judges are drawn. Judges are appointed from among lawyers after long and established practice. After their appointment judges continue to share social circles, especially within the various inns of court, with practising lawyers. Judges in this culture have sufficient practical experience of the standards expected of lawyers and also of the sort of frustrations which are likely to drive lawyers into uncharacteristic outbursts. In addition, there are alternative opportunities for aggrieved lawyers and judges to complain about each other's misbehaviour. The Lord Chancellor's office will take any complaints about judges with all seriousness as will the disciplinary committees of the Bar or the Law Society which deal strongly with lawyers' unprofessional behaviour, such as the scurrilous abuse of judges.

It is also clear that the Quintin Hogg case was the first in which the subject was addressed within the framework of human rights law. This was one of the few early cases in which arguments relating to the balance between freedom of expression on the one hand and the independence of the judiciary on the other were prominently canvassed. In their effort to define the appropriate balance between the competing liberal ideals, the judges in the Court of Appeal settled, once and for all, the bias in favour of freedom of expression. According to Lord Denning MR:

We [judges] do not fear criticism, nor do we resent it. For there is something far more important at stake. It is no less than free speech itself. It is the right of every man, in parliament or out of it, in the Press or over the broadcast, to make fair comment, even outspoken comment on matters of public interest. Those who comment can deal faithfully with all that is done in a court of justice. They can say that we are mistaken, and our decisions erroneous, whether they are subject to appeal or not. All we would ask is that those who criticise us will remember that, from the nature of the office, we cannot reply to their criticisms. We cannot enter into public controversy. Still less into political controversy. We must rely on our conduct to be its own vindication. Mr Quintin Hogg has criticised the court, but in so doing he is exercising his undoubted right.[31]

Lord Justice Salmon agreed fully with the balance struck by Lord Denning between freedom of expression and the independence of the judiciary. In his opinion:

The authority and reputation of our courts are not so frail that their judgements need to be shielded from criticism. Their judgements, which can, I think, safely be left to the care of themselves, are often of considerable public importance. It is the inalienable right of every one to comment fairly on any matter of public importance. This right is one of the pillars of individual liberty – freedom of speech, which our courts have always unfailingly upheld. It follows that no criticism of a judgement, however vigorous, can amount to contempt of court, providing it keeps within the limits of reasonable courtesy and good faith.[32]

Pressure groups with specialist focus on the administration of justice have also occasionally expressed strong views about the work of judges. There have, for instance, been recurrent outcries – often in immoderate language – about some judges' attitude and comments during trials, most commonly in relation to judges' comments about women during rape trials. Sharp criticisms about the insufficiency or inappropriateness of sentences, or indeed about the quality of trials as a whole, are not uncommon.[33] The recent miscarriages of justice involving the trials for terrorist activities in Birmingham (the so-called 'Birmingham Six')[34] and for the bombing of public houses in Guildford (the so-called 'Guildford Four')[35] have been the subject of continual criticism of the judges involved and of the judicial process as a whole. However, none of these criticisms has been prosecuted for being scurrilous. In fact, the contribution of these pressure groups in the review of the convictions has been acknowledged in decisions to quash the original judgments.

Judges have also been subjected to criticism during parliamentary debates. By convention, members of parliament are advised to desist from criticizing judges or their work except as part of a motion calling for their dismissal. This convention has, however, been honoured more in its breach than its observance.[36]

Rethinking the Offence

In English law, as in other jurisdictions such as Canada, there is a growing feeling that the special and extra protection for the judiciary does not need strict enforcement in order to uphold liberal ideals.[37] The English judge, Lord Diplock, for instance, has followed the trend of judicial thought set in the Quintin Hogg case and indicated that contempt of court arising from scandalizing the judiciary has become 'virtually obsolescent in the United Kingdom',[38] and, previously, another English judge had expressed the view that the citation and prosecution for contempt arising from critical comments about the judiciary and their work was not at all worthwhile.[39] This changing trend was again highlighted when, in the heat of the infamous UK Spycatcher[40] litigation (1987), the *Daily Mirror* newspaper was not prosecuted for contempt when it published upside-down photographs of all the members of the House of Lords who had granted an injunction prohibiting publications about the book under the headline 'YOU FOOLS'.[41] In a similar tone, James Dalrymple of *The Sunday Times* has written of judges: 'A few are guilty of jarring errors. Others, through comments of appalling crassness, seem to affront human reason. From the heights of buffoonery to the dark depths of gross prejudice, they blurt out their inanities.'[42] 'Corruption' he continued, 'is almost unknown in the brotherhood of judges, but stupidity, crassness and blatant prejudice especially against women are not.'[43]

Similarly, in a scathing article in *The Times* entitled, "When Judges Talk Too Much',[44] a column writer, Fenton Bresler, outlined a series of inappropriate remarks and decisions made by judges during the 1980s and 1990s upon which he commented as follows:

> Why do intelligent and able men, whose training as lawyers is to make them choose their words with care, sometimes do the exact opposite? In his Hamlyn lecture, Judge Leon suggested that one reason was that a judge 'is treated in court with a subservience and flattery which probably obtains nowhere else, and he probably gets a similar kind of treatment outside court; it isn't good for some of us'. That was 23 years ago. Judges no longer receive such fawning attention. Yet the tendency to pontificate persists. Why? I think there are three possible explanations: First, courtroom sycophancy still persists. 'Judgeitis', a disease that can afflict perfectly decent, modest lawyers the moment that they don the judicial ermine, giving them an exaggerated notion of their own importance, still continues. . . . Second, some judges become cynics . . . Third, some judges tend to accept too quickly everything that is told by the defence counsel when defendant pleads guilty. . . . What it boils down to is that all judges should remember that they are human and that not always, even by counsel, is the truth told in court. Discretion is not only the better part of valour, it is the better part of judging.

None of the above criticisms was prosecuted for scandalizing the court. In fact, the number of prosecutions for this sort of contempt in the United Kingdom have diminished considerably[45] and there has not been a successful prosecution for over half a century.[46]

Until recently, it was the conventional wisdom in the United Kingdom that judges had to be insulated from the controversies, and thus criticisms, of the day. This was publicly expressed in terms of the fact that judges were vulnerable in so far as they were not able to respond to criticisms. In reality, the truth lay in what has come to be known as the 'Kilmuir Rules' by the terms of which no judge was allowed to speak publicly without the prior approval of the Lord Chancellor's office. When Lord Kilmuir wrote the so-called Kilmuir Rules, in a letter to the Director-General of the BBC in 1955, he was far more transparent about the reason for keeping judges protected. He reasoned that 'So long as a judge keeps silent his reputation for wisdom and impartiality remains unassailable; but every utterance which he makes in public, except in the actual performance of his judicial duties, must necessarily bring him within the focus of criticism'.[47] The former Lord Chancellor, Lord Mackay of Clashfern, came to the conclusion that the facade sought to be built around judges was incompatible with the independence of the judiciary and abolished the 'Kilmuir Rules' in the late 1980s.[48] Today, the atmosphere in which judges operate is far more liberal[49] and judges take, and when appropriate, reply to criticism fairly well. The process of liberalizing the environment in which UK judges operate has just begun and, while it will admittedly take some time to reach a stage where criticism is taken for granted, it is inevitable that the liberalizing process will be irreversible.

With the coming into force of the Human Rights Act (1998), the UK law relating to scandalizing the court or any other offences arising from the criticism of judges will be affected considerably by the jurisprudence of the ECHR. According to s.2(1) of the Act:

> A court or tribunal determining a question which has arisen in connection with a Convention right must take into account any –
> - (a) judgement, decision, declaration or advisory opinion of the European Court of Human Rights.
> - (b) opinion of the Commission given in a report adopted under Article 31 of the Convention,
> - (c) decision of the Commission in connection with Article 26 or 27(2) of the Convention, or
> - (d) decision of the Committee of Ministers taken under Article 46 of the Convention
>
> whenever made or given, so far as, in the opinion of the court or tribunal, it is relevant to the proceedings in which that question has arisen.

The Strasbourg court's thinking in cases such as *De Haes and Gijsels* v. *Belgium*[50] and *Prager and Oberschlich* v. *Austria*[51] will therefore be of direct interest to the development of the common law in this field. So also will the general case law relating to freedom of expression under the convention.[52]

The UK courts will be called upon to use Strasbourg principles such as proportionality, common European standards, and what is considered necessary in a democratic society rather than ad hoc common law rules. The legal certainty which this new dimension is likely to introduce to the common law will be welcome.

It is also worth noting the special place accorded to freedom of expression under the Human Rights Act. Quite apart from incorporating Article 10 of the European Convention on Human Rights and the accompanying case law, s.12 of the Act provides specifically that:

(1). This section applies if a court is considering whether to grant any relief which, if granted, might affect the exercise of the Convention right to freedom of expression.

(2). If the person against whom the application for relief is made ('the respondent') is neither present nor represented, no such relief is to be granted unless the court is satisfied –

(a) that the applicant has taken all practical steps to notify the respondent; or

(b) that there are compelling reasons why the respondent should not be notified.

(3). No such relief is to be granted as to restrain publication before trial unless the court is satisfied that the applicant is likely to establish that publication should not be allowed.

(4). The court must have particular regard to the Convention right to freedom of expression and, where the proceedings relate to material which the respondent claims, or which appears to the court, to be journalistic, literary or artistic material (or to conduct connected with such material), to –

(a) the extent to which –

(i) the material has, or is about to, become available to the public; or

(ii) it is, or would be, in the public interest for the material to be published;

(b) any privacy code.

Conclusion

UK judges are part of a mature system of liberal democracy which has had the advantage of its long history in defining the place and responsibilities of its public officials. Judges have had sufficient time to earn the respect and confidence of the public even if occasionally they make inevitable errors which become the subject of vehement criticism. They have matured with considerable tolerance, which enables them to withstand such criticism. Today, we can say of the UK judges that they are not fragile flowers that will wither in the heat of controversy and hence they do not fear criticism nor need they seek to sustain unnecessary barriers to complaints about their operations or decisions.[53] This stable position is aided by the settled tradition among the press and the public to refrain from making scurrilous criticism of judges.

There have been recent public comments about judges generally and about the refurbishment of the official residence of the Lord Chancellor Lord Irving of Liarg in particular,[54] which confirms this increasing tolerance. In reality, this progressive development has been predictable, for, after all, judges in England and Wales have not been totally protected from criticism as long as the subject of the criticism is legitimate and the language used is not abusive.

However, the offence of scandalizing the court remains part of the law in England and Wales, although it is now hardly ever used. It is interesting to note that the last time there was a successful prosecution for this offence was in 1931.[55] The only other time it was used – unsuccessfully, it should be emphasized – was in the case against Quintin Hogg in relation to his comments in *Punch*.[56] While not entirely *passé*, the use of the common law to punish the criticism of judges is rare, and perhaps unlikely to happen in England except for the most extreme and abusive of circumstances.[57] In any case, the law will now be driven largely by the thinking in Strasbourg rather than in London, and the relative bias in the Human Rights Act towards freedom of expression will fall squarely in place with current developments in England and Wales.

Notes

1   Although this chapter focuses on the criticism of judges in England and Wales, there will be occasional references to political and legal principles which are applicable throughout the United Kingdom of which England and Wales are a part.

2   See on this, Supreme Court Act 1981, Judicial Pensions Act 1959 and the Courts Act 1971.

3   For a review of the scope of the offence of contempt of court in England and Wales, see, N. Lowe and B. Suffrin, *The Law of Contempt* (London: Butterworths, 1996).

4   The phrase 'scandalizing the court' is said to have originated in Lord Hardwicke's judgment in *St James's Evening Post* (1742) 2 Atk 469 but its modern representation is attributed to Lord Russell of Killowen CJ in *R. v. Gray* [1900] 2 QB 36 at p.40 who defined the offence as 'Any act done or writing published calculated to bring a court or a judge of the court into contempt or to lower his authority, is a contempt of court'. See, on this matter, Sir John C. Fox, *The History of Contempt of Court: The Form of Trial and the Mode of Punishment* (London: Professional Books, 1972). See also Douglas Hay, 'Contempt by Scandalising the Court: A Political History of the First Hundred Years', *Osgoode Hall Law Journal*, 25 (1987), p. 431.

5   David Pannick, *Judges* (Oxford: Oxford University Press, 1987) p. 105.

6   A definition per Lord Russell CJ in *R v. Gray* [1900] 2 QB 36 at 40.

7   Lowe and Suffrin, *The Law of Contempt, op. cit.*, p. 335. Similar sentiments had been expressed by Wilmot J in *R. v. Almon* (1765) Wilm 243 when he argued that:

> The arraignment of the justice of the judges ... excites in the minds of his (the King's) people a general dissatisfaction with all judicial determinations, and indisposes their minds to obey them; and whenever men's allegiance to the law is so fundamentally

shaken, it is the most fatal and most dangerous obstruction of justice, and in my opinion, calls out for a more rapid and immediate redress than any other obstruction whatsoever . . . To be impartial and to be universally thought so are both absolutely necessary for . . . justice. (p. 255)

8 [1936] AC 322.
9 Ibid., p. 335.
10 [1968] 2 All ER 319; [1968] 2 QB 150. See also Lord Russell CJ in the earlier case of *R. v. Gray* [1900] 2 QB 36 at p. 40 where he pointed out that 'Judges and courts are alike open to criticism and if reasonable argument or expostulation is offered against any judicial act as contrary to the law or the public good, no court could or would treat that as contempt of court'.
11 Ibid., at p. 155. See also the views of Lord Salmon in that case.
12 See Lord Hailsham's comments in *Badry v. DPP of Mauritius* to the effect that 'nothing encourages courts or Attorneys Generals [sic] to prosecute cases of this kind in all but the most serious examples, or courts to take notice of any but the most intolerable instances' [1982] 3 All ER 973 at 979.
13 See *R. v. Gray, op. cit.*, at p. 40 where a newspaper article described a judge as an 'imprudent little man in horse-hair' and as a 'microcosm of conceit and empty headedness' in reaction to a court order banning the publication of court proceedings.
14 See, for example, the case of *R. v. Editor of New Statesman, ex parte DPP* (1928) 44 TLR 301, in which Mr Justice Avory (a catholic) was accused of impartiality in the case against Dr Marie Stopes a well known advocate of birth control.
15 (1911) 12 CLR 280 at 286.
16 See, for example, the new Zealand case of *Solicitor-General v. Radio Avon Limited* [1978] 1 NZLR 225.
17 (1988) 47 DLR (4th) 213.
18 Ibid., at p. 241 per Cory JA.
19 Ibid., at p. 265 per Goodman JA.
20 See *Re Ouelet* (1976) 67 DLR (3rd) 73 where the scope of the impact of the language used was said to be diminished by the accused's bad command of the English language.
21 For a review of some of the forms of criticism see Pannick, *Judges, op. cit.*, p. 120 *et seq.*
22 In the Canadian case of *Re Ouellet* (1976) 67 DLR (3rd) 73 (Quebec CA) a Canadian federal minister was found in contempt of court for suggesting, *inter alia*, that a judgment was 'unacceptable' and 'silly' and a 'disgrace'. He also said that he could not 'understand how a judge who is sane could give such a verdict'. Hugessen ACJ commented that 'the position of the contemnor can sometimes be a critical factor. A scandalous comment by a private citizen might well pass unnoticed . . . the same comment by a person occupying a position of power and authority may create a serious and dangerous impediment to the independence and integrity of the judicial process' (ibid., p. 93). See also the Australian case of *Gallagher v. Durack* (1983) 45 ALR 53 where the official involved was a leading official of a trade union.
23 See Lord Denning in *ex parte Blackburn, op. cit.*, p. 321: 'We do not fear criticism, nor do we resent it. . . . All we would ask is that those who criticise us will remember that, from the nature of our office, we cannot reply to their criticisms. We cannot enter into public controversy'. See also the similar view expressed by Lord Justice Edmund-Davies in the same case at p. 320.
24 See Lord Morris in *Mcleod v. St Aubyn* (1899) AC 549 at p. 561.
25 [1951] 2 KB 164.
26 Ibid., p. 178, where in reference to previous landmark decisions he said:

If you read the great cases of *Ashby* v. *White* (1703) 2 Ld. Raym 938, *Pasley* v. *Freeman* (1789) 3 TR S1 and *Donoghue* v. *Stephenson* [1932] AC 562, you will find that in each of them the judges were divided in opinion. On the one side were the timorous souls who were fearful of allowing a new cause of action. On the other side there were the bold spirits who were ready to allow it if justice so required. ... It needs only a little imagination to see how much the common law would have suffered if those decisions had gone the other way.

See also Denning MR in *Chief Constable of Kent* v. *V and Another* [1982] 1 KB 34 at 41. Lord Denning was by no means the only judge who used the polite language of judicial opinion to criticize his colleagues. See, for example, Lord Bridge in *Attorney General* v. *Guardian Newspapers Limited & Others and Related Appeals* [1987] 3 All ER 316, especially at 346–47 on his colleagues' attitude to freedom of speech in a democratic society. In *Goose* v. *Wilson Sandford & Co. and Another*, (1998 unreported) the Court of Appeal was less courteous in its criticism of Harman J for a long delay in delivering a judgment. According to the Court:

> As the judge himself was the first to recognise, a delay of this magnitude [20 months] was completely inexcusable. ... Both parties were entitled to expect to receive judgement before Christmas 1994 at the very least. The fact that they were obliged to wait another year and a quarter, even allowing for the judge's illness, is wholly unacceptable. (Paragraph 109 of the Court's transcripts)

27   *Candler, op. cit.*, p. 195.
28   See H. Montgomerry Hyde, 'Diary of a Judge', *The Sunday Times*, 7 April 1963.
29   J.F. Oswald, *Contempt of Court*, 3rd edn, ed. G.S. Robertson (London: W. Clowes and Sons, 1910), p. 56
30   *Ex parte Blackburn (No. 2), op. cit.*
31   Ibid., p. 320.
32   Ibid.
33   In 1994 when a judge told a persistent joyrider who admitted aggravated vehicle taking that he regretted he (the joyrider) had not been injured in the crash involving the car he had taken, he was criticized by the Royal Society for the Prevention of Accidents for making unhelpful remarks. Judge Starford Hill QC is reported to have said to the joyrider, 'You put other people in the gravest danger of losing their lives. To my mind it is a thousand pities you didn't damage yourself in the crash'. The Royal Society responded to this by saying that 'Accidents and young people are a particular problem. But we would not wish injury on people. The answer is better education. These sort of remarks are not helpful': See 'Judge Rues Joyrider's Escape from Crash', *The Times*, 21 June 1994.
34   The original convictions in these cases were finally quashed in *R.* v. *McIlkenny* [1992] 2 All ER 417.
35   For the quashing of the convictions in this case, see *R.* v. *Richardson* and *R.* v. *Conlon and Others*, *The Times*, 20 October 1989.
36   On this matter see David Pannick, *Judges, op. cit.*, pp. 108–9.
37   See *Ex parte Blackburn, op. cit.*
38   *Secretary of State for Defence* v. *Guardian Newspapers Limited* [1985] AC 339, 347.
39   Per Lord Hailsham in *Badry* v. *DPP of Mauritius, op. cit.* In that case Commonwealth countries were urged not to punish for contempt for scandalizing the judiciary except for the most extreme forms of abuse.
40   *Attorney-General* v. *Guardian Newspapers Ltd (No. 2)* [1990] AC 109, [1988] 3 All ER 545 (HL).

41 Referred to in Geoffrey Robertson and Andrew Nicol, *Media Law* (Harlow: Longman, 1990), p. 298.
42 *The Sunday Times*, 13 June 1993.
43 Ibid.
44 *The Times*, 10 June 1993.
45 Clive Walker, 'Scandalising in the Eighties', *Law Quarterly Review*, **101** (1985), p. 359. See also Pannick, *Judges, op. cit.*, pp. 115–16 where he points out that:

> The continued existence of the offence [of scandalising the judiciary under English law], and the memory of successful prosecutions, inhibits journalists, who wrongly suspect that they have a legal obligation to speak respectfully and cautiously when discussing the judiciary. In fact, there is little danger of prosecution nowadays for criticising the judiciary, irrespective of the ferocity of the language used, unless one suggests that the court lacks impartiality.

46 Ibid., p. 359.
47 A.W. Bradley, 'Judges and the Media – The Kilmuir Rules', *Public Law* (1986), p. 383 at p. 385.
48 Lord Mackay of Clashfern, *The Administration of Justice* (London: Sweet & Maxwell, 1994), pp. 25–6.
49 In reply to a parliamentary question on the issues of public statements by judges, the Parliamentary Secretary at the Lord Chancellor's Department (Mr Streeter) reiterated the requirement under the principle of independence of the judiciary 'for each judge to decide individually whether to make public statements'. He confirmed that a copy of the Lord Chancellor's advice on the matter has been sent to every judge, and new judges will continue to receive the same advice on appointment. In a follow-up question, Mr Gordon Prentice asked if Mr Streeter did not feel that the independence of the judiciary would be compromised in circumstances such as when the Chairman of the Conservative party, Dr Brian Mawhinney, asked members of the public to write to judges and seek to intimidate them for handing down lenient sentences. Mr Streeter replied:

> That was a fairly extraordinary outburst. On appointment in 1987, my right hon. and noble friend the Lord Chancellor relaxed the rules to enable judges to speak out on issues of the day. It is important that experienced and senior judges speak out, express their opinions and take a full part in debates in the House of Lords. .... It is important that members of the public make their views known, if they feel that sentences passed in local communities are not appropriate, by going to see or writing to their Members of Parliament. That is what we call democracy. (Oral Answers, *Hansard*, 3 February, col. 1.

The author is grateful to Janet Tweedale of the Lord Chancellor's Department for drawing his attention to this statement.
50 (1997) 25 EHRR, 1.
51 Eur. Ct. HR Series A.313 (1995); 21 (1996) EHRR, 1.
52 See Chapter 15 in this volume, 'Article 10 of the ECHR and the Criticism of Public Officials'. See also D.J. Harris, M. O'Boyle and C. Warbrick, *Law of the ECHR* (London: Butterworths, 1995) ch. 11.
53 Similar sentiments have been expressed in relation to Canadian judges. See Cory JA in *R. v. Kopyto* 47 DLR (4th) 213 (1987).
54 Between February and April 1998, the newspapers were full of critical articles of the Lord Chancellor's decision to spend nearly £600 000 on refurbishing his official apartments in the Palace of Westminster.

55   In *R. v. Cosley Times*, 9 May 1931.
56   *Ex parte Blackburn, op. cit.*
57   See Lord Hailsham in *Badry* v. *DPP of Mauritius, op. cit.*

3   Criticizing Judges in Ireland

Mary Kotsonouris[1]

> But these judges in Ireland have other aspects . . . . Orders suppressing national, political and even literary organisations will be found over the signatures of members of this judiciary. So they have departed from the status of independence of the executive government by themselves taking a hand in its work. This has undoubtedly been a poison in the well of justice in this country.[2]

Introduction

In January 1922 the law adviser to the brand new Provisional government was advising the minister for home affairs that it should warn the judges that any interference in matters of state would be regarded as misconduct. As events turned out, the men thus impugned were to remain in office for another two and half years and to be succeeded by a judiciary constitutionally established and headed by the author of the opening quotation – Hugh Kennedy KC – as the first Chief Justice of Saorstát Éireann, the Irish Free State. Not only were His Majesty's judges to continue on suffrance and without the support of the British establishment, but they were to do so in competition with a rival and popular judiciary for a further seven months and on through a civil war followed by a long parliamentary debate on the bill which was writing them out of history. The Courts of Justice Act, under which the present Irish courts were established, did not become law until June 1924.

On the day of the judges' inauguration, the *Freeman's Journal* could not resist the temptation of some post-colonial glee:

> From the chambers of the old Privy Council where the practices of the old external tyranny were devised and directed, Ireland's own judges proceeded to the new Supreme Court where the oath of loyalty to the Free State and to the ideal of impartial justice was taken by the future administrators of Irish law. No department of the old order in Ireland was more poisoned in its effects upon Irish social life than the Department of Justice. In every conflict where the civic rights of the

common people conflicted with the interest of the dominant class, the scales were heavily weighted against the people.[3]

In fact, these were much the same sentiments as those expressed by Hugh Kennedy who, as Chief Justice, was now leading the procession to the Supreme Court to administer the oath to his brethren.

There was, however, nothing revolutionary about the law, procedure, dress or titles in the new Irish system which was, and is, governed by common law and statute, with one important difference – it is subject to a constitution. Ireland inherited the common law through conquest. The old Gaelic system of Brehon law remained in force up to the seventeenth century outside of Dublin and the surrounding counties where English administration and custom had taken root. What is known of it survives in law texts originating in the seventh and eighth centuries AD. In *A Guide to Early Irish Law*, Dr. Fergus Kelly says that judges or *breiteamh* were not of the *nemed* – the highest privileged group comprising kings, clerics and poets – but did rank next in importance.[4] A judge was required to give a pledge of five ounces of silver in support of his judgment. If that was wrongfully challenged, he was entitled to a hefty payment from the complainant in addition to his normal fee. It was believed that a judgment secured by bribery brought the wrath of God on a kingdom, and, perhaps even more persuasively for the office-holder, that a biased judgment visited unsightly blotches to the cheeks of the judge which would not disappear until he reversed it! However, it was not considered *lèse-majesté* to criticize a judge provided that you were prepared to pay him if you were proved wrong. Equally, only his knowledge of the law and impeccable fairness allowed him to continue in his calling, and these qualifications were subject to continuous scrutiny.

So much weight was placed on the Irish judicial system in the anti-Union cause as a primary source of 'all our ills' that it is difficult to judge what was deserved and what was propaganda. From early times, justices of the peace were appointed in Ireland specifically to enforce the King's peace by putting down rebellion. Around 1830, Robert Peel, as Chief Secretary for Ireland, created the office of Resident Magistrate. The invidious position of these men as a combination of judge and head of the local militia – generally former military or police officers without legal background holding office at the pleasure of the Viceroy – made them particularly hated because they were seen as the symbol of colonial power and the enforcers of repressive laws. When the secessionist party of Sinn Fein, which had won the majority of seats in the General Election of 1918, set up their own parliament – Dáil Éireann – in Dublin, it was only to be expected that the animus against the existing judicial regime would find expression in the creation of an overtly rival system of courts.[5] What was not anticipated, however, was its immediate and widespread success in winning litigants away from Crown Courts which, outside of Dublin and the Northern counties, were rapidly emptied of all but judges, court officials, police and lawyers – and it did not take long for the solicitors' branch of the profession to follow their clients into these intriguingly 'illegal' courts. Within a short time there was a hierarchy of Supreme, circuit, district and parish courts, the first two with only four professional judges between them. Of more interest in the present context is the lowest tier, because there was a court in every parish with its justices elected by a convention representative of local groups, and these parish justices may well have been the most fiercely criticized judicial figures in history! Moreover, because the Dáil minister for home affairs was anxious to ensure that he kept his consumer base, all complaints were attended to and investigated. However, even in the midst of guerrilla war and martial law, the justices stressed their independence and refused to be cowed into acquiescence by the Black-and-Tans, the gunmen, bureaucracy or, indeed, by clever lawyers. As one of them said to a sarcastic prosecuting solicitor, 'We may be simple men but we can distinguish between right and wrong'. Even all these years later, it is still quietly satisfying to reflect that, in fact, it was the lay justice who was legally correct, and not the solicitor – which perhaps accounts for his sarcasm!

The two court systems remained in operation to the detriment of the official courts, whose jurisdiction was largely ignored by litigants and unsupported by the Provisional government. However, at the beginning of the civil war, when a military prisoner applied successfully to the Dáil courts for a writ of *habeas corpus* the government moved swiftly to abolish them. As a result, over 5000 cases were plunged into limbo – and the unfortunate Dáil judge into prison without trial! It may well be that this crude manifestation of executive power left a residual trauma; when the Courts of Justice Bill creating the present judicial system was introduced in August 1923, the members of both the Dáil and Senate kept it in debate for over eight months in their determination to copperfasten the total independence of judges of the executive, most particularly those of the lower courts.[6] It was also strongly argued that to allow the salaries of the district justices to be paid at a level determined by a yearly vote in the Dáil from a source other then the Central Fund would allow deputies to use the occasion to criticize decisions of individual justices.

Public representatives were acquiring considerable expertise in debating such questions. The same year had seen the establishment of a judicial commission with extraordinary powers to hear cases and appeals pending in the Dáil courts at the time of closure and to register all their outstanding judgments. In 1925 the jurisdiction of these improvised and 'illegal' courts was transferred to the new High Court and so remains to this day. Thus, in the period between 1920 and 1924, Ireland had four distinct judicial regimes whose functions overlapped, clashed and criss-crossed – British (or imperial), Dáil Éireann, the Winding up Commission and constitutional.

Contempt of Court

The Constitution of the Irish Free State, which passed into law on 6 December 1922,[7] provided that judicial power would be exercised in public courts to be prescribed by law and that all judges would be independent in the exercise of their functions and be subject only to the Constitution and to the law. Under s.72 no person could be tried without a jury on any criminal charge save for minor offences or offences against military law triable by court martial or military tribunal. The Constitution also guaranteed freedom of speech, of assembly and of association 'for purposes not opposed to public morality'. The question of what constituted contempt of court, specifically with regard to the criticism of a judge, came up for decision early in the life of the new state and was rooted, as were other leading cases which followed, in its unhappy beginnings.

Three men had refused to plead when prosecuted for arms offences and the jury persistently claimed it could not agree on the question whether they were 'mute of malice'. An article in the *Nation* in February 1928 savagely criticized the trial judge for his reasonable conclusion that some jury members had acted in disregard of their oath and the law. The paper, which was the organ of the losing Republican side in the recent civil war, denounced 'the judge's insolence to jurors . . . who were sick of being called upon to assist the murderers of 8 December 1922 . . . men whose only crime was their faithful adherence to their Irish Republican convictions'. The editor, Sean T. O'Kelly, was prosecuted for contempt of court and a preliminary point was raised that, under Article 72 of the Constitution, the defendant was entitled to a jury trial.

All three judges of the High Court affirmed the inherent jurisdiction of the courts 'to punish on summary process the editor of a newspaper for contempt of court in publishing scandalous matter of a Judge with reference to his conduct in judicial proceedings' (Sullivan, P, quoting, in support, the decisions in *Gray*[8] and *R. v. The Editor of the New Statesman, ex parte DPP*).[9] His colleague, Hanna J, said:

> It was necessary that every court, no matter how established, should have the power to commit for contempt. The Courts of Dáil Éireann established under the decree of the first Dáil on June 29 1920 claimed this power. In my view, whether we are the grantees of the powers of the former Courts in the country through the operation of the statutory provisions referred to, or are the descendants of the Dáil Courts, or

were wholly created from the deliberations of our own Legislature, we are fully armed with this essential power.[10]

In other words, notwithstanding the constitutional provision that trials for criminal offences were to be held with a jury, the power to attach for scandalizing the court was inherent and survived intact. The later Constitution of 1937 also enacted that no person was to be tried on any criminal charge save in due course of law, but it also provided for the establishment of special courts for the trial of offences where '. . . the ordinary courts are inadequate to secure the effective administration of justice and the preservation of public peace and order'.[11]

We have seen that the *O'Kelly*[12] case was based on opposition to laws relative to the security of the state and, in two more recent cases, criticism of judges arose in the same arena – in fact, from the same trial in the Special Criminal Court. It is unfortunate that emergency-type legislation has been in place, in one form or another, almost contemporaneously with independence.[13] The Special Criminal Court comprises three judges who sit without a jury to decide cases brought under the Offences Against the State Act 1939 and subsequent legislation. While the majority of these would obviously be subversion-type offences, such as membership of an illegal organization or possession of arms and explosives, there have also been trials relating to kidnapping, bank robbery, and recently, drugs offences.

The legislation itself was the subject of the first case to be brought by an individual to the European Court of Human Rights, *Lawless* v. *Ireland*.[14] In 1957 Gerard Lawless, a member of the Irish Republican Army, had been detained under the Offences Against the State (Amendment) Act 1940 and held in a military detention camp for five months without trial. The Court found that, because of the 'public emergency . . . threatening the life of the nation', the Irish government was entitled to take measures derogating from its obligations under the Convention. In this respect, it is important to stress that the *Lawless* case centres on detention without trial and not trial without a jury.

However, in 1947, it was a question of a trial without professional judges in that the Court, at the time, was staffed by army officers. In *Attorney General* v. *Connolly*,[15] the editorial by Ross Connolly in a Sinn Fein publication had anticipated the outcome of the trial of one Henry White for the murder of a police officer: 'he awaits his death, which sentence will inevitably be passed on him after his mockery of a trial before the Special Criminal Court is over'. In his affidavit, the defendant fuelled the fires further by making allegations about the appointment, lack of justice and qualifications of the members of that Court. The defence, in the appeal against the conditional order, argued that the charge was one of a criminal nature not punishable by attachment and, moreover, that the judges of the Special Criminal Court were appointed and removable by the will of the government and hence were subject to criticism like any other department of state. The President of the High Court, George Gavan Duffy, was adamant that, given 'the old traditional distrust of the criminal administration that long pervaded the mind of the people during the British regime, it is essential to the rule of law in the new Ireland that the public should be convinced that justice is being truly administered in accordance with the law of the Irish people by the High Court of Justice established under our own Constitution'.

This was a theme understandably emphasized by judges following the establishment of the Irish Free State – that the administration of justice was now in native hands and that it was all the more important that it be accorded the people's obedience and respect. History has now shown that the difficulties encountered in this area are common in post-colonial societies, where it may have been a citizen's patriotic duty to disobey the law right up to the moment when it is time to obey it. It is not surprising, then, that contempt of court issues were particularly sensitive in Ireland, allied as they so often were to questions of territorial claims and the near irresistible temptation to ripe and righteous rhetoric. The President of the High Court said that the defendant's right of free speech was not a licence to undermine public order and quoted from Lord Aitken's famous 'cloistered virtue' judgment[16] that the right of criticism must not be exercised in malice or in an attempt to impair the administration of justice.

Interestingly, his remark that the charge was 'scandalising the Court, whether the actual trial was prejudiced or not' would appear to preclude a defence of justification. However in subsequent judgments, the allegedly impugned trial and decision has inevitably been reviewed, with observations to the effect that the comments were a gross misrepresentation of the facts or evidence given in court, which makes it difficult to isolate the issue of criticism of the judge. Even where the contempt consisted of rabble-rousing, bigoted abuse of a Protestant judge who had also served under the British administration, and the abuse directed solely at those personal elements only, as in *AG* v. *O'Ryan and Boyd*,[17] the High Court, in its review of the case, said that, if anything, the sentence imposed by the circuit court in the impugned trial was too lenient. Although, by then, the Irish Free State had been in existence for 25 years, Gavan Duffy spoke of the background against which the defamatory material should be judged and of the residual bitterness so easily stirred again. It was not possible to ignore the abuse as:

> ... the irresponsible rantings of an *exalté* ... this particular contempt is graver and even more reprehensible in Ireland than it might be in any other country .... There is no excuse for a man of influence who works upon the zeal and piety of a

Catholic community like the people of Waterford by stirring up public feeling against the Judge of the area who is not a Catholic, on the pretext that he had degraded his office by behaving in courts as a sectary and partisan.

He did go on to say that, when circumstances allowed, attacks on judges should be left to the discrimination of the public, that it was essential to preserve the right of fair criticism of the courts and that, consequently, the 'delicate jurisdiction over contempt of court upon summary application . . . should be leniently exercised to the benefit of a man who has no defence'. It would appear that, *mutatis mutandis*, judgments of the Irish courts which followed *O'Kelly* and *O'Ryan and Boyd* have done so also in essentials. There has been a refusal of defence applications for a trial by jury under the Constitution, a strong commitment to preserve the existing jurisdiction, lengthy, closely argued judgments separately delivered and a light punishment for the defendants, most of whom, it must be said, apologized profusely in the end. Moreover, every judgment has defended the right to criticize judges and courts and the establishment of the Special Criminal Court itself. Indeed, the principle has been so consistently restated that it would be difficult to argue that it constitutes nothing more than a conventional nod to a well-meaning sentiment. What follows is only a fraction of extracts from a variety of judgments, beginning with one from the nineteenth century:

I now come to the question of contempt of court. What is it? Is it insolvence used to a particular judge in his personal capacity? Is it the words that would be likely or calculated to induce a breach of the peace between the Judge and the person who speaks them? No such thing; it is not upon that ground that the Court acts. The Court acts, as stated in *R. v. Davison* and *ex parte Pater*, not out of regard for the particular judge. What it looks at is the dignity of the administration of justice and the acts, as for contempt against that which is aimed against the administration of justice and against what amounts to a defamation *of the Court* in the administration of justice.[18]

In upholding the current position to the extent of saying that it is for a judge and not for a jury to say if the established facts constitute a major criminal contempt, I would stress that, in both the factual and legal aspects of the hearing of the charge, the elementary requirements of justice in the circumstances would have to be observed. There is a presumption that our law in this respect is in conformity with the European Convention on Human Rights, particularly Articles 5 and 10(2) thereof.[19]

Freedom of expression which goes beyond acceptable limits is criticism which brings the administration of justice into disrepute and undermines the confidence which people should have in judges appointed under the Constitution to administer justice in the courts.[20]

The person producing the programme did not agree with the judgement but there is no suggestion that the Circuit Judge acted from improper motives or anything of that nature. . . . I do not see why a judgement cannot be criticised provided it is not done in a manner calculated to bring the court or the judge into contempt. If that element is not present there is no reason why judgements should not be criticised. Nor does the criticism have to be confined to scholarly articles in legal journals. The mass media are entitled to have their say as well. The public take a great interest in court cases and it is only natural that discussion should concentrate on the result of cases. So criticism which does not subvert justice should be allowed.[21]

Among certain groups the trial of persons supporting a political cause has been the subject of such strong emotion and condemnation of the Special Criminal Court process that it has led to action by the Director of Public Prosecutions. As already mentioned, one trial sparked off two separate prosecutions. In 1976 Noel and Marie Murray were convicted of the capital murder of Garda Reynolds, a police officer. Two letters were published in *Hibernia* which, in effect, accused the judges of bias in not entertaining evidence other than confessions and of a presumption of guilt. Kenny J, in delivering the judgment of the Supreme Court, pointed out that the three judges were of the High Court, the circuit court and the district court respectively and that the charges made against them were very grave:

The Court wishes to emphasise that criticism of the retention of death penalty of the Offences Against the State Acts or any of their provisions or of the establishment of the Special Criminal Court are not a contempt of court. These are matters which may validly be debated in public even if the comments made are expressed in strong language or are uninformed or foolish.[22]

He also pointed out that the Murray trial had been extensively reported and, therefore, that the editor should have known that statements in the letters were completely false and their publication was capable of being considered as contempt of court: 'Contempt of court also includes serious misrepresentation of the proceedings of a court.' Kenny J quoted Lord Hardwicke LC in *Read and Huggonson*, 'nothing is more incumbent upon courts of justice than to preserve their proceedings from being misrepresented.'

Another contempt of court hearing arising from the same *cause célèbre* did not reach the Supreme Court until 1981 and concerned a press release from an organization called the Association for Legal Justice, the burden of which was that the Special Criminal Court judges 'abused the rules of evidence as to make the court akin to a sentencing tribunal'. The DPP issued proceedings for contempt against the editor and the journalist of the *Irish Times* who had reported the statement which had been read over the telephone to the newspaper. They immediately apologized in court, but the chairman and secretary of the

Association, Walsh and Conneely, defended their action and appealed against the order of the High Court dismissing their application for a jury trial. Both the Chief Justice and Mr Justice Henchy of the Supreme Court delivered lengthy judgments which contribute much to the frequency with which *The State (DPP)* v. *Walsh* is referred: 'In short, the facts adduced in this application to commit for contempt (to which facts no rebuttal has been offered) constitute a classical example of the crime of contempt by scandalising a court'.[23] All the issues, which had also been raised in previous cases – jurisdictional and constitutional, as well as freedom of speech – were examined extensively. Irish, English and American decisions – 47 in all – were referred to; it even put to final rest the common law presumption that a wife acts under the coercion of her husband – too late to be of any comfort to the unfortunate Mr Bumble in *Oliver Twist*!

While cases such as the above are sometimes perceived as judges insisting on their dignity and high office, it should be remembered that there are often issues which involve individuals or the community, whose interest must deserve at least the same protection. We have seen in *AG* v. *O'Ryan and Boyd* that the court was particularly mindful of the local and historical background against which the inflammatory abuse of the circuit judge should be measured. Indeed, the judge himself had taken no action when the abusive letter was sent to him: it was this turning of the other cheek which enraged the writer into reading the missive aloud to the meeting of the county council two weeks later. There is also the issue of protection of family privacy and of children which is central to the judgment in *Re Kennedy and McCann*.[24] In 1976 a custody case was heard *in camera*, and an appeal by the mother to the Supreme Court was pending. A Sunday newspaper published her, understandably, one-sided view of the proceedings to date, included photographs of the children, and attacked the court and society as being hypocritical about morality and motherhood. The father brought an application to attach for contempt. It transpired that the journalist, Mr McCann, had not attended any of the court hearings and that Mr Kennedy, editor of the *Sunday World*, was unaware of the *in camera* ruling; both apologized. In his judgment, O'Higgins CJ referred to the account of the sorry state of a wrecked marriage, offensive references to the father, names, ages and photographs of the boys and their mother. He said that the article

> ... tore away the shield of privacy which the Court had erected ... exposed the children to the glare of publicity which can affect seriously their ordinary lives, companionship at school and their relationship with their parents ... The article further carried the direct implication, offensive to all judges and all courts in this country, that justice could not be obtained in Irish courts and that 'ours was a sick society which was hypocritical about motherhood, morality and the family'. ...

The right of free speech and the full expression of opinion are valued rights. Their preservation, however, depends on the observance of the acceptable limit that they must not be used to undermine public order or morality or the authority of the State.

Reform Proposals

In 1991 the Law Reform Commission published its *Consultation Paper on Contempt of Court*,[25] in which the question of the criticism of judge and the offence of scandalizing the court was examined at length. Irish leading cases, as well as those of other jurisdictions and commission reports on the subject in several countries, were extensively analysed. The members made several provisional recommendations and invited submissions to their proposals. A seminar was held some months later so that lawyers, academics, judges and media representatives could make their views known: the latter did so robustly. The Commission published its report in 1994[26] having first submitted it to the Attorney-General who, in 1989, had originally requested this examination of the law of contempt. It is difficult to summarize the recommendations, even in the specific area of scandalizing the court, and, moreover, there was no unanimity between the five members including the President, a former Supreme Court judge. However, very briefly, the recommendations were as follows:

- The offence of 'scandalising the court' should be defined by statute for prosecution purposes and should consist of imputing corrupt conduct to a judge or publishing a false account of court proceedings.
- The person must know there was a substantial risk, or be recklessly indifferent to the risk.
- Publication would bring the administration of justice into disrepute.
- There is an intention to publish a false account.
- The truth of the communication would render it lawful.
- There should be no legislative interference with the court's power of summary attachment.
- Abuse of the judiciary, even if scurrilous, should not constitute an offence.

Although there has been no move, as yet, to introduce laws giving form to these or any other of the proposals, a new Courts Service Commission, responsible for the administration of courts, established on 9 November 1999 in place of the Department of Justice, which has held this responsibility since 1924. It is understood that the Committee guiding this radical departure under Mrs Justice Susan Denham will soon be considering the whole question of the accountability of judges as a separate issue.

The potential conflict between the ideas of contempt of court and freedom of expression was explored in the MacDermott Lecture delivered at Queen's University in Belfast by Mr Justice Seamus Henchy of the Supreme Court in May 1981, which was subsequently published in the *Northern Ireland Legal Quarterly*.[27] Judge Henchy stressed that the circulation of information was as necessary to the body politic as fresh air is to an individual's well-being and that, equally, the right of the public at large to have the process of law preserved from debasement or frustration was vital to civil rights. He saw contempt of court as the common law remedy whose aim was to ensure that the administration of justice operated without undue interference: there was wide acceptance that the sanction of criminal law should attach to such conduct. However, it is his observations on *The Sunday Times* judgment of the European Court of Human Rights,[28] two years previously, that are of most interest in the present context. He saw it as having a profound and far-reaching importance.

> It may be that the European Court of Human Rights considers itself free to set and apply its own norms and criteria for determining when a valid domestic law must not be applied, even when the highest domestic court considers it to be necessary for the maintenance of the authority and impartiality of the judicial system of the state in question. It may be that in the future the frontiers between freedom of expression and contempt of court will, at least in certain cases, be drawn in Strasbourg, to the exclusion of domestic courts or the edicts of national parliaments.

Reading one of the most recent decisions from Strasbourg under Article 10 of the Convention, *De Haes and Gisjels* v. *Belgium* (1998),[29] one can see that the judge's forecast made 16 years previously was uncannily accurate. However, it would also be difficult not to agree with his conclusion that, because of the basic incompatibility which arises between a lawyer's view of the essential attributes of the administration of justice and those of freedom of expression which communicators believe to be necessary in an open democratic society, problems must continue to be solved empirically on a case-by-case basis.

Conclusions

All the foregoing has to do with the official or formal exposition of the law as governed by long-established practice, judicial precedents and by the Constitution but it is not at that level that the everyday legal affairs of the public are conducted. It is surely at least as important that people see their courts as the guardians of their civic rights and as tribunals where grievances are heard in a fairminded manner and that the conduct of proceedings is such as not to demean them. Given an adversarial system and the unequal terms in which they are confronted and surrounded by experienced lawyers speaking an archaic and mysterious language, it is incumbent on any judge to remain as reasonable and courteous as possible. It is here where scrutiny and critical comment could most benefit the community. Often it does not need comment: a factual account of a case which highlights bad behaviour on the judge's part should allow a reader to form his or her own opinion. Persistent rudeness, sarcasm, personal prejudice, impatience or downright laziness are failings which work to disillusion a person whose only experience of the living administration of justice may be one day in court when one or several of these characteristics were on prominent display. It will bring the process into disrepute as surely for that person as any libellous or malicious account of one decision which he or she may never read. A judge may be irritable or unfair or even bullying on occasion – a bad judge day – but persistence in unjudicial behaviour should not be tolerated in a free society.

Journalists and editors frequently remark that judges cannot be criticized and that they are accountable to nobody, but if one explores this issue with them, they seem to be confusing criticism with the *sub judice* rule, which regularly gets them into hot water. Judgments are constantly discussed, criticized, even denounced by columnists, commentators and the proverbial man-in-the-street in letters to newspapers or radio phone-ins. There have been furores about so many court cases in 1999 alone that it is impossible to single out one, yet nobody has been prosecuted for criticism or scandalizing, although several editors have been summoned to explain breaches of the *sub judice* rule. It was not always thus. While court proceedings provided the bulk of reporting in most provincial newspapers for years, atmospheric description rarely went beyond the sycophantic 'laughter in court', usually in response to a witticism from the Bench.

The end of deference was signalled in a series of 'colour pieces' by a young journalist which the *Irish Times* ran in the 1970s. In these articles, Nell McCafferty reported the happenings in the Dublin district court by way of a deceptively mild narrative which was not intended to conceal anger or wry amusement or pity.[30] The reality of grimy, dilapidated courthouses, judicial power and rudeness underlined by official indifference was brought home to the reader in a style for which the word 'inimitable' was invented. Moreover, there were no legal repercussions nor pressure on Donal Foley, the news editor who conceived the idea. The judges did not like it, neither did officialdom but the public did. Ms McCafferty threw windows open on a whole world that respectable society had heretofore ignored; thankfully, those windows have not been closed again. For some years now, Michael O'Toole, a columnist for the *Evening Herald*, has regularly scrutinized judges, judgments and procedures with a critical faculty honed by his early experience as a court reporter for a provincial paper and a keen knowledge of the law. Provided that a judge is not accused of corruption or bias in his or her professional conduct, none of the several journalists who write about court matters today could conceivably be the subject of a prosecution given the guidelines laid down by successive Supreme Court decisions.

Judges in Ireland appear to have escaped the generalized prejudice against lawyers. By and large, they are seen as the upholders of constitutional rights, as a welcome, if occasional, thorn in the side of the executive and, by successive judgments on constitutional issues, as effecting widespread social changes where timid governments have failed to lead. Privacy, contraception, health and religious equality are some of the many issues to have come before the Supreme Court and to have consequently caused a change in the law. This is not a role that judges particularly seek and they frequently rebuke the legislators for the lack of statutory remedies for issues which give rise to difficulties: at the time of writing, it is the quandary of the respective rights of adopted children and their birth mothers. When a particular judgment attracts publicity and partisanship, then criticism will centre on the remoteness of judges from 'real life', their social background and the fact that they cannot be criticized – even while they are! Within days, some other judgment is welcomed as a triumph of common sense – and, arguably, this is the way things should be in a democracy. Irish people are remarkably well informed in the law; they do not consider judges as superior beings, but take judicial independence as a given. Neither do they question for a second their democratic right to criticize the whole process relentlessly.

In the final analysis, the most effective criticism of a judge lies in the power of a superior court to review his or her decisions. One might be found to have been wrong in the interpretation of the law but it must be far more of a rebuke – and justifiably so – to have one's decision set aside because a party was not granted a full opportunity to put his or her case, or a summing up was unfair, or some fundamental duty was overlooked. Apart from delivering a judicial and public slap on the wrist, this process has the inestimable advantage of having the power to right the wrong – the modern equivalent, perhaps, of removing the blotches from the face of the unjust judge in the more immediately perceived cause and effect according to Brehon Law! However, the increasing use of judicial review does not detract at all from the need and desirability to subject the judiciary and the administration of the law to examination and comment from a free press. That there will always be tension in the exercise must be accepted as a given and not be allowed to develop into bullying by one side or the other. For a small country which achieved its independence only in the twentieth century, and where, previously, the nature of the legal process was overwhelmingly biased towards maintaining the status quo, the lively interest and the quizzical eye on all things under the law are not only inevitable but a sophistication to be rejoiced in. That the eye may be cast a little more warily on government rather than the judges is equally understandable in a people who saw their own amateur and painfully constructed courts destroyed by their first government within six months of attaining power. This gives them all the more reason, therefore, to keep their judges up to scratch in the service of the people.

Notes

1   In the preparation of this chapter the author spoke and corresponded with judges, journalists, academics, editors, senior executives of the Law Society and of King's Inns, lawyers, officials of the Departments of Justice and of the Law Reform Commission, archivists and friends. They were extremely generous with their interest, patience and time, and the author wishes to express her gratitude. The opinions expressed herein are, however, those of the author alone.

2   UCD Archives, Kennedy Papers, P/4 272, Kennedy to Duggan, 18 January 1922.

3   *Freeman's Journal*, 12 June 1924.

4   Fergus Kelly, *A Guide to Early Irish Law* (Dublin: Institute for Advanced Studies, 1981); see also Liam Breathnach, 'Lawyers in Early Ireland' in D. Hogan and W.N. Osborough (eds), *Brehons, Serjeants & Attorneys*, Dublin 1990.

5   Mary Kotsonouris, *Retreat from Revolution* (Dublin: Irish Academic Press, 1994).

6   The Courts of Justice Act 1924.

7   Saorstat Eireann Public Statutes 1922.

8   [1900] AC All ER 59.

9   (1928) 44 *Times Law Reports*, 301.

10   [1928] *AG v. O'Kelly*, IR 308.

11   Constitution of Ireland, Art.38.

12   Ibid.

13   Colm Campbell, *Emergency Law in Ireland 1918–1925* (Oxford: Clarendon Press, 1994).

14   (1960) *Lawless v. Ireland (No.1)* 1 EHRR, 1.

15   [1947] *AG v. Connolly*, IR 213.

16   *Ambard v. Attorney General for Trinidad and Tobago* [1936] AC 322 at 335.

17   [1946] *AG v. O'Ryan and Boyd*, IR 70.

18   Chief Baron Pallas in *Ex parte Tanner M.P.* [1889] Judgements of the Superior Courts in Ireland, 343. Emphasis in original.

19   Henchy J in *The State (DPP) v. Walsh* [1981] IR 440 (Sup. Ct).

20   Chief Justice O'Higgins in *Re Kennedy and McCann* [1976] IR 386 (Sup. Ct).

21   Carroll J in *Weeland v. RTE* [1987] IR 666.

22   In *Re Hibernia National Review* [1976] IR 388 (Sup. Ct).

23   Henchy J in *The State DPP v. Walsh, op. cit.*

24   [1976] IR, 382.

25   *Law Reform Commission Consultation Paper on Contempt of Court* (Dublin: Law Reform Commission, 1991).

26   *Law Reform Commission Report on Contempt of Court* (Dublin: Law Reform Commission, 1994).

27   'Contempt of Court and Freedom of Expression', *Northern Ireland Law Quarterly*, 33 (4) (Winter 1982), p. 326.

28 *Sunday Times* v. *United Kingdom No.1*, 2 EHRR, 245.
29 25 EHRR, 1–125.
30 Some of the articles were later published; Nell McCafferty, *In the Eyes of the Law* (Dublin: Poolbeg Press, 1987).

PART III
THE ORDINARY LAW

4 Criticizing Judges in Germany

Michael Bohlander[1]

Introduction

The German[2] law and practice on criticizing judges and the ways in which they may react to criticism differ considerably from those in the so-called common law countries. Here I will only look at criticism of judges insofar as it relates to their judicial office. Judges do not enjoy any special protection as far as their private lives are concerned, and thus criticism or defamation with regard to purely private matters are of no interest in this context.

The Constitutional Position of Judges and the Court Hierarchy

The Constitutional Position

The German Constitution, the *Grundgesetz*, regulates the law of the judiciary in Article 97, which is almost a verbatim copy of the relevant provisions of the Weimar Constitution of 1919.[3] Article 97 provides that judges are independent and only subject to the law.[4] The constitutional provision is complemented by an Act of Parliament, the *Deutsches Richtergesetz* (German Judiciary Act) for federal judges, which, to some extent, applies also to state judges, and by the corresponding laws of the individual states of the Federation.

Judicial Independence

In its modern sense this doctrine is a creation of nineteenth-century German legal history. Before that time judges could be dismissed from office by order of the government if their behaviour in some way seriously displeased the government of the day. Even after the first judiciary acts had been passed,

Ludwig I of Bavaria stated in 1847: 'I do not favour the separation of the administration of justice from the executive in the lowest tiers of the hierarchy; it weakens the influence of the government.'[5] However, these promising beginnings suffered a setback under the Bismarck regime when judges were discriminated against in matters of pay, promotion, rank and social standing, as opposed to civil servants within the executive branch of government and the military.[6] The Weimar Republic saw great distrust against the partially still monarchistic judiciary, especially in politically sensitive trials, which sometimes even provoked physical attacks against judges.[7] In 1937 the Nazis abolished all judiciary acts passed so far, and Hitler proclaimed himself supreme judge.[8] The independence of the judiciary was reinstated after the Second World War by the Allied Powers.[9]

Judicial independence is commonly divided into two separate aspects:

- personal independence (*persönliche Unabhängigkeit*) and
- independence in judicial decision-making (*sachliche Unabhängigkeit*).

The first means that judges who have been appointed for life – as opposed to probationary judges in the first three to five years of their career – may not be removed from office or moved to another court without their consent unless one of the disciplinary provisions allows such a sanction. There are some ramifications to this concept which do not concern us here.[10] The latter means that judges are not subject to any directives or orders from others as far as their genuine judicial function is concerned. This is what is normally understood by judicial independence. It does not apply to administrative functions, which judges also sometimes have – for example, as presiding judge of a court district.[11] This part of judicial independence is the area where conflicts with the disciplinary control by the state Court of Appeal and the ministry of justice mostly occur.

Court Hierarchy

The courts are divided into state and federal courts. The states regulate their judiciaries by their own laws.[12] For the sake of simplicity I will only look at the federal law which is congruent to the state law in the matters which concern us here. There is no federal jurisdiction of first instance, save for the *Bundespatentgericht*, which decides in matters of patents. There are five different jurisdictions: ordinary, administrative, social, industrial and fiscal. Figure 4.1 gives an example of the hierarchy in the ordinary jurisdiction. Disciplinary control is exercised by the ministers of justice, the presiding judges of the state Courts of Appeal and the presiding judges of the lower courts. There is no federal disciplinary control over state judges. The federal

BUNDESVERFASSUNGSGERICHT (FEDERAL
CONSTITUTIONAL COURT)
*Constitutional complaints after ordinary appeal process has been
exhausted.*

BUNDESGERICHTSHOF (FEDERAL COURT OF APPEAL)
Civil: appeals on points of law only from the *Oberlandesgerichte* and on
leapfrog from the *Landgerichte*.
Criminal: appeals on points of law from the *Landgerichte*.

FEDERAL JURISDICTION
STATE JURISDICTION
OBERLANDESGERICHTE (STATE COURTS OF APPEAL)
Civil: appeal on points of fact and law from the *Landgerichte* as courts of
first instance.
Criminal: appeals on points of law from the *Landgerichte* and on leapfrog
from the *Amtsgerichte*.

LANDGERICHTE (DISTRICT COURTS)
Civil: courts of first instance where value in dispute exceeds 10 000 DM,
and appellate court for decisions of the *Amtsgerichte*.
Criminal: appeals on fact and law from the *Amtsgerichte*; first instance for
serious crime.

AMTSGERICHTE (COUNTY COURTS)
Civil: courts of first instance where value in dispute is under 10 000 DM,
and other, non-contentious jurisdictions.
Criminal: petty to intermediate crime.

Figure 4.1   The court hierarchy in Germany: ordinary jurisdiction

judges of ordinary jurisdiction are under the disciplinary control of the
Federal Ministry of Justice and the presiding judge of the *Bundesgerichtshof*.[13]

Judicial Freedom of Expression

Judges, like every other citizen, enjoy the right to free speech emanating from
Article 5 of the Constitution. They are, however, subject to certain restrictions,
especially when they speak in their official capacity. These restrictions are

laid down in s.39 of the Deutsches Richtergesetz (DRiG) in connection with provisions concerning the civil service.[14] That provision states that:

> A judge shall, in his official capacity as well as privately and when engaging in political activities, behave in such a manner that the trust in his independence is not jeopardized.

The concept of independence used in this provision is wider than the two aspects just mentioned.[15] It means an inner independence not only from the other two branches of government, but also from ideological and economic associations and powers within society in general – for example, media, trade unions and political parties – although judges may be active members of the latter. Whether a judge's behaviour is in violation of this rule must be determined by an objective bystander test – that is, by a test regarding the foundations of the dispute as seen by an objective and reasonable third person not party to the dispute.[16] It is clear, however, that the concept of independence, in its wide applicability, lacks sharp features.

Not surprisingly there is a great volume of literature and numerous court rulings[17] on the topic. One of the standard works is an article by the former presiding judge of the Federal Administrative Tribunal, Horst Sendler,[18] who distinguishes between utterances in the hearing, in the wording of the judgment,[19] public discussion in (legal) journals, parliamentary hearings and the media in general. He urges judges to use '*Pietät und Takt*', meaning moderation and non-offensive language. The more public interest there is in a matter, the more careful a judge should be when stating his opinion on a certain issue.

In 1984 the *Deutscher Richterbund* (German Judges' Association) published guidelines for its members on what judges and public prosecutors should take into account when making or reacting to public statements. They may serve as an example of what is probably the prevailing opinion within the judiciary today:

1. Statements about own decisions

1.1. When informing the public about the contents and reasons of judicial decisions, the rules laid down by the respective procedural laws should be heeded. Insofar as they expressly provide for manners of publication only these should be used.

1.2. If a judge or prosecutor are personally criticized for a decision, it is the duty of the administration [20] to protect them from such criticism.

1.3. If the public reporting of a decision is inaccurate, the administration should, especially on request by the judge or prosecutor, seek a correction.

1.4. For each court or prosecutor's office a press spokesperson should be appointed. It is his sole duty to inform the press about judicial and prosecutorial decisions. Only where this appears to be impracticable or unfeasible and where grave errors must be corrected, which could undermine the public's trust in the administration or justice, a statement by the judge or prosecutor concerned himself may be appropriate under certain circumstances.

1.5. Public criticism by a judge of decisions of his own court is usually inappropriate and, if the secret of deliberation is violated, unlawful.

2. Statements about the decisions of others

2.1. Judges and prosecutors may state their opinions on contemporary decisions of other judges and prosecutors, which capture the public's interest, and bring their experience into the debate. This follows from their responsibility as citizens.

2.2. Judges and prosecutors must not allege facts which have not been proven when making statements, they must exercise self-restraint in evaluations and respect the presumption of innocence as well as procedural safeguards in general. Such self-restraint is especially important in pending proceedings; the public's trust in the administration of justice must not be jeopardized.

3. Statements about issues of legal policy and general politics

3.1. Judges and prosecutors, as well as their professional organizations, may participate vigorously and in an outspoken fashion in the public discussion of matters of legal policy and general politics.

3.2. Demagogism and incitement to disobedience of the law are unlawful.

4. Professional title

Judges and prosecutors may add their title when making statements.[21]

Criticism by Parties and Lawyers

As with any other state subscribing to some form or other of the rule of law, parties to the proceedings before a certain judge and their counsel may criticize the judge for the way in which he handles the case. Especially important in this respect is the right to recuse a judge for fear of bias or to lodge a formal complaint (*Dienstaufsichtsbeschwerde*) with his superior judge. It is not necessary for a recusal motion to show that the judge is actually biased, but only that a reasonable, objective bystander in the same position as the petitioner would have sufficient reason to believe that the judge is biased.

It should be noted that a party's or lawyer's own behaviour (for example, when counsel insults the judge) cannot usually be reasonable grounds for a recusal, because then the parties would have the power to recuse any judge whom they disliked. The judge may answer this form of criticism by lodging a criminal complaint or suing the contemnor, and in the case of a party's, witness's or spectator's misbehaviour he may also impose summary sanctions, which remain, however, far below the contempt powers granted to judges in common law countries. German law does not recognize contempt powers for acts committed outside the courtroom.

A rather unique feature of the German law is that obstreperous counsel cannot be held in contempt at all when they appear before the judge in the proceedings and not merely as spectators or witnesses. They may not even be forcibly removed from the courtroom, unless they create a most severe disturbance; and, to my knowledge, the appellate courts have not yet decided such a case in favour of a judge. The only avenue left open to the judge is to file a complaint with the Bar Associations (*Rechtsanwaltskammern*) of which each lawyer must be a member, although the *Bundesrechtsanwaltskammer* has recently informed me that such complaints are few and far between: only one out of every 100 complaints about lawyers comes from courts.[22]

Nor are prosecutors subject to this sanctioning power, because, in respect of complaints of judges, they answer to their own superiors, and the system there seems to be efficient, given the teutonic penchant for obeying superiors.

Criticism in Disciplinary Proceedings/Impeachment

Judges, like any other civil servants, are subject to disciplinary control which may be invoked *ex officio* or by aggrieved persons through a formal complaint. This is regulated by s.26 of the DRiG:

(1). The judge shall be subject to disciplinary control only insofar as his independence is not infringed.

(2). Subject to subsection (1) the disciplinary control shall also cover the power to criticize the judge for the way he conducts his business and to urge him to conduct his business in an orderly and expeditious manner.

(3). If a judge alleges that a disciplinary measure infringes his independence, a court to be instituted by special act shall, on his motion, decide the dispute.

There is a mass of case law and literature on the issue and it is impossible to give even an outline of the practice, but suffice it to say that the courts responsible for hearing such disputes have traditionally taken a rather broad view of what violates judicial independence.[23] Thus, subsection (2) of s.26 of the DRiG might appear to be devoid of any substance, as recent decisions have held that a judge may not be blamed for the (lack of) speed with which he disposes of his cases, unless there is a clear indication that he does so out of laziness or lack of professional ethics. In my opinion, this sometimes goes too far, because judges are also assessed regularly on their professional performance and it can become very difficult for a disciplinary superior judge to put anything meaningful into such as assessment if the judge concerned tends to overstress his independence.

What happens in practice – according to the judicial grapevine – therefore is that superiors do, of course, evaluate the quality of the judge's work, including matters which fall squarely into the realm of his independence, and that promotions are decided in the sphere of informal meetings of the presiding judges and the ministry. It is traded as an open secret among judges, for example, that even though placements for promotions must be advertised so that any judge may apply for the post, the choice will usually have been made before the advertisement is published and that the desired candidate has already been asked to put in his application and will receive an assessment which cannot be beaten by any other contender.[24] The lack of meaningful criticism which sometimes applies to judicial job performance may therefore be a reason for clandestine nepotism.[25]

Fully tenured judges may be removed from office for administrative reasons mentioned in s.21 of the DRiG and, according to s.24, for misconduct, but only after a final court order stating the misbehaviour and sentencing the judge to imprisonment of more than one year for an intentional and not merely negligent offence or for treason, to loss of eligibility to public office or to forfeiture of a *Grundrecht* – that is, a civil right under the Constitution. The tenure ends automatically when such a judgment becomes final.

The German Constitution provides for an impeachment procedure in Article 98, subs. 2 of the *Grundgesetz*. A federal judge may be impeached by a motion of the Bundestag before the *Bundesverfassungsgericht* (Federal Constitutional Court) on an allegation that he has violated the federal constitution or that of one of the *Länder*. The *Bundesverfassungsgericht* may then decide, on a two-thirds majority, that the judge may be transferred to another court or retired; if the court finds that the violation was intentional it may also order removal from office. Similar provisions exist for state judges. This procedure has never been used.[26]

Criticism by the Media

Sometimes the most trying attacks for a judge can be those made by or through the media. The media enjoy an almost unfettered freedom under Article 5 of the Constitution and it is a formidable task for anyone hit by media criticism to retaliate or protect his honour. The *Bundesverfassungsgericht* and the federal courts have traditionally held strongly in favour of the press and the media when politicians or matters of public interest have been involved. The latter is almost always, but not necessarily only, the case with judicial or prosecutorial decisions in high-profile cases. Judges are in no different position from private citizens when they want to react to media criticism of their behaviour in their official capacity. For them, the general principles of the civil and criminal law apply.

The victims of criticism by the media may institute civil proceedings for libel and slander or bring the offender before a criminal court for the same offences. A severe obstacle for any action against the media is the defence of *'Wahrnehmung berechtigter Interessen'* (acting in justified interests) which means that the media may report on any issue which is, or might be, of interest to the public and should therefore be brought to its attention. This defence goes a long way. And even if there is no objective defence in a certain case, the offender may be exculpated if he has used the necessary care and diligence in his research for the publication, and it is difficult, if not impossible, for the aggrieved party to obtain the research materials used by the offender in order to demonstrate that he did not use such diligence. The law on this matter is extremely complicated and cannot be fully explained in this short introduction.[27]

Criticism by the Government or Political Parties

The judiciary is only one of the three branches of government. Its actions often collide with the interests of the executive or, to a lesser extent, the legislature and, through them, with those of the political parties. The judiciary is, of course, not exempt from criticism by the other two powers for politically unpopular decisions, as the judges of the *Bundesverfassungsgericht* have frequently discovered in recent years – examples are the abortion issue, whether the soldiers of the *Bundeswehr* may be called 'murderers'[28] and the issue of a Bavarian law prescribing that a crucifix must be installed in every public school classroom.[29] The government may legitimately express its dissatisfaction with a court ruling but, especially in recent years and with politically sensitive matters, such criticism has sometimes gone too far – so far that, in some cases, judges and prosecutors have more or less explicitly been accused of perverting the course of justice.

A blatant example is the 1996 case of the search and seizure of confidential official documents in newspaper offices and radio stations in the North German city state of Bremen, where a report of the official auditing authority (*Rechnungshof*) of the city had been leaked to the media because it contained incriminating material against one of the top officials of the government, a member of the Social Democratic Party, about serious mismanagement of taxpayers' money.[30] The president of the *Rechnungshof* lodged a criminal complaint with the prosecution service, after he had been confronted with a complete copy of the report during a radio interview. The prosecution applied for judicial search warrants for some newspaper offices and radio stations where the copies were supposed to have been sent, and the court granted them. The offices were searched and the copies found and seized.

Legally, the whole procedure was legitimate,[31] yet the city parliament (called the *'Bürgerschaft'*), consisting of members of the Social Democrat and Christian Democrat Parties, in a quite unprecedented move, distanced itself from the prosecution and the examining judge, calling the searches 'attempts at intimidation' of the freedom of the press. The prosecutor-general was threatened with disciplinary proceedings for not informing the minister before the searches were carried out – which he was not at all obliged to do under the existing law– but these were eventually dropped; nevertheless, he was sacked from his post as press spokesman of the administration of justice. The parliament even went so far as to issue the statement, that 'notwithstanding the legal evaluation' of the search, 'it violated the principle of proportionality'.[32] This shows, by the way, the quality of the statement because, according to German constitutional theory, this principle is one of the fundamental aspects of the rule of law.

The media, of course, eagerly joined in the hue and cry and the *Deutscher Journalistenverband* (German Journalists' Union) in an act of fierce criticism of the administration of justice demanded that 'it was high time that prosecutors and judges be shown their limits'.[33] The Social Democrat party whip called the responsible prosecutor 'crazy'.[34] There is no report that any of the judges or prosecutors involved took action against this massive intimidation by the parliament and the political parties, apart from the joint protest by the presiding judge of the Court of Appeal and the prosecutor-general. It would have been useless, anyway, in my opinion.[35]

Conclusion

I am a judge and I therefore cannot claim to hold totally unbiased views about how the criticism of judges should be treated. In fact, I would like to see something like the power to cite for contempt of court that judges have in the USA or England implemented in the German system. I may be rather isolated in this respect, probably even amongst my colleagues. While it is true that German judges may generally say much more in public on matters of general politics than their British or American counterparts would consider appropriate, does this really compensate for being unable to sanction intrusions by other branches of government, by political parties, the media and disruptive counsel? I often have doubts. Few judges make use of the right of freedom of expression to begin with. If a judge does say anything in court, in his judgments or in public, the consequences depend on whether anybody takes offence at his words and who takes offence: those few with power and members of organizations with a large lobby have powerful weapons with which to retaliate and they are *de facto*, and sometimes even *de jure*, exempt from court sanctions. German law-makers may find it worthwhile to reflect on whether a judiciary armed with sanctions to punish contemptuous behaviour and severe intrusions on the functionality and integrity of the courts might also not be one of the 'highest goods of a free society',[36] because people, after all, want judges to be independent and free of subalternism of any kind. They are meant to guarantee that the system of checks and balances works in practice and is not undermined by private interests and connections. I believe that, apart from the fact that judges already do so through their judgments, they need at least a dormant, but readily available, power to react to intrusions which cannot be dealt with by sanctions under the current law, but require the individual judge or prosecutor to take on the offenders like a private citizen. Such a situation does not do justice to the fact that they have been attacked as representatives of the only impartial branch of government, and not as private citizens. It is difficult to understand why attacks on police officers should be the object of a separate criminal offence, while there is no counterpart for judges – for example, in the form of a contempt provision.

Of all countries, the socialist German Democratic Republic in its last days, after civil disobedience of the *Wende* and many bitter experiences with regard to the intimidation of judges and meddling with the administration of justice by the party and executive, introduced a provision in its criminal code which made it an offence to intimidate or obstruct judges in the execution of their duty. This provision was retained by the Unification Treaty for the new East German states, but has been scrapped by the last criminal law reform, the reason being that, in the new system dedicated to the rule of law, such a provision is no longer necessary. One wonders if the judges in Bremen, for instance, would subscribe to that view.

Notes

1   The views expressed in this chapter are my own and do not represent those of the UN or ICTY. For reasons of simplicity I have used the male pronoun throughout the text. I would like to thank Peter Marqua of the *Deutscher Richterbund* and the *Bundesrechtsanwaltskammer* for making materials available to me.

2   By *German* I mean the law of the Federal Republic which came into force in the five new *Länder* after reunification. For a discussion of the law of the GDR and the transition period after 1990 see Michael Bohlander, 'United We Stand: The German Judiciary after the Unification', *Anglo-American Law Review*, **21** (1992), p. 415 and Schmidt-Ränsch, *Deutsches Richtergesetz, Commentary*, 5th edn, (1995), pp. 53-62 with references.

3   Articles 102–104 (*Reichsgesetzblatt* 1919, 1383).

4   The text reads *Gesetz* (act), but according to the prevailing opinion this also covers unwritten law; see, for example, R. Herzog in Maunz, T. Dürig, G. and R. Herzog, *Grundgesetz, Commentary*, Vol. IV (Munich: C.H. Beck, 1996), Article 97, paras 13–32 and Schmidt-Ränsch, *Deutsches Richtergesetz, op. cit.*, s.25, para. 11 with references.

5   Cited after A. Wagner, *Der Richter* (Karlsruhe: C.F. Müller, 1959), p. 68.
6   Ibid., p. 72.
7   Ibid., p. 74.
8   Ibid., p. 76.
9   On the process of reform and a view of the time see E. Schiffer, *Die deutsche Justiz; Grundzüge einer durchgreifenden Reform* (Munich: Biederstein Verlag, 1949).
10 For further reference see the bibliography in Schmidt-Ränsch, *Deutsches Richtergesetz, op. cit.*, s.25, at the beginning.
11 See for the distinction and some examples, ibid., s.25, paras 5–10.
12 References to the state judiciary acts can be found in ibid., Anhang Nr.7.
13 For the other jurisdictions see ibid., s.26, paras 8–16.
14 See ibid., s.39, para. 2.
15 Ibid., s.39, para. 5.
16 Dienstgerichtshof Celle, *Neue Juristische Wochenschrift* (1990), p. 1498.
17 See the references at Schmidt-Ränsch, *Deutsches Richtergesetz, op. cit.*, s.39.
18 *Neue Juristische Wochenschrift* (1984), p. 689.
19 Each judgment must contain a reasoned explanation of the court's ruling, stating the facts deemed proven and the law applied.
20 Meaning the presiding judge or committee of the court and the superior judges, the prosecutor general and the ministry.
21 Published by *Deutsche Richterzeitung* (1984), p. 116; author's translation. Further examples may be found in the article by K. Rudolph, 'Öffentliche Äusserungen von Richtern and Staatsanwälten', *Deutsche Richterzeitung*, **55** (1987), p. 33.
22 The legal profession interprets this as proof of the impeccable ethical nature of Germany's lawyers. I and many of my colleagues tend to see it as a sign that judges have given up trying to get the Bar to take care of their own black sheep. Another reason may be that there is too much comity between lawyers and judges, something about which the 1970 report by the American Bar Association, Special Committee on Evaluation of Disciplinary Enforcement, *Problems and Recommendations in Disciplinary Enforcement* [the so-called 'Clark Report'] had already complained of in the United States.
23 See, for example, the references in Schmidt-Ränsch, *Deutsches Richtergesetz, op. cit.*, s.26.
24 No presiding judge or minister would publicly admit this, however.
25 A striking example for this is the patronage by political parties for posts at the federal supreme courts. A friend of mine, Christian Latour, who is an attorney, and I have recently undertaken a survey among the judges of the *Bundesgerichtshof* on this subject with the consent of the court's presiding judge. About 50 of the 121 judges replied to our questionnaire and the results showed a tendency that judges who are members of political parties are, on average, appointed faster than non-party members and that their professional qualifications are on average lower than those of the others. A German summary of the survey has been published in the *Zeitschrift für Rechtspolitik* (1997), p. 437.
26 However, one judge of the *Landgericht* in Mannheim recently came very close to being the first to be impeached because of the way in which he formulated the reasons of a judgment against a leader of a neo-fascist party, Deckert, when the division sentenced him for inciting racial hatred. The reasons of the judgment drafted by Judge Orlet expressed a certain amount of sympathy for the defendant's ideological views and caused an outrage amongst the media and the legal public in Germany. See, on this case, G. Bertram, 'Entrüstungssturm im Medienzeitalter – Der BGH und die Auschwitzlüge', *Neue Juristische Wochenschrift*, **47** (1994), p. 2002 and 'Noch einmal: Die Auschwitzlüge – Anmerkungen zum Urteil der 6. Grossen Strafkammer des Landgerichts Mannheim vom 22.6.1994' at

p. 2397; also G. Wasserman, 'Richteranklage im Fall Orlet?', *Neue Juristische Wochenschrift*, **48** (1995), p. 303 – each with further references. The sentence was quashed by the Bundesgerichtshof and the case remanded to another Landgericht of the same judicial district, Karlsruhe, which finally sentenced Deckert to 3 years' imprisonment. Orlet still sits in the same court.

27   For an excellent treatise of the whole area of law see M. Löffler and R. Ricker, *Handbuch des Presserechts*, 3rd edn, (Munich: C.H. Beck, 1994), chs 16, 17, 41–44 and 53.

28   They may. See the judgment in *Amtliche Sammlung der Entscheidungen des Bundesverfassungsgerichts*, vol. 93 (Cologne: Heymanns Verlag), p. 266 with a dissenting opinion by Judge Haas at p. 313. The decision, which was passed with a majority of five to three judges, caused widespread public outrage and has led to a bill for the introduction of a special criminal provision protecting the integrity of the armed forces. See H. Tröndle, *Strafgesetzbuch, Commentary*, 48th edn (Munich: C.H. Beck, 1997), s.193 paras 14n–14p with references.

29   It was held to be unconstitutional, but Bavaria is now trying to circumvent the decision by introducing a new law which provides for the possibility of taking them down if a pupil opposes the practice.

30   See on this the article by K.-H. Kunert, 'Recht, Presse und Politik – Von einer unglücklichen Dreierbeziehung in Bremen', *Deutsche Richterzeitung*, **75** (1997), p. 325.

31   Although there has been some criticism from another judge, Christian Zorn, in his letter to the editor in *Deutsche Richterzeitung* (1997), p. 526. See also the comment by Helmut Waller, a former prosecutor-general, in *Deutsche Richterzeitung* (1997), p. 527.

32   Kunert, *Deutsche Richterzeitung, op. cit.*, at p. 327.

33   Ibid.

34   *TAZ*, 29 August 1996.

35   This example shows quite clearly, why I cannot accept the statement of Barend van Niekerk in his book, *The Cloistered Virtue: Freedom of Speech and the Administration of Justice in the Western World* (London: Praeger, 1987), p. 71, that a fiercely criticized judiciary is one of the highest goods of a free society. Such criticism almost invariably is instrumentalized through the media and more often than not by people who have a political axe to grind without having regard to the damage they might cause of other fundamental values of society, or the personal harm they inflict on their victims for purely political gains. There is no fair opportunity for the criticized to state their point of view with the same amount of publicity as their opponents, because that would mean using the forum of the very people they want to criticize in turn. In my experience, at least in high-profile cases, the media must often be forced, through the courts, to give their victims a platform to voice their view of the affair and they try everything in their power to prevent it, invoking the freedom of the press. Thus, not without some justification, they have been called 'The fourth branch of government'.

36   Ibid., p. 71.

5   Recusing Judges in Austria

J. Michael Rainer and Thomas Tschaler

Introduction

If the expression 'criticizing judges' is understood strictly, every form of criticism of judges falls within this term. However, in the context of the following discussion, it should not be overlooked that the challenging and questioning of decisions made by a judge, regardless of whether this is of purely procedural or factual nature, is to be distinguished from the questioning of the judge as a person. The opportunity to challenge decisions of a judge in his official capacity can usually be found, to a satisfactory extent, in the rules of procedure of all countries with a constitutional order and an obligation to respect human rights[1]. In modern and effective laws of procedure the availability of judicial remedies and different stages of appeal afford the possibility of challenging decisions which may be annulled or modified as a result.[2]

All human beings are fallible in their actions, and so is the judge. Decisions and orders can be wrong, incomplete or defective. Findings of such a nature infringe not only the legally protected position of the parties but they also endanger the effectiveness of the whole legal system in so far as the public interest in the administration of justice opposes wrong decisions.[3] Only by having the possibility of challenging judges' decisions may the quality of decisions and the guarantee of a uniform application of the law be achieved.[4]

The issue to be analysed in this chapter is, however, not the judicial remedies available to oppose a legal decision but, primarily, the possibilities of preventing a situation in which a judge whose impartiality and other attitudes towards the case are doubtful and therefore to be questioned, is involved in decisions. The problems to be dealt with here are, first, the disqualification of a judge on the grounds of bias or public discredit and, second, the protection of the judge against an unjustified exclusion from the case. These two cases, which have to be located in the preliminary stages of proceedings, are to be distinguished from those situations in which the controversial judge has already made a decision, leading to the question of how this decision can be challenged. Another differentiation has to be made in terms of when the reasons for the distrust in the concerned judge occurred and were revealed. If the reasons for objection occurred after the proceedings, they cannot be held to have affected the proceedings. Alternatively, facts may have occurred before the start of the proceedings but were not, or could not, be brought to the attention of the court. In these cases a decision already made without a motion of disqualification prior to the proceedings may be challenged as the only way to reveal the grievance relating to the judge in question. The appeal against the judgment then also represents the objection to the judge.

The Court System in Austria

Basic provisions on the Austrian court system can be found in the Constitution and several federal statutes.[5] According to Article 10, subs. 6 of the Bundesverfassungsgerichtsgesetz (B-VG) both the legislative and executive power in the areas of civil law and criminal law and therefore also procedural matters in these areas fall within the exclusive competence of the federation. Exceptions to this principle, allowing the federal states to legislate in the areas of civil and criminal law, exist only to a very limited extent, based on a special competence laid down in Article 15, s.9 of the B-VG. Further fundamental provisions can be found in Articles 82–94 of the B-VG. Some of these provisions concerning the position of the judges are of particular importance for the issues dealt with in this chapter.

The jurisdiction forms part of the enforcement and is the counterpart of the administration. These two areas of implementation are separated from each other in all instances.[6] According to Article 82 of the B-VG all jurisdiction emanates from the federation. It follows that there are only courts of the federation and none of the federal states,[7] although this does not exclude the obligation of these courts to apply state law. According to this Article no one may be removed from the jurisdiction of his or her lawful judge. This rule is valid not only for the jurisdiction but also, contrary to the wording, for the administration.[8] Through this principle everybody has the constitutionally guaranteed right to a decision by the competent state organ – competent both in respect of the subject matter and as an entity.

From statutory provisions[9] follows the allocation of the jurisdiction to district courts, state courts, higher regional courts of appeal and the Supreme Court as final instance[10]. Not all proceedings start before a district court and end before the Supreme Court. The sequence of stages of appeal depends on the subject matter in civil proceedings and the severity of the offence in criminal proceedings. The procedural laws also provide for especially established committees and senates as instances of complaint for certain acts.[11] All these institutions serve to guarantee constitutional and lawful proceedings and effective judicial remedies.

Judicial Independence

A functioning and independent apparatus of execution for the area of jurisdiction can only be guaranteed if the institutions set up for this purpose, or the administrators who exercise the organ's functions, have a firm and strengthened position. One feature of the so-called judicial guarantees is the position of the judge in Austria. Judges are appointed to an established post.[12] From the time of appointment they are protected by judicial guarantees which include, according to Article 87, s.1 of the B-VG, the judge's independence. However, he enjoys independence only in exercise of his judicial function – that is, when he handles any of the judicial duties assigned to him by law and the assignment of business and any of the issues of legal administration that are, by law, to be dealt with by senates and commissions.[13] The nature of judicial independence is made up of the comprehensive freedom not to take directives in any of the areas mentioned above.[14] Judges' security of tenure (they are not to be dismissed or transferred) is also an attribute of judicial independence, although they must retire, on a pension, at the age of 65.[15] Also a judge can and may be transferred to another post or into retirement or removed from his office against his will only in cases and forms specified by law and subject to a formal decision.[16] Removal from office is a contrary act to appointment; transfer means the move from one judge post while at the same time being appointed to another established judge post; and transfer into retirement means that, while the title of judge is formally retained, the judge involved is released from the duty of further service.[17] Non-transferability means that the judge may neither be ordered to serve at another court, nor may his area of competence at his original court be changed without his consent.[18] The guarantees described above are enjoyed by all judges.[19]

Article 87, s.3 of the B-VG constitutionally establishes the rule that the assignment of business for every judge is fixed in advance for the calendar year according to objective criteria; this provides for securing factual independence of influence in respect of the assignment of business for every judge.[20] To ensure that cases are assigned randomly to judges, the common practice in Austria is to distribute cases to judges alphabetically, using the first letter of the plaintiff's surname in civil cases and the first letter of the accused's surname in criminal cases.[21] Therefore, it is impossible for a court clerk or the federal minister of justice to doctor the distribution of cases and give certain cases to certain judges or, indeed, for a certain judge to pick which cases he deals with.[22] Inconsistencies regarding the question as to which judge gets which case therefore automatically do not arise.

In civil proceedings, according to para. 477, s.1, subs. 2 of the Zivilprozessardnung (ZPO), the participation of a judge who participates in a case which has not been appointed to him by the assignment of business constitutes a reason for annulment on the grounds of improper constitution of the court. However, this type of procedural mistake does not automatically render the judgment void, but can only be used as a reason to annul a decision either *ex officio* or if the parties to the case formally objected to the judge's presence at the beginning of the oral hearing of the case.

In contrast to civil proceedings in which the infringement of the assignment of business is regarded as a ground for annulment, even if only a relative one, the rule is different for criminal proceedings. In the opinion of the Oberster Gerichtshof (OGH), deviations from the assignment of business do not account for an improperly constituted court within the meaning of para. 281 s.1, subs. 1 of the Strafprozessordnung (StPO)[24]. Accordingly, in criminal proceedings there is no possibility of correcting a disregard of the assignment of business by means of legal remedies.[25]

The Consequences of Judicial Independence

The judgeship is a two-edged issue in this respect. On the one hand, the legal guarantee of freedom from directives[26] and the judge's non-removability and non-transferability[27] provide for their independence and impartiality. On the other hand, these guarantees might protect the judge from attacks which may be justified in terms of the administration of justice or which might be admissible and even useful in terms of finding out the truth and the law. Concrete examples might be activities undertaken outside judicial work that influence the judge's opinions and may drive him to a biased consideration of evidence, to preconceived opinions (for example, xenophobia, hostility towards women and so on) to a certain sociopolitical or partisan viewpoint or to a deeply-rooted belief in certain stereotypes. There undeniably exists an area of conflict between the level of protection necessary for judicial work and an excessive protection that has a negative, rather than positive, effect on the administration of justice. This raises the question as to whether the provisions for the disqualification and exclusion of judges laid down in the Austrian rules of procedure are satisfactory to sufficiently safeguard the impartiality of judges without excessively narrowing down the freedom of decision and discretion necessary for a judge to perform his duties properly.

Being independent, different judges can arrive at different conclusions on the same set of facts. Everybody is different. For this reason, even if the same law is being applied the decision is influenced fairly significantly by the judge's personality, his experiences, his world-view and even by his personal mood. The constitutional guarantees of the judgeship can only secure the judge's independence and impartiality in the abstract but cannot prevent his bias in an individual case.[28]. However, abstract independence and impartiality is of no interest to the parties. They desire a more concrete independence since, otherwise, no correct judgment can be expected. In other words, only the non-existence of any sort of relationship with the legal case to be decided or with any of the parties, and therefore only concrete objectivity, is of practical importance. Consequently, specific attention need not be directed towards the constitutional bases here but towards preventing judges from making decisions preconceived by the nature of the case or its background and therefore operating on the basis of biased opinions. The instrument of disqualification and exclusion of judges secures concrete objectivity.[29] In this context, therefore, the options available to the parties and their legal representatives to take legal action against a judge who, in whatsoever form, is impaired in his objectivity towards a specific case, and how this relates to the issue of protecting the judge, has to be explained.

The Recusing of a Judge

Unfortunately, the law of civil procedure does not contain a descriptive list of possible grounds of bias.[30] According to the wording of the law any adequate reason is sufficient to assume bias and, hence, to call into question the judge's impartiality.[31] As this succinct statutory statement is not very helpful, its contents have to be put into more concrete terms. According to the established practice of the courts, a judge is to be considered biased if circumstances are known which, after an objective and impartial examination and assessment, justify the questioning of his impartiality.[32] The nature of the bias is irrelevant if it *prima facie* hinders impartial decisions. Generally, it is considered a sufficient reason within the meaning of the provision if the judge has quarrelled or is friendly with one of the parties, if he is, or was, engaged to one of them or to one of their closest relatives, if he is a partner of a company or cooperative or a member of a club involved in the proceedings, if he makes irrelevant personal remarks to the parties or their legal representatives, if he gives them (legal) advice or if there are personal disagreements with the parties' legal representatives.[33]

A judge's membership of a political party is no reason for bias unless he has already publicly declared his position on the decisive issue of the lawsuit.[34] Further examples can be found in Fasching's *Zivilprozeßrecht.*[35] Austrian databases contain more than 1000 documents on the topic of judges'bias.[36] The examples given above are therefore only an illustration.

Reasons for Recusing a Judge

Unlike the grounds for bias, for which there is no detailed statutory provision, the reasons for disqualification are laid down in para. 20 of the Jurisdiktionsnorm (JN) and para. 537 of the ZPO. The lists are exhaustive.[37] Judges are, amongst other things, excluded from sitting on the bench in civil proceedings[38] in actions to which they themselves are a party or in regard of which they and one of the parties are jointly entitled, jointly obliged or jointly liable to recourse and in actions involving their spouses and other persons to whom they are related. On this topic, too, many cases and materials can be found, although the volume of material is relatively small as a result of the detailed statutory provision.

In civil proceedings the grounds for disqualification can be enforced upon application of the parties (that is, the parties can instigate exclusion of the judge), as well as *ex officio*.[39] If the judge considers himself prejudiced he has to inform the head of the court and, until a final decision has been made, is allowed to carry out only those judicial activities which cannot be delayed.[40] If it is evident that the intention behind challenging judge is merely to delay the proceedings the judge concerned may continue to sit on the case, but is not entitled to make a final decision on the matter until the application for disqualification has been finally rejected. If the application for reclusion is carried, the judicial acts of the judge involved have to be declared void.[41] The judicial acts of the judge involved carried out between the time of the application for recusion and the time at which the decision becomes final are held in abeyance.[42]

The Appeal Against a Decision made after an Application for Recusion

If a disqualified judge has made a decision before the application for recusion has been finally decided, the decision to appeal against this decision is to be made only after the final decision on the motion for disqualification.[43] If the motion is carried, bringing an appeal is not necessary[44] as, in this case, the legal consequence of the successful motion is to render the decision null and void, thereby making an appeal redundant. If, however, the motion for disqualification is rejected, the judge's decision is not void, but at most defective, which, however, does not affect its validity and which, consequently, is not to be considered in subsequent appeal proceedings.[45] The right of the party who challenged the judge to bring an appeal is, hence, dependent on the final decision on the motion for disqualification. Whether or not the judge's decision is void is to be declared only after the decision on the motion.[46] This legal opinion is supported by para. 477, s.1, subs. 1 of the ZPO. According to this provision, a judgment in the delivery of which a challenged judge took part must be declared void if the challenge has been confirmed as justified. However, it would be incorrect to assume that the mere fact that there is doubt about the position of the judge in a case constitutes a procedural irregularity that can lead to the case being annulled. The law orders the annulment of the judgment only if the motion for disqualification is finally carried and leaves the challenged judgment unaffected if the motion remains unsuccessful. Until the decision on the challenge the effectiveness of the decision – as already mentioned above – is held in abeyance. The cited provision would not make sense if the challenged judge's decision could be quashed before the decision on the disqualification on the grounds of procedural irregularities. This would anticipate the consequence of annulment on the grounds of the formal rejection of the judge. The Court of Appeal, therefore, has to wait for the final decision on the motion for disqualification before deciding on the question of nullity within the meaning of para. 477, s.1 subs.1 of the ZPO.

To summarize: if a motion for disqualification is rejected, a challenge of the final decision merely on the grounds of the judge's bias will involve significant difficulties since it is not the existence of a ground for bias itself but only the final decision for exclusion on the grounds of bias that results in the judicial acts carried out by the disqualified judge becoming null and void. A consequence is that grounds of bias concerning the initial proceedings, but revealed only after the decision on the disqualification has become final, cannot be considered any more and therefore cannot form the basis of an action for annulment.[47]

The Appeal Against a Decision made Without Previous Application for Recusion

With regard to this situation one must distinguish strictly between the subsequent revelation of reasons for bias and the subsequent revelation of reasons for exclusion. Reasons for exclusion are peremptory and have to be enforced *ex officio* as grounds for nullity in every stage of proceedings, including subsequent appeal proceedings, and they are enforceable even after the decision has become final due to an action for annulment.[48] Revealed reasons for bias, on the other hand, must be put forward immediately – that is, by the end of the main hearing before the court of first instance – as it is inadmissible to put forward grounds for bias which were known already during the procedure before the court of first instance during the proceedings on appeal against this decision.[49] If the reason, or reasons, for the sitting judge's bias were already known at the beginning of the proceedings – or, at least, become known before the end of the hearing before the court of first instance – and if nevertheless no formal application to reject the judge concerned was lodged, then the appearance in court of the party who is in full knowledge of the reasons of bias is to be considered as a tacit waiver of their enforcement.[50] In these cases a later enforcement, especially in appeal proceedings against the decision of the court of first instance, is precluded.

If reasons that could justify the disqualification of the judge in the lower instance only become known after the end of the hearing before the court of first instance – in other words, if they become known only during the appeal proceedings – they have to be put forward before the court of first instance by means of a special application for rejection. The appeal proceedings then must be suspended until the final decision on the motion for disqualification has been made. If the motion of disqualification is carried, the proceedings carried out by the challenged judge, including all decision issued in the course of it, will be declared void and the proceedings in process will be terminated as without object.[51] In such cases, therefore, a judge can also be disqualified after the end of the hearing and after passing judgment.[52]

Like the law of civil procedure, the law of criminal procedure also does not contain any satisfactory regulations concerning the disqualification of a judge on the grounds of bias. In the Code of Criminal Procedure only a vague general formulation can be found. According to the wording, a judge (and any other member of the court) can be challenged if there are reasons which are likely to call the full impartiality of the person concerned into question.[53] Therefore reasons for disqualification are all circumstances which impair the receptiveness of the judge to all incriminating and exonerating arguments or which at least give the impression that the judge lacks the due openness.[54] A specific suspicion that the judge will actually be led by considerations other than legally relevant ones – that is, unlawful ones – is not necessary.[55] The fact that the judge holds certain legal opinions,[56] has participated in the sentencing of an accomplice,[57] has drawn up a draft judgment before the main hearing or, has, with justification, indicated his preliminary opinion,[58] does not represent a reason for rejection. In other respects concerning the contents of the provision on grounds for bias in criminal proceedings, one can refer, due to the similar wording, to the explanations given above on the corresponding provision in the Code of Civil Procedure.

Certain similarities to the law of civil procedure can also be found with regard to the reasons for exclusion. In criminal proceedings, too, unlike the reasons for bias, the reasons for exclusion are laid down exhaustively in the law.[59] For appropriate examples see Bertel.[60]

In civil proceedings both the reasons for bias and the reasons for exclusion are to be enforced either upon application of the parties or *ex officio*.[61] Here again, if the judge considers himself prejudiced he has to come forward on his own initiative.[62] If a judge who is later excluded did not fulfil this obligation and took part both in the proceedings and in the delivery of a judgment, the judgment is void. The same is true if a disqualified judge, who was not himself aware of the circumstances, delivers a judgment or takes part in the proceedings.[63] If an application for rejection is wrongfully refused, the judgment is void as well.[64] Evidence taken by the excluded judge can be void.[65] If the evidence is nevertheless used in the main hearing the judgment is void, too.[66]

Known reasons for disqualification or exclusion in the person of the deciding judge have to be put forward before the main hearing or immediately after its beginning; reasons for disqualification or exclusion in the person of the appellate judge have to be put forward at the latest during the appeal proceedings.[67] Reasons for disqualification and exclusion which have occurred or have been revealed only subsequently have to be asserted immediately.[68] In criminal proceedings there are no absolute time limits and, contrary to civil procedure, there is no presumption that the accused has waived his or her right to have the case retrospectively annulled if he or she submits to the jurisdiction of the court.

Other Expressions of Disapproval with Regard to the Person of the Judge by the Parties or their Legal Representatives

Apart from the formal disqualification of a judge it remains to be examined how other expressions of disapproval by the parties and their representatives are dealt with and, in particular, which limits are set by the rules of procedure to protect the judge.

In order to maintain order and prevent disturbances the court has the authority to condemn breaches of the rules of order. This task of presiding over a hearing includes the power to impose certain sanctions. Anybody whose conduct during a civil proceedings hearing is unbecoming and who continues to disturb despite calls of order can be removed from the courtroom. In addition to this, a disciplinary fine can be imposed on all persons with the exception of lawyers and notaries who are subject to their professional code of conduct.[69] Consequently, any open criticism of the judge is permissible only as long as it takes place in a way regarding the due respect towards the court.

In criminal hearings any expressions of approval or disapproval are prohibited.[70] This rule is primarily targeted at spectators, but it can be assumed that the parties and their representatives are also obliged to behave in correspondence with the occasion and the dignity of the court, even if they have objections against the judge. The defendant can be removed during the hearing if he or she continues to disturb despite repeated warnings.[71] Other parties, such as the plaintiff in a private prosecution case or other privately involved persons, are likewise bound by the rules of procedure with respect to the proper conduct in the courtroom.[72] The possibilities of imposing sanctions on the legal representatives of parties depend on whether or not they are subject to the disciplinary powers of the professional authority. Whereas against the former only the sanction of refusing to grant the right to speak is admissible, the latter can be fined.[73] In criminal proceedings the possibilities of expressing disapproval are likewise very small. They are limited to formally challenging the judge as provided for by the rules of procedure and, if applicable, to protesting against his conduct.

Conclusion

Despite the possibility of disqualifying and excluding a judge and the fact that the rules of procedures provide for certain sanctions, the specially protected position of the judge appears to be all-powerful in relation to that of the parties. This is mainly because it is primarily the parties' responsibility to demonstrate the facts for the grounds of exclusion and bias and because the parties have to bear all disadvantages deriving from their inability to demonstrate the necessary facts. Despite the fact that this procedural situation is unsatisfactory from the parties' viewpoint, the protection which the judge enjoys is nevertheless indispensable in the interests of a well functioning justice system.

Notes

1   Article 6, s.1 of the ECHR, stating that 'everyone is entitled to a fair and public hearing within a reasonable time by an independent and impartial tribunal established by law'; paras 461 to 547 of the ZPO and paras 280 (proceedings involving lay judges), 340 (proceedings involving a jury), 463 (proceedings before the BG) and 489 of the StPO (individual judges at the court of first instance).
2   H.W. Fasching, *Zivilprozeßrecht*, 2nd edn (Vienna: Manz Verlag, 1990), point 1659.
3   Ibid.
4   Article 7 of the B-VG and Article 2 of the StGG.
5   For a general overview see Fasching, *Zivilprozeßrecht*, *op. cit.*, point 39 *et seq.*
6   Article 94 of the B-VG.
7   Fasching, *Zivilprozeßrecht*, *op. cit.*, point 81.
8   Ibid.
9   For an overview see ibid., point 40 *et seq.*
10   However, the OGH is established by the Constitution; cf. Article 92 of the B-VG. Its powers are guaranteed by Article 6 of the ECHR.
11   The chamber of the council set up by para. 12 of the StPO.
12   Concerning the requirements of qualification to become a judge, cf. Fasching, *Zivilprozeßrecht*, *op. cit.*, point 140.
13   On the exceptions cf. ibid., point 141.
14   R. Walter and H. Mayer, *Grundriß des Bundesverfassungsrechts*, 7th edn (Vienna: Manz Verlag, 1992), point 770.

15 Article 88, s.1 of the B-VG.
16 Article 88, s.2 of the B-VG.
17 Walter and Mayer, *Grundriß, op. cit.*, point 772.
18 VfSlg 8523.
19 VfSlg 1687, 1985.
20 Fasching, *Zivilprozeßrecht, op. cit.*, point 142.
21 C. Bertel, *Grundriß des österreichischen Strafprozeßrechts*, 4th edn (Vienna: Manz Verlag, 1994), point 192.
22 Fasching, *Zivilprozeßrecht, op. cit.*
23 Ibid., point 143.
24 SSt 56/31 and SSt 41/71.
25 Bertel, *Grundriß des Strafprozeßrechts, op. cit.*, point 192.
26 Article 87 of the B-VG.
27 Article 88 of the B-VG.
28 Fasching, *Zivilprozeßrecht, op. cit.*, point 160.
29 Ibid.
30 Ibid., point 164.
31 Para. 19, subs. 2 of the JN.
32 EvBl 1988, 43.
33 Fasching, *Zivilprozeßrecht, op. cit.*, point 164.
34 OGH in EvBl 1988, 43.
35 Fasching, *Zivilprozeßrecht, op. cit.*, point 164.
36 The result of a search in the RDB with the term 'Ablehnung von Richtern' ('disqualification of judges').
37 Fasching, *Zivilprozeßrecht, op. cit.*, point 163.
38 For a complete overview of the grounds for exclusion consult the cited provisions.
39 Fasching, *Zivilprozeßrecht, op. cit.*, point 161.
40 Para. 25 of the JN.
41 Fasching, *Zivilprozeßrecht, op. cit.*, point 161.
42 OGH in SZ 41/164.
43 Ibid.
44 The last sentence of Para. 25 of the JN.
45 OGH in SZ 41/164.
46 Ibid.
47 Fasching, *Zivilprozeßrecht, op. cit.*, point 162.
48 Ibid., point 161; OGH in SZ 43/104.
49 Fasching, *Zivilprozeßrecht, op. cit.*
50 Ibid.
51 Ibid.
52 OGH in SZ 43/104.
53 Para. 72, s.1 of the StPO.
54 Bertel, *Grundiß, op. cit.*, point 202.
55 Ibid.; cf. OGH in AnwBl 1989, 158.
56 EvBl 1980/160.
57 SSt 52/29.
58 Bertel, *Grundiß, op. cit.*
59 Paras 68 and 69 of the StPO.
60 Bertel, *Grundriß, op. cit.*, point 194 *et seq.*
61 Ibid., point 203.
62 Para. 70, s.1 and para. 72, s.2 of the StPO.

63   Para. 281, s.1, subs. 1 and para. 345, s.1, subs. 1 of the StPO.
64   Para. 281, s.1, subs. 4 and para. 345, s.1, subs. 5 of the StPO.
65   Para. 71 of the StPO.
66   Para. 281 s.1, subs. 1 of the StPO.
67   Bertel, *Grundriß, op. cit.*, point 203.
68   SSt 25/77.
69   Fasching, *Zivilprozeßrecht, op. cit.*, point 790 *et seq.*
70   Para. 233, s.3 of the StPO.
71   Para. 234 of the StPO.
72   Para. 235 of the StPO.
73   Para. 236 of the StPO.

6   Criticizing Judges in Belgium

Dirk Voorhoof

To be accused of bias is the worst possible insult that can be levelled at a magistrate.[1]

The freedom of the press to impart – in a way consistent with its duties and responsibilities information and ideas on political questions and on other matters of public interest – undoubtedly includes questions concerning the functioning of the system of justice, an institution that is essential for any democratic society. The press is one of the means by which politicians and public opinion can verify that judges are discharging their heavy responsibilities in a manner that is in conformity with the aim which is the basis of the task entrusted to them.[2]

Introduction

Discussion on the issue of criticizing judges in Belgium is a fairly recent phenomenon. The judgment of the European Court of Human Rights in the case *De Haes and Gijsels* v. *Belgium*[3] has highlighted the polemic nature of the issues which place journalists and judges in antagonistic positions. On the one hand, the media emphasize their freedom of expression, especially the right to critically report judicial affairs, which also includes the right to criticize judgments and hence directly or indirectly criticize judges. On the other hand, the judges, in view of their institutional position within a democracy under the rule of law, tend to draw attention to the responsibility of the media and the restrictions needed on the freedom of expression in order to maintain the authority and impartiality of the judiciary. The media are expected not to undermine public confidence in the administration of justice. In the last few years the media have reported critically on the functioning of the administration of justice in general and criticized some individual judges or magistrates in particular, some of whom have claimed (additional) protection against destructive attacks in the media.[4]

While the (sporadic) case law of the last 10–15 years in Belgium seemed to emphasize the need to protect the reputation of judges and the importance of maintaining the authority of the judiciary against critical attacks in the media, the European judgment in the case of *De Haes and Gijsels* made clear that this jurisprudence risks neglecting, or has even manifestly neglected, the freedom of expression guaranteed by Article 10 of the European Convention on Human Rights. The 'condemnation' of Belgium for not respecting the freedom of expression in the *De Haes and Gijsels* case was even more revealing because, at the same time, the European Court came to the conclusion that the applicant journalists in their case against four Belgian magistrates did not receive a fair trial. According to the European Court, Article 6 of the Convention was breached because the principle of equality of arms between the plaintiff judges and the defendant journalists was not respected by the Belgian courts.[5]

The criticism of judges has become a central issue in Belgium not only because of the *De Haes and Gijsels* case, but also because, in the last few years, it has become apparent that the judicial system is in crisis. Particularly since the *Dutroux* case,[6] the judiciary has had to undergo a great deal of criticism, and public confidence has diminished to an unprecedented level. Individual judges investigating magistrates, members of the public prosecutor's offices and members of the judicial police have also been compromised. During the last few years discussion on the reform of justice has constantly been on the political agenda, and this has fostered the media's interest in the actual functioning or disfunctioning of the administration of justice. Last but not least, in the context of the commercialisation of the media and the daily battle to win more readers, viewers or listeners, it has been demonstrated that reporting on crime and judicial affairs is an important news category, and judges are becoming more prominent figures in this emerging trend. At the same time, the general public wants the administration of justice to become more transparent, and the members of the judiciary to justify themselves and be responsible for their actions and role in a modern democratic society.[7]

This chapter will focus on the applicable legal provisions and the procedures that can be used to protect the reputation of judges and the authority of the judiciary against destructive attacks in the media. Following this, some recent case law applying this legal framework will be analysed.

Freedom of Expression and Press Freedom

The Constitution

Article 19 of the Belgian Constitution guarantees freedom of expression,[8] the scope of which is determined by the competence of parliament to define by law what content or speech is to be considered a criminal offence. It is up to the courts to apply this legislation in the light of the constitutional provision: the courts have the competence to restrict or punish the abuse of the freedom of expression in so far as there is a law which provides such restriction or sanction. Criminal law, for example, punishes incitement to racism and xenophobia, public acts which offend morals and sexuality, libel and defamation.[9] Similarly, Article 25 of the Constitution also protects freedom of the printed press and explicitly excludes any form of censorship.[10] This implies that prior restraint is unconstitutional, although it is not clear how this is to be interpreted precisely with regard to the possibility of the seizure of publications or the use of injunctions by the president of the court.[11]

The second paragraph of Article 25 organizes a 'cascade' system for criminal complicity in printed press offences. This means that, in principle, only the writer or the author of an article or a book can be held responsible for its criminal content. The publisher, the printer or the distributor cannot be prosecuted in the case where the author is known and has his domicile in Belgium. This 'cascade' system was introduced in the Constitution of 1831 as a guarantee against private censorship by the publisher, the printer or the distributor: as they were not responsible for the content, they had no legal arguments to interfere in the content of journalistic articles, books or other writings. In a judgment of 31 May 1996 the Court of Cassation ordered that the 'cascade' system also applies for civil liability.[12]

The printed press is also protected in a special way by Article 150 of the Constitution which installs the jury (Assize Court) for printed press offences, as well as for political offences and criminal cases. The exclusive competence of the Assize Court in cases of criminal press offences has resulted, in practice, in fewer prosecutions as, for several reasons, no criminal press cases are brought before this Court.[13] Instead, procedures are initiated before the civil courts: the courts of first instance.

The Criminal Law

Belgian criminal law complements the constitutional provisions on freedom of expression in so far as the penal code provides what is to be considered a criminal offence and punishes abuse of freedom of expression – for example, in order to protect the reputation of others. However, there is no special protection under the criminal law for judges. In the absence of an offence of contempt of court or any specific provisions to protect the authority of the judiciary, the general provisions of the Criminal Code are to be applied.

In criminal law a distinction is made between several offences that can damage the reputation of others. The crimes, qualified as calumny, defamation and malicious divulgence, all concern the allegations of precise facts. Allegations which do not refer to concrete facts may be qualified as offences ('injuries'). And in the case of insulting public persons in their presence, the criminal offence of affront (slander, contempt) ('outrage') is applicable. The qualification of these crimes demands an *'animus injurandi'* (malicious intent) which means that good faith avoids criminal liability.[14]

Calumny, defamation and malicious divulgence   In principle, calumny and defamation towards persons performing a public function, such as judges, or towards public institutions (the so-called 'constituted bodies'), can be prosecuted and punished in the same way as calumny and defamation towards private persons.[15] This principle is enshrined in Article 4 of the Decree on the Press of 20 July 1831 stipulates that:

> Calumny or abuse towards public officials, or towards bodies or agents exercising public authority, or towards any other constituent body, will be prosecuted and punished in the same way as calumny or abuse directed against individuals, except for cases detailed in clauses below.[16]

A rather similar provision is reflected in Article 446 of the Criminal Code which provides that 'Calumny and defamation towards any constituent body will be punished in the same way as calumny or defamation directed against individuals.'[17] According to the Criminal Code, criminal 'calumny' arises if the alleged fact is not proven. 'Defamation' concerns the allegation of certain facts which are not susceptible of proof. If such allegations that harm the reputation of other persons are made public – for example, by the press – while the alleged fact amounted to defamation *or* calumny, the responsible persons (that is, the author or the journalist) can be punished following a complaint by the victim. According to Article 443 of the Criminal Code:

> Anyone who, in such cases as indicated hereinafter, has maliciously imputed to a person a precise fact that is of a nature to undermine the honour of that person or to expose him to public contempt and that is not proved as required by law is guilty of calumny if the law accepts the proof of the alleged fact, and of defamation if the law does not accept the proof. . . . If this proof is sufficient, the imputation will not give rise to any repressive proceedings.[18]

The Criminal Code itself has indicated which legal means can be used as a proof. Facts in relation to the performance of the function of a person exercising public authority can be proven by all legal means. Allegations regarding the private life of an individual, even if he performs a public function, are legally more difficult to prove before the court; in such a case one has to rely on a judgment or an official (authentic) document in order not to be punished.

Article 447 of the Criminal Code provides that:

> The person accused of a calumnious offence for having made allegations relating to the functions of either depositories or agents of public authority, or any person who is a public figure, or to any constituent body will be asked to provide by any ordinary means proof of such alleged details. If it is a question of a fact which deals with private life, the author of the allegation cannot use in his defence any proof that does not arise from a judgement or any authentic act.[19]

This means that the author of a press article or the person responsible for a radio or TV programme criticizing judges and making specific factual allegations can be prosecuted and punished under these articles of the Criminal Code if:

- the allegations inflict damage on the honour or reputation or expose to public disapproval
- the allegations are not or cannot be proven
- the allegations are made public maliciously, with an *animus injurandi* – that is, with the intention to defame or to harm.

Defamation and calumny are punished by imprisonment of between eight days and one year or by a fine. However, if the allegations can be proven, but they are made public not for the benefit of any private or public interest but solely with the aim of damaging another person's reputation, the Criminal Code punishes such allegations as 'malicious divulgence'. In Article 449, the Criminal Code provides that:

> When there is at the time of the crime a legal proof of the alleged details (or facts), if it is established that the accused made the allegations without any public or private interest and solely with the aim to damage the other person's reputation, he will be punished, as guilty of malicious divulgence, with imprisonment of between eight days and two months and with a fine . . .[20]

Offences Baseless allegations, opinions or value judgments which are considered damaging to another person's honour or reputation are to be qualified as 'offences' under Article 448 of the Criminal Code which provides that:

> Anyone who has offended a person either by deeds, written words, images or emblems in one of the circumstances mentioned under Article 444 will be punished by imprisonment of between 8 days and two months and by a fine . . . . Also punishable in this way is anyone who, under the circumstances indicated in Article 444, has offended by words anyone in his or her quality as, or as a result of his function as, an agent of public authority or the police or who is a public figure.[21]

In such cases there is no possibility of proving the correctness or truthfulness of the allegations, because no reference is made to precise facts. Article 444 of the Criminal Code is explicitly applicable when the offences dishonour public figures in the exercise of their public function.

Affront　The provisions of Articles 275 and 276 of the Criminal Code specifically deal with what could be described as 'insults' towards ministers, members of parliament and other persons exercising public authority, including members of the judiciary. These facts are qualified as 'affront'. The criminal offence of affront applies when the insult relates to the exercise of an official function and when the insults are divulged maliciously in the presence of those persons exercising public authority. These insults according to Article 275, para. 1 can be punished by imprisonment of up to six months or a fine. Article 275, para. 2 provides for more severe sanctions should the insult take place in the courtroom. In such circumstances insults against judges can be punished with an imprisonment of up to two years. These provisions of the Belgian Criminal Code can be compared with 'contempt in the face of the court' when insulting the bench (misconduct in courtroom).[22] This kind of contempt however falls outside the scope of criticising judges by the press as it is analysed in this contribution.

Civil Law

As there are no specific provisions for civil liability by the press, the general principle of tortuous liability is applicable to the media and journalism. Articles 1382[23] and 1383[24] of the Civil Code accordingly provide a basis for civil proceedings for abuse of the freedom of the press and open the possibility for an action for damages against journalists. These articles apply when a 'fault' has been established and if, at the same time, there is damage with a sufficient level of causal connection between the fault and the damage. A publication is regarded as being a fault leading to civil liability when it breaches a criminal provision such as, for example, defamation or calumny.

Apart from any application of a criminal provision, tortuous liability arises in the case of dissemination of ill-considered accusations without sufficient evidence or when gratuitously offensive terms or exaggerated expressions are employed. An action for damages on the basis of Articles 1382–1383 is also possible when a press article fails to respect an individual's private life. These elements are clearly developed in Belgian case law. In its judgment of 13 September 1991 the Court of Cassation confirmed the legality of the reasoning of the Brussels Court of Appeal in application of Articles 1382–1383 of the Civil Code. The Court agreed on the fact that:

the Court of Appeal based its decision that the appellants had abused the freedom of expression secured in Article 10 paragraph 1 of the Convention . . . not only on the need to protect the respondents' private life but also on the unchallenged grounds that the accusations made had not been proved; the criticism had been directed towards named judges; the matters relied on were irrelevant to the decisions that had been taken and the accusations had been inspired by a desire to harm the respondents personally and damage their reputation.[25]

According to the case law of the civil courts, the press can be held liable if journalists are considered not to have been careful, prudent and diligent. Articles which include factually incorrect information, insufficiently checked facts, unnecessarily insulting or aggressive speech, intentionally damaging comments or invasion of privacy can lead to civil liability. It is standard case law that the constitutional freedom of the press does not restrict the principle enshrined in Article 1382 of the Civil Code.[26] Press cases on civil liability are handled before the court of first instance, sitting with three professional judges.[27]

Of course, these civil cases can only lead to civil damages. In many cases, a civil damage of one franc may be ordered, although more substantial damages can be awarded. These damages awards are essentially restitutive. They may not have a punitive character. The highest damages on civil liability by journalists concerned an award of 500 000 francs.[28] Another possible type of 'sanction' which is imposed frequently in these civil cases is a publication order of the judgment in one or more journals or magazines. The costs of the publication are to be borne by the culpable journalist.

An often heard criticism is that the decision in cases of civil liability often comes too late, only months or years after the erroneous or defamatory article has been published. The finding of culpability in relation to civil liability is therefore not capable of restoring the damage to the victim's reputation. This explains why, in some cases, procedures have been tried out in order to obtain a court order preventing the distribution of a press article or the broadcasting of a TV programme. An injunction order by the president of a civil court sitting in matters of special urgency[29] is to be regarded, however, as a preventive measure in breach of Article 25 of the Belgian Constitution and is otherwise difficult to reconcile with Article 10 of the Convention.[30]

Finally, just like any other citizens, judges can invoke a right of reply in application of the Law of 23 June 1961 (revised on 4 March 1977). The basic condition for a right of reply is that one's name is mentioned or that an article or broadcast programme implicitly refers to an identifiable person.[31] If the text of the right of reply meets all the conditions of the law, the newspaper, magazine or broadcasting organization is obliged to publish or communicate the reply in full and without undue delay.

Other Possible Ways of Complaining about Criticizing Judges in the Media

The Flemish Council of Disputes on Radio and Television

A very specific procedure is available only with regard to radio and television, and only within the Flemish community. In applying Article 79 (Article 116 octies decies) of the Broadcasting Decree after a complaint, the Flemish Council of Disputes on Radio and Television can investigate whether there has been a breach of the journalistic ethics in a litigious radio or TV programme. The Council of Disputes is composed of judges, academics and professional journalists. If the Council establishes that there has been an infringement of journalistic ethics, it can make a declaration to that effect or issue a warning, as well as requiring its decision to be broadcast.[32] So far, the Council has not had occasion to adjudicate on matters relating to judicial reporting or criticizing judges.

The Council of Ethics of the AGJPB/AVBB

Similarly, within the organization of professional journalists in Belgium (Association Générale des Journalistes Professionnels de Belgique, AGJPB – Algemene Vereniging van Beroepsjournalisten in Belgique, AVBB) the 'Council of Ethics' can receive complaints concerning the alleged non-application of the professional ethics of journalists. Membership of the AGJPB/AVBB implies that the national and international codes of ethics are to be applied by the member journalists. This means, *inter alia*, that the press must strive to respect for the truth, that it will not be gratuitously offensive and will respect the privacy of individuals.[33] The Council of Ethics is an internal body, within the private organization of professional journalists with competence over its own members of the AGJPB/AVBB. Complainants and respondents before the Council of Ethics have equal rights to be informed of the Council's decision.[34] A College of Ethics acts as an appeal chamber.

A summary of the decision is published in the annual report of the Council, and in the AGJPB/AVBB magazine, *Le Journaliste/De Journalist*. The Council's decisions have no juridical effects. The most far-reaching measure that could be taken is that a professional journalist could temporarily or definitively lose his or her membership of the AGJPB/AVBB. In other words, the impact of the Council's decisions is purely moral. Recently, the Council of Ethics decided in a case concerning the defamation of a judge.[35] According to the Council, the defendant journalists in some press articles had defamed the public prosecutor of the court of Brussels in a way that breached their professional ethics.

Case Law

The principle that freedom of expression also applies to judicial reporting is clearly recognized and emphasized in Belgian case law. In a recent judgment of the court of first instance of Nijvel, it was considered that:

> ... the press has notably the right and the duty to indicate abuses and excesses when this is in the public interest; and that among the issues of public interest that the press has a responsibility to report are undoubtedly those which deal with the functioning of the law and the forces of order.[36]

In a judgment of the Court of Cassation of 5 April 1996 it is recognized that the reporting by the press of cases before the courts is protected by the principle of freedom of expression and information: 'that as far as publicity is concerned, dissemination by the media is a consequence of freedom of expression and communication.'[37]

The criticizing of judicial decisions by the press is considered as an inherent part of the freedom of judicial reporting:

> ... that the freedom of the press carries with it the right to exercise control over the judicial work of the magistracy, including judgments which fall in the public domain through their reading in hearings and which can then be the object of appraisal and discussion; that just because a case has been definitively judged does not mean that it can no longer be criticized.[38]

In the same way, the president of the court of first instance of Brussels in a decision of 1 March 1996 observed:

> ... a judgment is a public act open to criticism as anyone is free to express himself in the manner which he considers the most effective through any form of media.[39]

In a 1986 case[40] the city magazine of Bruges, *Kan't*, published two articles under the title 'Hoe word ik rechter' ('How do I become a judge?'). Both articles described the influence of political parties on the appointment of magistrates in the courts of Bruges. Some concrete examples were given and some names of magistrates were published, with reference to their political background. It was also argued that the political affiliation seemed much more important than the professional skills or legal competence of some recently nominated magistrates. The author of the article, as well as the publisher, were sued under civil law by a substitute public prosecutor (a 'substitute-procurer') who was mentioned explicitly as an example of the latter category. The author and the editor were cited for affecting the good name and reputation and for potentially damaging the career of the plaintiff by means of the allegations in the article.

In its judgment of 17 April 1989 the court of first instance of Bruges was of the opinion that the defendants were liable for civil offence ('injuries') under Article 1382 of the Civil Code and Article 448, para. 2 of the Criminal Code. According to the judgment, the author and the publisher had undoubtedly committed an offence by directly and personally affecting the integrity and invading the privacy of the substitute-procurer. The court considered, *inter alia*, that the defendants had acted maliciously and that the comments and critics in the article had nothing to do with press freedom or freedom of expression. The allegations with regard to the applicant substitute-procurer were qualified as 'insulting writings' and as a 'flagrant fault' which failed to respect any elementary feeling for journalistic ethics. The court decided that the defendants had to pay 200 000 francs in moral and material damages and ordered the judgment to be published in two newspapers and two regional weekly magazines, as well as in the city magazine itself.

The De Haes and Gijsels Case

There is also the internationally renowned *De Haes and Gijsels* case.[41] In 1986 Leo De Haes was the editor of the weekly magazine, *Humo*, on which Gijsels worked as a journalist. Between June and November 1986 they published five articles in which they firmly criticized the judges of the Antwerp Court of Appeal for having, in a divorce case, awarded custody of the children to the father, Mr X, a notary. The three judges of the Antwerp Court of Appeal, together with the advocate-general were criticized in the articles for not having protected the children and for being biased in favour of notary X.[42]

The three judges and the advocate-general instituted civil proceedings against Mr De Haes and Gijsels and against *Humo*'s editor, publisher, statutory representative, printer and distributor. On the basis of Articles 1382–1383 of the Civil Code they sought compensation for the damage caused by the statements in the articles in question – statements that were described as very defamatory. The court of first instance of Brussels was asked to order the defendants to pay nominal damages of one franc each in respect of non-pecuniary damage and to publish the judgment in *Humo* and in six daily newspapers at the defendants' expense.

In its judgment of 29 September 1989 the Brussels court positively answered the request, although only the case against the two journalists was withheld because of the 'cascade' system of responsibility. The court was of the opinion that the two journalist defendants 'committed a fault in attacking the plaintiff's honour and reputation by means of irresponsible accusations and offensive insinuations'.

On 5 February 1990 the Brussels Court of Appeal affirmed this judgment, holding, *inter alia*, that the two *Humo* journalists had 'commented on a court case and besmirched the honour of magistrates without being in possession of all the necessary information, and this makes the complete irresponsibility of their malicious attacks even more flagrant'. Furthermore the judgments considered that:

> ... the words used and the insinuations and imputations made in the articles and passages in question are extremely virulent and dishonouring, since the original plaintiffs, referred to by name, were accused of having been biased as senior magistrates, and it was gratuitously insinuated ... that they came from an extreme-right-wing background and belonged to the circle of friends of the children's father ... all this without any serious and objective evidence whatever being adduced or existing to show the accusations against these magistrates had any factual basis.

It was emphasized that 'false reports of this kind, however, caused the original plaintiffs irreparable damage, since to be accused of bias is the worst possible insult that can be levelled at a magistrate'. The Court also referred to the magistrates' special position:

> Given the discretion incumbent upon them by virtue of their office, magistrates cannot defend themselves in the same way as, for example, politicians, if certain newspapers, apparently hungry for lucrative sensational stories, attack them and drag them through the mud.

Mr De Haes and Gijsels applied to the Court of Cassation, which dismissed their appeal on 13 September 1991. Hence the liability of De Haes and Gijsels was confirmed. For lack of due care (Article 1382 of the Civil Code) they were ordered to pay one symbolic franc of damages and to bear the cost of the publication of the judgment.

In its judgment of 27 February 1997 the European Court of Human Rights was of the opinion, however, that these judgments amounted to an interference with the journalists' exercise of freedom of expression in breach of Article 10 of the European Convention on Human Rights.[43] According to the European Court, the articles were indeed based on a mass of detailed information which itself was based on thorough research. The Court also took into consideration the fact that Mr De Haes' and Mr Gijsel's comments were undoubtedly severely critical, but that they nevertheless appeared proportionate to the stir and indignation caused by the matters alleged in their articles.

The Doutrèwe Case

The Doutrèwe judgment of 16 December 1997 of the court of first instance of

Brussels was brought by Mme Doutrèwe (an investigating magistrate) against Philippe Brewaeys/*Le Soir Illustré*.[44] In January 1997 *Le Soir Illustré* published an article focusing on the investigative judge Martine Doutrèwe of Liège in the *Dutroux* case, involving the killing of two little girls, Julie Lejeune and Melissa Russo, whose dead bodies were found in August 1996. Mme Doutrèwe was heard several times by the parliamentary commission investigating the disfunctioning of justice in this case. Some questions were raised on the way Mme Doutrèwe handled the case of the missing children. While the hearings of the parliamentary commission were taking place, the weekly magazine, *Le Soir Illustré*, published an article on Mme Doutrèwe under the title 'Une demoiselle sur une balançoire' ('A young lady on the swings'), accompanied by a photograph of Mme Doutrèwe in a bathing suit taken at the holiday villa of a certain Mr Schevenels, in the south of France. Part of the article focused on the relationship between the Doutrèwe and the Schevenels families. At the time of the article's publication Mr Schevenels and Mme Doutrèwe's husband, Mr Guy Wolf, were inculpated for fraud in the *Comuele* case.

With regard to the revelations on the relationship between the Doutrèwe family and Mr Schevenels, the Court was of the opinion that this information was relevant and factual. It was argued that this information in the article was protected by the right of the journalist to criticize and comment on actual matters of public interest and on the administration of justice. The judgment recognized that 'a person involved in a judicial case in the news can be the object of more criticism and comments from journalists than the man in the street'.[45]

With regard to the publication of the photograph and to some other allegations and commentary, the Court, however, came to the conclusion that there was an infringement of Mme Doutrèwe's right to privacy. The Court considered, *inter alia*, that:

> This was not a topical photo where the plaintiff might, for instance, have been photographed carrying out her function as investigative judge in a media case or at the time of her testimony to the 'Dutroux' commission; that the fact that Mme Doutrèwe has been subjected to the glare of the media as a result of her office in the case in point is immaterial because it is precisely and undoubtedly a private photograph.

> That if journalists can reveal matters relevant to the private life of individuals who, as here, are in the news momentarily, it goes without saying that these matters must be superfluous and must fit the public's need for information; that in this case the publication of the photograph in question does not fit with the need for information in the article. . . .

> Given that, on top of this, the invasion of the right of her image ('*droit à l'image*') is coupled with an incorrect attack on her private life. . . .

The link between the plaintiff's holidays and her professional activity made by the journalist in his comments with regard to the photo was wrong; that in fact the nature of the comments suggested, without any proof to back it up, that the manner in which she conducted the investigation entrusted to her was affected by these holidays taken beforehand.[46]

The defendant journalist was ordered to pay 500 000 francs in moral damages to Mme Doutrèwe, while at the same time an order was made to publish the judgment in two newspapers (*Le Soir* and *La Libre Belgique*), as well as in *Le Soir Illustré* itself.

The Court of Appeal of Brussels, in a judgment of 5 February 1999,[47] confirmed that the publication of the photograph of Doutrèwe neglected the right of her image and was an intrusion of her privacy. With regard to the content of the litigious article the Court noted that the article as such, and some of the information it referred to, was not problematic. As a matter of fact, the journalist was reporting on the functioning of the administration of justice and of individual judges. The Court emphasized that 'il s'agit d'informations exactes que la presse peut divulguer parce qu'elle sont nécessaires à l'information du public quant au fonctionnement de la justice et à la personnalité des magistrats qui la rendent'. The Court, on the other hand, was of the opinion that the journalist had not sufficiently proven the truthfulness or correctness of some allegations against Doutrèwe. According to the Court, the journalist has acted with 'une légèreté coupable'. Nevertheless, the Court considered this 'light fault' was not a sufficient basis to apply civil liability of the journalists in relation to the content of the litigious article. With regard to the publication of the photograph that neglected the investigating judge's right of image and right of privacy, the Court decided to reduce the award of damages to one symbolic franc, emphasizing that civil awards of damages for a victim 'doivent toutefois réparer son préjudice et non punir l'auteur de l'atteinte'. At the same time, it confirmed the order to publish the judgment in two newspapers and a weekly magazine.

In a case against the journalist C. Moniquet, Judge Doutrèwe complained of damage to her honour, reputation and right of privacy. Shortly after she appeared before the parliamentary commission on the Dutroux case, her personal notes made in preparation for the commission hearing were published, without her consent, in the weekly magazine *Ciné-Télé-Revue*. The Brussels court, in a judgment of 23 March 1999, was of the opinion that the publication of these personal notes was a violation of the right of privacy while the critical comments added by the journalist overstepped the freedom of expression principle.[48] The Court ordered an award of damages of 500 000 francs and the publication of the judgment in the magazine *Ciné-Télé-Revue*.

The journalist M. Bouffioux, in another case, was not found liable with regard to an article that contained some criticism towards Judge Doutrèwe.

The judgment of the court of first instance of Brussels of 23 March 1999 refers, *inter alia*, to some considerations of the Strasbourg Court in the *De Haes and Gijsels* case. The court also emphasized that the journalist's aim was to inform the public on a matter of general interest, while he had acted in due care and diligence.[49]

In a judgment by the court of first instance of Brussels of 23 December 1999 another journalist was considered liable in terms of defamatory comments towards the investigating judge, Mme Doutrèwe. Steve Polus, the editor-in-chief of *Le Soir Illustré* had criticized the judgment of 16 December 1997 in which his journalist colleague, Philippe Brewaeys, was held liable for the infringement of Mme Doutrèwe's privacy and for damaging her reputation without sufficient proof of the allegations.[50] In his article, Mr Polus repeated some of the allegations which were originally published in the Philippe Brewaeys article. In its judgment of 23 December 1999 the Brussels court concluded that:

> Under the pretext of what he describes as a criticism of the judgment of 16 December 1997, the journalist widely spread insidious considerations about the applicant; this leads one to believe that the journalist's actual aim was to discredit the applicant's professional life.[51]

The judgment also emphasized that Mme Doutrèwe, who had become a public figure because of the *Dutroux* case, had had her professional reputation as a judge especially damaged by Mr Polus's litigious article in which Mme Doutrèwe was presented as incapable of guaranteeing fair justice. In the words of the court:

> That the applicant [who] became a public figure when the facts [of this case] attracted the attention of an entire country is because of the insinuations and the lies set out in the attacked article, which harmed her in her private life as well as in her professional life being presented as unable to guarantee fair justice.[52]

The court also stressed that the defendant journalist in his article did not merely analyse the principles under discussion in a judgment and that the right of criticism by the media is to be exercised within the limits of a certain correctness.[53]

After considering the fact that Mr Polus had repeated some of the allegations published earlier by Mr Brewaeys, although he had been warned by the judgment of 16 December 1997 that these allegations were defamatory towards Judge Doutrèwe, the court decided that the editor-in-chief of *Le Soir Illustré* 'went over the threshold of acceptable criticism within the context of the freedom of expression; his aim is to belittle the applicant with an insulting article'.[54] As a consequence of this reasoning, the court ordered an award of moral damages of 750 000 francs. The court explicitly disagreed with the Brussels Court of Appeal which had earlier decided, in its judgment of 5 February 1999, that moral damage can only lead to an award of one symbolic franc.[55] In the view of the court of first instance of Brussels:

> Compensation given to a victim whose honour is damaged does not amount to punishing the author of the harm. [Monetary] damages are meant to repair the harm in the most complete manner.[56]

Finally the defendant journalist was also ordered to publish the full text of the judgment in two newspapers (*Le Soir* and *La Libre Belgique*) and in the magazine *Le Soir Illustré* itself.[57]

A recent decision of the Council of Ethics concerns a complaint by the public prosecutor (*Procureur-des-Konings*) at the court of Brussels, Benoit Dejemeppe. The magistrate complained about three articles published in *De Morgen* with titles such as 'Dejemeppe linked to prostitution' and 'Public prosecutor leads a brothel'. The articles are to be situated in a broader context in which the public prosecutor of Brussels was encountering a great deal of criticism because of his alleged responsibility in the case of Loubna Benaïssa, the young girl, who disappeared some years ago and whose dead body was found in 1997. Based on the information from only one source *De Morgen* had revealed that Dejemeppe and his family had contact with the prostitution business in Brussels. This allegation led to a complaint by Mr Dejemeppe at the Council of Ethics of the AGJPB/AVBB.

After a hearing with Ludwig Verduyn (the journalist) and Yves Desmet (the editor-in-chief of *De Morgen*), the Council of Ethics came to the conclusion that *De Morgen* could not rely on sufficiently trustworthy information to publish the allegations on Dejemeppe. The allegation published in *De Morgen*, according to which Dejemeppe and his family had contact with the prostitution business in Brussels, seemed to be based on only one source which was not very reliable. The Council concluded:

> 1. The accusations made by *De Morgen* against the prosecutor Dejemeppe are very serious. Even after a careful reading of the text, the message remains that there are links between the highest magistrate in the Brussels Public Prosecutor's office and the world of prostitution.
> 2. The chief editor and the journalist maintain that other elements support the accusations. That is what they say should come out of the confidential documents that they have given to the Council of Ethics. The Council has examined the documents but can only record that they can be interpreted in different ways. In any case, they do not confirm the accusations against Benoit Dejemeppe that he was maintaining links with the world of prostitution.[58]

The Council also took into consideration that *De Morgen*, in the days following publication, made no reference to the fact that Dejemeppe had written a letter protesting against the content of the articles.

In its conclusion the Council decided that *De Morgen* acted inaccurately by publishing such serious allegations against the public prosecutor. According to the Council the grievous accusations seriously compromised the dignity of the public prosecutor and his family:

> 4. The Council of Ethics is consequently of the opinion that *De Morgen* has acted in a negligent manner in this affair. The newspaper has published extremely serious accusations against the public prosecutor and this in a sensational and unilateral manner (notably on the front page and in the editorial). The accusations undermine the dignity of the prosecutor and that of his family.[59]

This case demonstrates that magistrates can complain about inaccurate or harmful information published by the media and that the Council of Ethics is taking its moral competence seriously in evaluating the application or non-application of professional ethics by its members.

Furthermore, it must be emphasized that the decision of the Council of Ethics in the *De Morgen* case was published together with an editorial in which the editor apologized because of the erroneous information *De Morgen* had published and which compromised the Brussels' public prosecutor. This voluntary publication of the decision by *De Morgen* in full, the fact that *De Morgen* explicitly confirmed the moral authority of the Council's decision, together with the apologies offered to the public prosecutor in the editorial, made clear that the self-disciplinary instrument of the Council of Ethics can also be an important tool in finding a balance between the freedom of the press and critical judicial reporting on the one hand, and responsible and accurate journalism, with respect for the rights of others, on the other.

Conclusions

It has been indicated how general provisions in the criminal law (calumny, defamation, malicious divulgence, offence by the press) and in civil law (Articles 1382–1383 of the Civil Code) can be the legal basis, in Belgium, for action against media criticism of judges. For many decades criminal prosecution against the press did not take place in Belgium. The exclusive competence of the Assize Court in cases of criminal press offences has resulted in a factual criminal impunity as no criminal press cases were brought before the Court of Assizes. Instead, as is illustrated by reference to some case law, procedures are initiated before the civil courts. This means, however, that press cases are deliberated by professional judges of the civil courts and not by the lay judges of the Assize Court jury. As professional magistrates have to decide on the conflicts between journalists and judges in some cases, the media (and the public) may have the impression that the courts will pay more attention to the need for protection against destructive attacks on members of the judiciary than on the principle of freedom of expression and information.

A solution might be to bring these cases before the Assize Court. In such a procedure, the infringement in the media's freedom of expression is not dependent on a judgment by professional judges, but on a verdict by the jury. The procedure before the Assize Court is to be reformed, however, in order to open a realistic perspective for such kind of a criminal procedure in cases of press offences.

Another way of avoiding a decision by professional judges, as the case *Dejemeppe v. De Morgen* made clear, is to complain to the Council of Ethics. Such a procedure has the advantage that a judge is not complaining before a court in which fellow judges have to decide on an issue in which the judges institutionally are involved, or at least concerned. The disadvantage, however, is that the plaintiff judge also might not have much confidence in bringing his case before the Council of Ethics, as this Council is exclusively composed of professional journalists. In the (near) future, however, the Council of Ethics might be replaced by a Council of Journalists with a mixed composition of journalists, editors and publishers under the presidency of a magistrate and completed with other members or experts who are not journalists (for example, university professors in ethics, philosophy, communication sciences or law).[60] The Flemish Council of Disputes on Radio and Television already has such a mixed composition.

Anyway, it should be stressed that, in a procedure before the civil courts, the professional judges considering the civil liability of a journalist, have to take into account the perspective of Article 10 of the European Convention and have to apply the Strasbourg case law. This means that the Belgian civil courts, more as they did in the past, have to give more weight to freedom of expression and information in so far as there is a sufficient factual basis for the allegations against, or criticisms of, judges published by the media. Journalists, for their part, must be aware that criticizing judges requires accurate and correct reporting and that allegations should be based on sufficient and pertinent facts, taking into account also the general context of a court case.

In a modern democracy the courts cannot operate in a vacuum; this means that critical reporting, discussion and disputes on pending court cases, including the criticizing of judges, must be tolerated.

Notes

1   Court of Appeal, Brussels, 5 February 1990, *Rechtskundig Weekblad* (1989–90), p. 1464.
2   *Prager and Oberschlick* v. *Austria* (1995) Eur. Ct. HR, Series A.313; (1996) 21 EHRR 1, para. 34.
3   (1997) 25 EHRR, 1
4   See, for example, J. Delva, 'De onafhankelijkheid van de Belgische rechter ten aanzien van de uitvoerende macht', *Tijdschrift voor Bestuurswetenschappen en Publiek Recht* (1988), pp. 242–43 and J. Velu, 'Beschouwingen over de europese regelgeving inzake betrekkingen tussen gerecht en pers', *Rechtskundig Weekblad* (1995–96), pp. 273–308. On this issue, see also P. Deltour, *Man bijt hond. Over pers, politiek en gerecht*, (Antwerp: Icarus, 1996) and J. Clement and M. Van de Putte, 'De vierde macht', *De gespannen driehoeksverhouding tussen media, gerecht en politiek* (Groot-Bijgaarden: Globe, 1996).
5   The Brussels Court of Appeal rejected the journalists' request to admit in evidence the documents referred to in the impugned articles or to hear some witnesses. The Strasbourg Court was of the opinion that the rejection of this request had put the journalists at a substantial disadvantage *vis-à-vis* the plaintiff judges and that therefore there was a breach of the principle of equality of arms.
6   This was a shocking case in which minors were sexually abused and murdered. A parliamentary commission investigated the failures of the judiciairy system. Over 300 000 people demonstrated in the streets of Brussels in October 1996 against the lack of action by the police and the judiciary in this case. See also F. Tanghe, *Het spaghetti-arrest. Recht en Democratie* (Antwerp/Baarn, Hadewijch, 1997).
7   See D. Voorhoof, *De relatie tussen Media en Justitie* (Brussels: Koning Boudewijnstichting, 1998).
8   'Freedom of worship and its public exercise, together with the freedom to manifest opinions on all subjects, are guaranteed, save for the punishment of offences perpetrated in exercising those freedoms.'
9   See J. Velaers, *De beperkingen van de vrijheid van meningsuiting* (Antwerp/Apeldoorn: Maklu Uitgevers, 1991) and D. Voorhoof, *Actuele vraagstukken van mediarecht. Doctrine en jurisprudentie* (Antwerp: Kluwer Rechtswetenschappen, 1992).
10 'The press shall be free; there shall never be any censorship; no security can be demanded of writers, publishers or printers.'
11 See J. Velaers, 'De actuele toepassing van de grondwettelijke waarborgen inzake de vrijheid van de media', *ICM-Jaarboek Mensenrechten 1995–1996*, (1996), pp. 83–98; M. Hanotiau, 'La censure de la presse écrite par le juge des référés', *Auteurs & Media*, (1997), pp. 203–12 and D. Voorhoof, 'De doorwerking van publiekrechtelijke beginselen in de civielrechtelijke aansprakelijkheid voor informatie via (multi-)media', *Publiekrecht. Doorwerking van het publiekrecht in het privaatrecht. Referaten van de Postuniversitaire Cyclus Willy Delva 1996/1997* (Ghent: Mys & Breesch, 1997), pp. 485–523. See also D. Voorhoof, 'Interdiction de diffusion d'un livre sur l'affaire Dutroux: censure illicite ou mesure nécessaire?', *Auteurs & Media*, 2 (1999), pp. 250–59.
12 Court of Cassation, 31 May 1996, *Recente Arresten van het Hof van Cassatie*, 1996/9, 389, note D. Voorhoof.
13 D. Voorhoof, 'Drukpersmisdrijven en de bevoegdheid van het Hof van Assisen' (note under Court of Cassation, 7 February 1995), *Algemeen Juridisch Tijdschrift*, (1995–96), pp. 249–50. Offences which do not include a punishable opinion, however, do not enjoy the application of Article 150 of the Constitution: for example, the reporting of the hearing in a divorce case, which infringes Article 1270 of the Code of Procedure; the disclosure of the identity of victims of certain sexual offences, which infringes Article 378 *bis* of the

Criminal Code; the reporting on hearings before the youth court, in breach of Article 80 of the Act of 30 April 1965 concerning the protection of the youth. Press publications infringing these provisions can be prosecuted in the criminal court, sitting with professional judges. Due to a revision of Article 150 of the Constitution on 7 May 1999, printed press offences which are inspired by racism or xenophobia are explicitly exempted and can also be prosecuted now in a criminal court, sitting with professional judges. See D. Voorhoof, 'Vacature met racistische inhoud en de kwalificatie "drukpersmisdrijf"', *Algemeen Juridisch Tijdschrift* (1999–2000), pp. 6–7; and also E. Francis, 'Bedenkingen bij de "correctionalisering" van racistisch geïnspireerde drukpersmisdrijven', *Rechtskundig Weekblad* (1999–2000), pp. 377–94.

14   For a general overview, see P. Arnou, 'Aanranding van de eer en goede naam van personen', in *Om deze redenen. Liber Amicorum A. Vandeplas* (Ghent: Mys & Breesch, 1994), pp. 49–90.

15   The constituted bodies are installed and organized by law and perform a public service. Through their members but not through the institutions themselves they can claim their rights in court.

16   'La calomnie ou l'injure envers des fonctionnaires publics, ou envers des corps dépositaires ou agents de l'autorité publique, ou envers tout autre corps constitué, sera poursuivie et punie de la même manière que la calomnie ou l'injure dirigée contre les particuliers, sauf ce qui est statué à cet égard dans les dispositions suivantes.'

17   'La calomnie et la diffamation envers tout corps constitué seront punies de la même manière que la calomnie ou la diffamation dirigée contre les individus.'

18   Article 443 reads as follows:

Celui qui, dans les cas ci-après indiqués, a méchamment imputé à une personne un fait précis qui est de nature à porter atteinte à l'honneur de cette personne ou à l'exposer au mépris public, et dont la preuve légale n'est pas rapportée, est coupable de calomnie lorsque la loi admet la preuve du fait imputé, et de diffamation lorsque la loi n'admet pas cette preuve . . . . Si cette preuve est rapportée en insuffisance, l'imputation ne donnera lieu . . . à aucune poursuite répressive.

19   Article 447 of the Criminal Code which provides:

Le prévenu d'un délit de calomnie pour imputations dirigées, à raison des faits relatifs à leurs fonctions, soit contre les dépositaires ou agents de l'autorité ou contre toute personne ayant un caractère public, soit contre tout corps constitué, sera admis de faire, par toutes les voies ordinaires, la preuve des faits imputés. S'il s'agit d'un fait qui rentre dans la vie privée, l'auteur de l'imputation ne pourra faire valoir, pour sa défense, aucune preuve que celle qui résulte d'un jugement ou de tout autre acte authentique.

20   Article 449 of the Criminal Code provides:

Lorsqu'il existe au moment du délit une preuve légale des faits imputés, s'il est établi que le prévenu a fait l'imputation sans aucun motif d'intérêt public ou privé et dans l'unique but de nuire, il sera puni, comme coupable de divulgation méchante, d'un emprisonnement de huit jours à deux mois et d'une amende . . . .

21   Article 448 of the Criminal Code provides:

Quiconque aura injurié une personne soit par des faits, soit par des écrits, images ou emblèmes, dans l'une des circonstances indiquées à l'article 444, sera puni d'un emprisonnement de huit jours à deux mois et d'une amende . . . sera puni des mêmes peines, quiconque, dans l'une des circonstances indiquées à l'article 444, aura injurié par paroles, en sa qualité ou en raison de ces fonctions, une personne dépositaire de l'autorité ou de la force publique, ou ayant un caractère public.

22   See, for example, Article 759–763 of the Code of Procedure. See also Article 452 of the Criminal Code:

> Ne donneront lieu à aucune poursuite répressive les discours prononcés ou les écrits produits devant les tribunaux, lorsque ces discours ou ces écrits sont relatifs à la cause ou aux parties. Les imputations calomnieuses, injurieuses ou diffamatoires étrangres à la cause ou aux parties pourront donner lieu soit à l'action publique, soit à l'action civile des parties ou des tiers.

23   'Any act committed by a person that causes damage to another shall render the person whose fault the damage was caused liable to make reparation for it.'

24   'Everyone shall be liable for damage he has caused not only through his own act but also through his failure to act or his negligence.'

25   Court of Cassation, 13 September 1991, *Rechtskundig Weekblad* (1991–92), p. 464 and *Arresten van het Hof van Cassatie* (1991–92), p. 46. See also D. Voorhoof, *Actuele vraagstukken*, *op. cit.*, p. 276 *et seq.*; J. Velaers, 'Schrijven over rechters. Enkele beschouwingen over de grenzen aan de gerechtsverslaggeving', in X., *Liber Amicorum Alfons Vandeurzen* (Ghent: Mys & Breesch, 1995), pp. 307–28 and D. Voorhoof, 'De grenzen aan de kritiek op (leden van) de rechterlijke macht', *Recht en Kritiek* (1989), pp. 280–301.

26   For a general introduction on the civil liability of the press, see J. Milquet, 'La responsabilité, aquilienne de la presse', *Annales de Droit de Louvain*, **1** (1989), pp. 33–86; H. Vandenberghe, 'Over persaansprakelijkheid', *Tijdschrift voor Privaat Recht* (1993), pp. 843–83; and D. Voorhoof, 'De rechtsbescherming in geval van misbruik van de persvrijheid: overzicht van rechtspraak (eerste deel)', *Droit de la Consommation/Consumentenrecht*, **19** (1992–93), pp. 199–243.

27   Article 92, para. 1, s.2 of the Code of Procedure.

28   See also F. Jongen, 'Responsabilité, de la presse: la fin du symbolisme?' (note under Court of first instance of Brussels, 16 December 1997), *Journal des Procès*, **341** (1998), p. 30. More recently, higher amounts of damages were awarded by the Brussels court of first instance. Two journalists were sentenced to pay damages of 2 200 000 francs for criticizing, in a defamatory way, some members of the police: Court of first instance of Brussels, 16 November 1999, *Auteurs & Media*, **1–2** (2000), p. 117. See also P. Deltour, 'De X-files. Justitie houdt lelijk huis onder gerechtsjournalisten', *De Journalist*, **5** (1999), pp. 8–9; and S.P. de Coster, 'Les jugements Bouffioux-Van Heeswijck et Brewaeys-DelIège', *Auteurs & Media*, **1–2** (2000), pp. 123–29.

29   'Référé/kort geding' (summary proceedings): Article 18, s.584 of the Code of Procedure.

30   M. Hanotiau and M. Kadaner, 'Le référé dans la presse écrite et dans l'audiovisuel', *Revue de Droit de l'ULB* (1993), pp. 147–92; D. Voorhoof, 'Beperkingen op de expressievrijheid via de kortgedingrechter: een omstreden rechtsmiddel', *Auteurs & Media* (1997), pp. 168–71 and J. Velaers, 'De actuele toepassing', *op. cit.*, pp. 86–98. For some recent applications, see President of the court of first instance of Brussels, 9 January 1997, *Auteurs & Media*, **2** (1997), p. 197; Brussels Court of Appeal, 12 June 1997; *Jurisprudence de Liège, Mons et Bruxelles* (1998), p. 764; and Brussels Court of Appeal, 27 June 1997; ibid., p. 768.

31   See D. Voorhoof, 'Het recht van antwoord', *Mediagids/Mediarecht*, **3** (1995), pp. 27–36.

32   See also D. Voorhoof, 'De Vlaamse Geschillenraad voor radio en televisie', *Mediagids/Mediarecht*, **8** (1997), pp. 69–76.

33   P. Juusela, *Journalistic Codes of Ethics in the CSCE Countries*, (Tampere: University of

Tampere, 1991). See also the 4th European Ministerial Conference on Mass Media Policy, *The Media in a Democratic Society*, Resolution no. 2, Journalistic freedoms and human rights, MCM, **20** (94), 7–8 December 1994 and Steering Committee on the Mass Media, *Journalistic Freedoms and Human Rights in the Member States of the Council of Europe: Information Submitted by Experts* (Strasbourg, 1994), MM-S-JF (94), p. 13.

34   See also D. Voorhoof, 'De titel van beroepsjournalist en de bewaking van de journalistieke deontologie door de AVBB', *Mediagids/Mediarecht*, **9** (1997), pp. 59–70.

35   Raad voor Deontologie, 11 February 1998, *Auteurs & Media*, **2** (1998), p. 160.

36   '. . . que la presse a notamment le droit et le devoir de signaler les abus et les excès dans l'intérêt général; que parmi les thèmes d'intérêt général sur lesquels il incombe à la presse de communiquer des informations et des idées figurent sans nul doute ceux qui concernent le fonctionnement de la justice et les forces de police'. See court of first instance of Nijvel, 11 September 1997, *Auteurs & Media*, **2** (1998), pp. 157. See also Brussels Court of Appeal, 3 December 1997, *Auteurs & Media*, **3** (1998), pp. 255.

37   'Qu'en ce qui concerne la publicité . . . la diffusion par les médias constitue un corollaire de la liberté d'expression et de communication.' See Court of Cassation, 5 April 1996, *ICM-Jaarboek Mensenrechten 1995–96* (1996), p. 429.

38   'Que la liberté de la presse emporte le droit d'exercer son contrôle sur l'oeuvre juridique de la magistrature, en ce compris des jugements, tombés dans le domaine public par suite de leur lecture à l'audience, et qui peuvent faire l'objet d'une appréciation et d'une discussion; qu'il ne suffit pas qu' une cause soit définitivement jugée pour qu'elle ne puisse plus être critiquée.' See court of first instance of Brussels, 29 June 1987, *Journal des Tribunaux*, 1987, p. 685.

39   'Un jugement est un acte public ouvert à critique, chacun étant libre de s'exprimer de la manière qu'il estime la plus adéquate, par la voie de n'importe quelle media.' See president of the court of first instance of Brussels, 1 March 1996, unpublished, no. 95/1992/C, *SA Sierra 21* v. *RTBF*.

40   D. Voorhoof, *Actuele vraagstukken van mediarecht, op. cit.*, p. 253.

41   Court of first instance of Brussels, 29 September 1989, '*W, X, Y and Z* v. *De Morgen and Humo*', *Recht en Kritiek* (1989), p. 302; Court of Appeal of Brussels, 5 February 1990, *Rechtskundig Weekblad* (1989–90), p. 1464 and Court of Cassation, 13 September 1991, *Arresten van het Hof van Cassatie* (1991–92), p. 46. See also D. Voorhoof, 'Die grenzen aan de kritick op (leden van) de rechterlijke macht', *Recht en Kritiek* (1989), pp. 280–301.

42   Articles with an analogue content at that time also were published in the newspaper, *De Morgen*. The editor-in-chief, as well as the journalists, were held liable for lack of due care, just as in the case against De Haes and Gijsels. The journalists of *De Morgen*, however, did not complain in Strasbourg.

43   See D. Voorhoof, 'Het Humo-arrest: scherpe kritiek op rechters geoorloofd', *Mediaforum*, **4** (1997), pp. 68–69.

44   Court of first instance of Brussels, 16 December 1997, *Journal des Procès*, **341** (1998), p. 24.

45   '. . . une personne mêlée à l'actualité judiciaire puisse faire l'objet de plus de critiques ou de commentaires de la part du journaliste que le premier venu.' See also court of first instance of Brussels, 29 June 1987, *Journal des Tribunaux* (1987), p. 625.

46   'Qu'il ne s'agit pas d'une photo d'actualité où la demanderesse aurait, par exemple, été photographiée dans l'exercice de ses fonctions de juge d'instruction dans le cadre d'une affaire médiatique ou lors de son témoignage devant la commission "Dutroux"; que le fait que Madame Doutrèwe ait été, de par sa fonction, projetée sous les feux de l'actualité est en l'espèce indifferent dans la mesure où il s'agit précisément et indubitablement d'une photographie privée . . .'

'Que si les journalistes peuvent révéler des éléments relatifs à la vie privée des individus qui comme c'est le cas en l'espèce accèdent momentanément à l'actualité il va de soi que ces éléments ne doivent pas être superflus et doivent être nécessaires aux besoins de l'information; qu'en espèce, la publication de la photographie litigieuse n'est pas nécessaire aux besoins des informations diffusées dans l'article . . . .'

'Attendu que, surabondamment, l'atteinte au droit à l'image se double d'une atteinte fautive au respect de la vie privée . . .'

'L'amalgame fait par le journaliste dans le cadre des commentaires figurant en regard de la photo entre les vacances de la demanderesse et son activité professionelle est fautif; qu'en effet la nature des commentaires laisse entendre sans qu'aucun élément ne soit apporté à l'appui de cette thèse que la manière dont elle aurait instruit le dossier d'instruction qui lui fut confié aurait été affectée par ces "vacances" prises antérieurement.'

47   Court of Appeal of Brussels, 5 February 1999, *Auteurs & Media*, 2 (1999), pp. 274 (with note by F. Ringelheim, pp. 278–80). Other recent case law applies and develops the principles of civil liability of journalists while criticizing members of the police or judicial inquiries: Court of first instance of Brussels, 30 March 1999, *P. De Baets and A. Bille* v. *S. Jourdain, Auteurs & Media*, 1–2 (2000), p. 102; 'Court of first instance of Liège, 21 September 1999, *R. Brose* v. *J.F. Deliège, R. Hurbain, SA Rossel & Cie and Ph. Brewaeys, Auteurs & Media*, 1–2 (2000), p. 155; Court of first instance of Brussels, 28 October 1999, *J.L. Duterme* v. *M. Bouffioux, M.J. Van Heeswijck and SA Mediaxis, Auteurs & Media*, 1–2 (2000), p. 113 and Court of first instance of Brussels, 16 November 1999, *P. De Baets, A. Bille and others* v. *Ph. Brewaeys and J.F. Deliège, Auteurs & Media*, 1–2 (2000), p. 117.

48   Court of first instance of Brussels, 23 March 1999, *M. Doutrèwe* v. *C. Moniquet, Algemeen Juridisch Tijdschrift*, (1998-99), pp. 1004. The Court considered:

'Que le journaliste par la présentation et les commentaires outrageantes de cet article a dépassé son droit à la liberté d'information correcte du public; que par la divulgation des notes personnelles, par le titre tapageur et les commentaires inopportuns et superflus l'équilibre entre le respect de la liberté d'expression et le respect des droits d'autrui est compromis.'

49   Court of first instance of Brussels, 23 March 1999, *M. Doutrèwe* v. *M. Bouffioux, Algemeen Juridisch Tijdschrift*, (1998–99), pp. 1001. The Court considered:

Attendu que le but du défendeur apparaît avoir été d'informer sur une question d'intérêt général le citoyen qui se devait d'être éclairé sur cette douloureuse affaire qui est devenu un fait majeur de société . . . . Que l'article litigieux ne vise pas à jeter le doute sur l'honorabilité de la demanderesse mais à montrer aux citoyens les défaillances constatées à l'occasion de l'affaire dit Julie et Melissa et la volonté des autorités d'analyser des dysfonctionnements d'y remédier; que le journaliste a fait preuve de sérieux dans ses commentaires élaborés dans l'article litigieux; qu'il ne peut être reproché aucune faute au défendeur qui a agi comme un journaliste normalement avisé et prudent et a assumé de manière adéquate son rôle d'informateur.

50   Court of first instance of Brussels, 23 December 1999, *La Libre Belgique* (21 January 2000), p. 9.

51   '. . . sous le couvert de ce qu'il qualifie de critique du jugement du 16 décembre 1997, le journaliste se répand en considérations gravement insidieuses à l'égard de la demanderesse; que tout porte à croire que le véritable dessein du journaliste fut de jeter le discrédit sur la vie professionnelle de la demanderesse.'

52 '... que la demanderesse, devenu personnage public lors de faits qui ont retenu l'attention de tout un pays est, par les insinuations et les allégations mensongères figurant dans l'article incriminé, atteinte non seulement dans sa vie privée mais dans sa vie professionnelle puisqu'elle est présentée comme n'étant plus garante d'une bonne justice.'

53 '... que l'article incriminée ne se borne pas à analyser les principes en jeu dans une décision de justice; que le droit de critique doit s'exercer dans les limites d'une certaine correction.'

54 '... a dépassé le domaine de la critique admissible dans le cadre de la liberté d'expression; qu'il poursuit le but de déconsidérer la demanderesse par son article injurieux.'

55 See Court of Appeal of Brussels, 5 February 1999, *Auteurs & Media*, 2 (1999), p. 274.

56 '... si les dommages et intérêts alloués à une victime d'atteinte à son honorabilité ne doivent pas punir l'auteur de l'atteinte, ceux-ci doivent cependant réparer le dommage moral de la manière la plus complète.'

57 Court of first instance of Brussels, 23 December 1999, *La Libre Belgique* (21 January 2000), p. 9.

58 '1. Les accusations portées par De Morgen à l'encontre du procureur Dejemeppe sont trés lourdes. Même après une lecture attentive du texte des articles, le message reste qu'il existe des liens entre le plus haut magistrat du parquet de Bruxelles et le milieu de la prostitution . . .
2. Le rédacteur en chef et le journaliste affirment que d'autres éléments viennent soutenir les accusations. C'est ce qui doit ressortir des documents confidentiels qu'ils ont fournis au Conseil de déontologie. Ce dernier a examiné les documents mais ne peut que constater qu'ils peuvent être interprétés de différentes manières. En tout cas, ils ne confortent pas les accusations à l'encontre de Benoit Dejemeppe, à savoir qu'il entretiendrait des liens avec le milieu de la prostitution.'

59 '4. Le Conseil de déontologie est dès lors d'avis que De Morgen a agi de manière négligente dans cette affaire. Le journal a publié des accusations extrêment graves à l'encontre du procureur et ce, de manière unilatérale et avec grand fracas (notamment la première page et le commentaire). Les accusations portent gravement atteinte à la dignité du procureur et à celle de sa famille . . .'; Raad voor Deontologie, 11 February 1998, *Auteurs & Media*, 2 (1998), p. 160.

60 See D. Voorhoof, 'Naar een Raad voor de Journalistiek?', *Samenleving en Politiek*, 4 (1998), pp. 22–26 and 'Journalisten Zonder Grenzen?', *Auteurs & Media*, 1–2 (2000), pp. 36–48.

7 Contempt of Court in French Law: A Criminal Offence

Hélène Lambert

Introduction

Article 10 of the European Convention on Human Rights (1950)[1] guarantees freedom of expression to everyone, but this freedom is not absolute and it may be subject to limitations provided by domestic law in order to guarantee the administration of justice and its impartiality.[2] One such restriction is the general notion of contempt of court (*atteintes à l'autorité de la justice*) provided under French penal law. Until 1992 provisions regarding contemptuous acts (*outrage*) against judges (and jurors) were to be found in Articles 222 and 223 of the Napoleonic Penal Code of 1810. In 1958 the offence of discredit brought upon a decision or an act of a court was added, in response to increasingly aggressive journalism.[3] These provisions have since been incorporated in two articles of the new Penal Code 1994: Article 434-24 relating to contemptuous acts against judges and Article 434-25 relating to the discredit brought upon an act or a decision of a court.[4] Moreover, Articles 30, 31 and 33 of the Act of 29 July 1881 on the freedom of the press may also become relevant in cases of defamation or insult committed by the press.

The origins of the concept of contempt of court in French law can be found in Roman law. Contempt, then, was divided into *injuriae verbis* (oral offence) and *injuriae re* (physical offence). When directed against a judge or a civil servant, the offence, whether *verbis* or *re* fell into the category of *injuriae atroces* (severe offence) and was thus subject to more severe penalties. The French Napoleonic Penal Code of 1810 was inspired by these provisions. Referring to the basic distinction between contemptuous acts (that is, oral offences) and violent acts (that is, physical offences), Articles 222–227 of the 1810 Penal Code expanded the notion of contemptuous acts (*outrage*) in order

113

to protect both the administration of justice and the person of the judge or civil servant. As a result, contemptuous acts were to be punished not only when directed against judges in the performance of their duties, as representatives of the authority of justice, but also when directed against such persons, outside public office, for acts performed within their duties. Since 1810 the scope of these articles has been enlarged to include, in particular, protection against contemptuous acts in unpublished writings or drawings against a judge or a juror.

Contemptuous Acts Against a Member of the Court

According to Article 434-24 of the new Penal Code 1994:

> . . . any person who commits a contemptuous act, either orally, or by gestures or menaces toward, or in unpublished writing or drawing of any nature, or by sending any objects to a judge, a juror or any judicial officer in or because of the performance of their duties and, tending to reflect upon their dignity or the respect attached to their duties, shall be punished by one year imprisonment and a fine of 100 000 FF.
>
> If the contemptuous act has been committed in court or tribunal, the penalty shall be a two-year imprisonment and a fine of 200 000 FF.[5]

It is generally accepted by the doctrine and the French courts that any abusive, insulting or defamatory expression addressed to a person representing public authority in the performance of his or her duties, and aiming at undermining the respect of this official, thereby also infringing the respect due to his or her duties, constitutes a contemptuous act.[6] A contemptuous act must therefore be distinguished from a rebellion or an act of violence, understood more as a physical act. It must also be distinguished from certain insulting, abusive or defamatory acts committed by the press, and strictly covered by the Act of 29 July 1881 relating to the freedom of the press, although, in practice, this distinction is often difficult to make.[7]

The offence provided in Article 434-24 of the new Penal Code can be characterized by four elements: the protected person, the material act of contempt, the link between the act and the exercise of duties, and the intention. First, according to Article 434-24, protected persons are the *magistrats de carrière*, the jurors of the Assize Court and any persons sitting in a judicial capacity (for example, members of the commercial courts). The term *magistrat de carrière* refers to any professionals whose permanent task is to guarantee the administration of justice, whether in ordinary or in administrative courts. Included in this category are members of the Court of Cassation,[8] Courts of Appeal, regional courts or district courts, the Council of State (*Conseil d'Etat*), administrative courts, the auditor's general department, the jurisdiction court, and the prosecution (law officers). Registrars, however, seem to be unprotected against contemptuous acts under Article 434-24, except for those from commercial courts.[9] Second, as far as the act of contempt itself is concerned,[10] it must tend to undermine the dignity of the person concerned or the respect attached to his or her duties. However, the act does not need necessarily to aim directly at the duties performed. For instance, the assertion that a judge exercised a 'justice based on class' and then that, in performing his duties, he demonstrated 'bad faith', was found to constitute such an act.[11] Nor does the act need to aim directly at the person concerned; it can also be indirect – that is, when addressed to a third person rather than the judge. Thus, the use of bad language or words such as 'coward', 'pauper' or 'braggart' to describe a judge constitute contemptuous acts, as do mere attitudes, threats or the tone of voice used, combined with otherwise perfectly neutral words.[12] It is for the Criminal Section of the Court of Cassation to verify not only that the act reached the victim but also that this was the intention of the author of the act.[13] Finally, French courts have long recognized as contemptuous the act of reporting imaginary facts to a judicial or administrative authority, provided such information leads to unnecessary research. This practice was finally codified in Article 434-26 of the new Penal Code.[14] In addition, the contemptuous act must be expressed by some positive, visible means; it cannot be implied. According to Article 434-24, words, in whatever language, including boos and shouts, constitute such means, but also gestures or menaces, unpublished writings or drawings or, any sent objects. This list is exhaustive. For instance, throwing a fruit, spitting or sitting with your back turned to a judge would constitute contemptuous acts against judges. However, any really severe gestures would be considered as violence and fall under Article 222-12 of the Penal Code.[15] In another instance, the Criminal Section of the Court of Cassation held that a letter addressed to a judge and providing that: 'we note that you have deliberately blocked our criminal complaint . . .', constituted a contempt of court under Article 434-24 and found the writer of the letter to be an accomplice, while the intellectual instigator was found to be the principal author of the wrongful act.[16] Similarly, a defendant was fined 6 000 FF, under Article 222 of the new Penal Code, for sending a personal letter to a Mr K, criticizing certain judges and requested K to start an investigation on the person of the judges. The Court found that, although the letter was personal, the defendant could not ignore that the contents of the letter would be made known to the judges, for them to be able to justify their acts.[17] However, published writings or drawings would be covered by the Act of 29 July 1881 on the freedom of the press. Third, Article 434-24 of the Penal Code does not extend protection against contemptuous acts to judges acting as individuals in their private capacity.[18] Indeed, judges are only protected against contemptuous acts when performing their duties or when outside the performance of their duties, if in connection with such performance.[19] Thus a retired judge criticized for reasons of the duties that he or she used to perform is protected by Article 434-24 of the Penal Code.[20] Finally, criminal intent presupposes that the author of the act was fully aware of its wrongfulness and that he or she deliberately acted in full knowledge of this wrongfulness. Contempt is a criminal offence and it is a general rule of penal law that criminal offences shall be intentional as a matter of principle.[21] However, only mere intent is presumed and under Article 434-24 proof of a qualified intent is required – that is, a specific motive.[22] It is for the courts to appreciate the circumstances leading them to believe that the author was fully aware of his or her acts and for the Court of Cassation to ensure that reasons were given by lower jurisdictions.[23]

Contemptuous acts directed against persons protected under Article 434-24 – that is, judges – are subject to more severe penalties than if the same act was directed against a person protected under the more general provision of Article 433-5 – that is, the president of the Republic, members of the government and prefectures, mayors and deputy mayors, and police superintendents. A distinction nevertheless must be made depending on whether the offence took place during or outside a hearing. Where the contemptuous act against a judge takes place outside a hearing (for example, at the general meeting of a tribunal concerned with discussing administrative matters or at deliberations), its author may be punished with imprisonment of a maximum of one year and a fine of a maximum of 100 000 FF. Where the offence takes place during a hearing against a judge (or law officer) present at the hearing or against the court as a whole, the penalty increases to a maximum of two years' imprisonment and a 200 000 FF fine.[24] The immunity provided by Article 41 of the Act of 29 July 1881 does not apply to contemptuous acts against judges, whether during a hearing or not.[25]

Discredit Brought upon a Decision of a Court

While there may still be an important element of truth in the statement that 'France offers the rare example of a legal system moving in the opposite direction [to that, in particular, of Germany or the United Kingdom] through the creation of new formal legal restrictions on legal free speech by putting the administration of justice on a different footing to other concentrations of power',[26] these conclusions may nevertheless be moderated since the entry into force of the provisions of the new Penal Code on 1 March 1994. Article 434-25 of the new Penal Code, though recapturing the main provisions of Article 226 of the old Penal Code, has considerably limited its scope of application. Moreover, the offence has become subject to a three-month time limit, just like offences committed by the press.[27]

According to Article 434-25 of the new Penal Code:

> Any person who publicly by any acts, words, writings or drawings of any nature, seeks to bring discredit upon an act or a decision of the courts, so as to impair the authority or the independence of the administration of justice, shall be punished by six months' imprisonment and a fine of 50 000 FF.
>
> The foregoing provisions are not applicable to purely technical commentaries nor to acts, words, writings or drawings of any nature seeking to reverse, quash or review a decision.
>
> When the offence is committed by the press or media, the particular provisions on these matters shall apply in order to determine the person responsible.
>
> Criminal proceedings are subject to a three-month time limit running from the day the offence took place, provided no measure of investigation or step was taken during that time.

The discredit brought upon a decision of a court may be characterized by three elements: the means used to bring the discredit; the notion of discredit and act or decision of a court; and the wrongful intention. First, as under Article 434-24, the words 'acts, words, writings or drawings' under Article 434-25 must be interpreted widely so as to encompass, in particular, the expression of thoughts through the media, television, cinema, records, tapes, theatre, songs, speeches, shouts or threats but also press articles and leaflets, books, journals, posters, brochures or letters addressed to large groups of undesignated people – even drawings, pictures and photographs – and, finally, acts such as protests and fund-raising against a decision of a court.[28] The crucial characteristic is that the means used be subject to publicity – that is, either in a public place or in the presence of a public.[29] Thus, the discredit brought upon a court's decision during a private conversation or a private meeting or by means of a private letter addressed to a designated person does not constitute a criminal offence. Moreover, Article 434-25, para. 2, further provides that 'purely technical commentaries' or 'acts, words, writings or drawings of any nature seeking to reverse, quash or review a decision' shall remain outside the scope of Article 434-25. Thus, any commentaries providing a legal discussion on a technical subject, provided that the critical examination of the decision or the act is limited to the work itself and does not extend to the author of the act or the decision, may not be considered a criminal offence under Article 434-25, even if it brings discredit upon the act or decision on which it is commenting.[30] Arguably, some journalists have used this justification to write sensational articles, arguing that a decision on appeal is to come. A solution to this problem, as suggested by André Vitu, would be to require that such written articles be concurrent to the accepted application for appeal.[31]

Second, the notion of 'discrediting' is quite vague. In its general sense, it means loss of repute or loss of credibility (from the latin word *credere*, which means to believe, to trust).[32] The notion of discredit therefore goes beyond objective criticisms or mere malicious gossip. It implies the wilful intention to ruin the authority of the act or decision itself but also the authority of its author, thereby also affecting the trust and independence generally attached to the judicial function. Article 434-25 is indeed clear on this point; the discredit must aim at impairing the authority or the independence of the administration of justice as a whole. For instance, the Court of Cassation held that abusive statements resulting in questioning the impartiality of the judges who adopted the decision subject to discredit, and in presenting the judges' attitude as an illustration of 'judicial injustice', constituted a criminal offence under Article 434-25 of the Penal Code.[33] In addition, the discredit brought upon the judges, and indeed the whole system of justice, must either aim at an act or a judicial decision. The expression 'judicial decisions' refers not only to decisions from criminal jurisdictions but also to decisions from any jurisdictions.[34] Since the term 'judicial' refers only to a decision, 'an act' is to include any act of justice, whether written or oral, and whether originating from the judges and law officers (that is, prosecutors) or from members of administrative jurisdictions, including mere citizens (for example, jurors or members of a commercial court or an industrial tribunal). Thus, the scope of Article 434-25 is to be interpreted widely so as to include the protection of any acts carried out or any judicial decisions adopted by any competent members of any judicial organs. This interpretation, which aims at extending the protection of Article 434-25 to acts or judicial decisions carried out by other members of the courts or tribunals than the judges, did not, however, prevail without some hesitation from the Court of Cassation and even judgments to the contrary by lower jurisdictions.[35]

Finally, it is the duty of the prosecutor to establish that the author of the criminal offence acted in bad faith. As under Article 434-24, mere criminal intent, which is always presumed, is not sufficient; a particular motive must be shown. In particular, the fact that the author of the discredit acted 'so as to impair' (or *dans des conditions de nature à porter atteinte*) the authority or the independence of the administration of justice, must be established. This is a difficult requirement to prove, especially since the person who commits the offence often carefully avoids bringing discredit upon the administration of justice as a whole.

The criminal offence of bringing discredit upon an act or a judicial decision is punished by six months' imprisonment and a fine of 50 000 FF. In addition, the penalty may be advertised in the conditions provided by Article 131-35, as referred to in Article 434-44 of the new Penal Code.[36] The public prosecutor alone is competent to bring proceedings against the author of an offence of discredit upon an act or a judicial decision; civil actions may not be brought.[37] The time limit to bring a criminal action under Article 434-25 is three months, starting from the day the offence was committed.[38]

Since most of the offences under Articles 434-24/25 are being committed by the press, it is the aim of the next section to consider the relevant provisions of the law relating to the freedom of the press.

Defamation of Judges under the 1881 Act on Freedom of the Press

The Act of 29 July 1881 subjects the exercise of the freedom of the press to certain restrictions considered to be necessary for the protection of the reputation and the rights of others, in accordance with Article 10 of the European Convention on Human Rights (1950).[39] Articles 30, 31 and 33 of the 1881 Act, in particular, provide that defamatory acts (libellous or slanderous) and insults committed against a court, a tribunal, or a public official, such as a judge, shall be punished by one years' imprisonment and/or a fine of 300 000 FF (in the case of defamation against a court or tribunal), or three months' imprisonments and/or a fine of 80 000 FF (in the case of defamation against a judge or insults of a court, tribunal or judge).[40] Article 29 of the Act defines 'defamation' as 'any allegation or accusation of an act which would result in attacking the good reputation or respect of the person or the body to which the act is charged to'.[41] It must nevertheless be distinguished from insults which refer to 'any abuses or contemptuous expressions or wordings not containing accusations of any act'.[42] However, whether the act is constitutive of a defamation or an insult, its criminal intent is always presumed. It is therefore up to the defendant to bring evidence of his or her good faith.[43] It follows that defamatory or insulting acts under Articles 30, 31 and 33 of the 1881 Act are not easily distinguishable from offences under Articles 434-24/25 of the Penal Code.

Furthermore, Article 23 of the 1881 Act provides very similar, although not identical, means by which the offence of defamation may be committed to those listed under the Penal Code. Under Article 23, these means may either be speeches, shouts or menaces made in public places or public meetings, or writings, prints, drawings, engravings, paintings, signs, pictures or any other means of supporting writings, words or drawings sold or distributed, for sale or exhibited in public places or public meetings, or posters for the public, or by any other means of audiovisual communication – that is, tapes, records and CDs. For the purpose of this Act, a 'public place' was interpreted to mean a place whose *raison d'être* is to get the public together – for example, a city hall or a café, but not a staircase nor the entrance of a building.[44] The element of publicity constitutes, therefore, an essential characteristic of the offence of defamation or insult under the Act of 1881. For instance, this element was found to exist in a case where information was distributed, in return for money, to diverse categories of people sharing no common interest, and who would receive this information in a non-confidential way with the intention of passing it on to new categories of people.[45]

Since most of the offences under Articles 434-24/25 of the new Penal Code are committed by the press, provisions of the Penal Code on contempt and provisions of the 1881 Act on defamation do overlap considerably. While Article 434-25 makes explicit reference to 'the particular provisions on these matters . . . in order to determine the persons responsible for it' in cases where an offence is committed by the press or media, it remains silent on which provision should be applied in situations covered by both articles.[46] Article 434-24 is equally silent on the matter. The practice of both the Court of Cassation and the doctrine reveal that no satisfactory solution reconciling these two provisions has yet been found. Soon after the 1881 Act was adopted, both the doctrine and the jurisprudence agreed that the relevant provisions of the old Penal Code were to remain unaffected.[47] As a result, the courts were faced with the problem of which of the two texts to apply in cases where, for instance, an abusive behaviour constitutes, at the same time, a contemptuous act against a judge under the Penal Code and an act of defamation against a judge under the 1881 Act. This overlapping situation, which has existed since the 1810 Penal Code, remains unsettled under the new Penal Code of 1994.[48] The stake is important since, under the Code, offences of contempt are principally subject to the general rules of law whereas, under the 1881 Act, the same offence would be subject to certain particularities – that is, a time limit of three months, provocation as a ground for exemption from punishment, different penalties and so on.[49]

We shall first consider the courts' answer to the potential conflict existing between Article 434-24 on contemptuous acts against judges and Articles 31 and 33 on acts of defamation and insults against judges, when the offence is committed by the press. Although Article 434-24 does not explicitly refer to offences committed by the press, the Court of Cassation has dealt with many cases of contemptuous acts committed by the press. Considering the scope of the conflict, this may be put in terms of three elements: the persons that these provisions seek to protect; the means of expression of the act of defamation or insult constituting a contemptuous act; and the link between the act and the duties performed by the victim. Taking each element in turn, it seems that a conflict between Articles 31 and 33 of the 1881 Act and Article 434-24 of the new Penal Code may only arise where the victim is a judge or a juror. Moreover, no conflict may arise involving contemptuous writing and drawing: if they have not been made public, Article 434-24 is applicable, if they have been made public, Article 31 or 33 of the 1881 Act becomes applicable. Potential conflict may only exist in cases of words, gestures or menaces made in public. So far as sent objects are concerned, as provided by Article 434-24, they would need to be found as constituting a means of supporting writings or drawings and be publicised in order to fall under both articles. Finally, only in cases where the act tends to undermine the dignity of the person concerned outside the performance of his or her duties but in connection with such performance may a conflict take place.[50] In cases where the act tends to affect the victim in the performance of duties because of the respect attached to the duties of the person concerned, Article 434-24 is solely applicable. Thus, a typical, and in fact quite frequent, scenario would be the case of a defamatory act considered contemptuous, committed by spoken words, gestures or menaces made in public against a judge (outside the performance of duties but for reason of such performance) or a juror.

A constant jurisprudence of the Courts of Cassation, more than 100 years old, reveals that Article 434-24 of the new Penal Code[51] prevails over the provisions of the 1881 Act. This jurisprudence has raised repeated criticisms on the part of the doctrine not the least because it fails to give reasons for this preference. Thus, today, one finds the doctrine splits between partisans of the application of the rule of plurality of legal classifications, which under general French law gives priority to the text which provides the most severe penalty,[52] and partisans of the application of the 1881 Act in accordance with the adage *lex specialis generalibus derogat*. It follows that, in the view of the doctrine, whichever way the problem is viewed, the solution is that Articles 31/33 of the 1881 Act should prevail over Article 434-24 of the new Penal Code.[53]

A conflict between Article 343-25 of the Penal Code and Articles 30 and 31 of the 1881 Act is equally conceivable, particularly when a judicial decision is being discredited by the press, whether by written or audiovisual means. Both sets of provisions – Article 434-25, on one hand, and Articles 30 and 33, on the other – do indeed seek to protect the respect and reputation of the administration of justice in general. The term 'judicial decisions' in Article 434-25 refers to any jurisdictions, thereby meeting with the terms used by Article 30, and referred to in Article 33, of the 1881 Act of 'court' or 'tribunal', including any organs performing judicial functions.[54] The solution adopted by the Court of Cassation with regard to contemptuous acts against judges committed by the press was extended to offences of discredit, including defamation and insult, of the administration of justice committed by the press. The particular provisions of the 1881 Act concerning responsibility are nevertheless applicable in accordance with Article 434-25, para. 3. Thus, Articles 42 and 43 of the 1881 Act, which provide for the responsibility 'in succession' for authors of such acts, shall apply instead of the general rules of law concerning responsibility as under Article 434-24. As a result, when the editor of the journal can be identified, he or she is regarded as the principal author of the offence, and the writer as accomplice. But when the editor cannot be identified, the writer, or short of one, the printer, becomes the principal author. In addition, the offence of discredit brought upon a judicial decision by the press is subject to a second rule of procedure which is particular to the 1881 Act – namely, a time limit of three months for bringing proceedings. Despite these two particularities and the fact that it is committed by the press, the offence is not considered a press offence; it remains punished by Article 434-25.[55]

Conclusion

The mechanisms discussed in this chapter were created with one main purpose in mind – that is, the protection of the administration of justice and its impartiality – thereby reflecting the spirit of Article 10 of the European Convention of Human Rights. However, efficient guarantee of this protection largely depends on the independence of the judiciary from outside influence. This is a characteristic of the status of judges in France which is difficult to guarantee. French judges are career judges and act as bureaucrats rather than professionals (such as in the United Kingdom).[56] They are selected on *concours* and their training takes place within the judiciary. Until recently, the Minister of Justice (or *Garde des Sceaux*) was the sole guarantor of the judges' independence in France. This state of affairs resulted in poor safeguards for judicial independence, as illustrated by the Giresse affair in 1985. According to his 'memoirs', André Giresse, President of the Paris Court of Assizes 1975–85, was forced to resign from his judicial functions as a consequence of a conspiracy against him organized by the judiciary, supported by politicians and facilitated by the press and the media. He was discredited as the most repressive and inquisitorial judge in France. *Libération* wrote on 30 November 1985:

> For the last ten years that M. Giresse has presided at the Court of Assizes of Paris, how many accused have been convicted to five, ten or twenty years' imprisonment, just because they were unlucky enough to be judged by such a character?[57]

Despite the fact that this article was bringing discredit upon the administration of justice – namely, the authority and impartiality of the Court of Assizes of Paris – no proceedings were brought by the public prosecution under Article 226 of the old Penal Code. Giresse explained that:

> It would have been futile to turn to my hierarchy or the service of the press, Place Vendome, in order to defend myself. I knew that I would face a wall of indifference

and standstill. Even worse, I would be denied the right to answer these contemptuous accusations, i.e., the right of expression, on the ground that I was obliged to exercise reserve. Should I have taken hits and be discredited in silence?[58]

And that same year, in 1985, he wrote:

> . . . a judge should be free from anyone. No political, executive or legislative powers, economic or financial pressures, public opinion, philosophical schools, spiritual powers, social classes should influence his/her decision . . . .[59]

Following the adoption of the Act of 5 February 1994 relating to the creation of the Supreme Council of Judges (*Conseil Supérieur de la Magistrature*), judges are no longer appointed solely by the president of the French Republic; half of them are now appointed by their peers. This should be seen as an improvement but not as a means of guaranteeing complete judicial independence. The Giresse affair shows that the *raison d'Etat* can sometimes win over the independence of judges, thereby undermining the entire system of protection of authority and impartiality of the administration of justice. The bottom line is that provisions of the French Penal Code and of the 1881 Act on contempt of court may only be applicable to protect judges if judges themselves are willing to protect their own peers.

Notes

1 Paras 1 and 2.
2 France is a monist country; thus, the European Convention on Human Rights (1950) does not require incorporation into national law to become applicable in French courts; like all international treaties duly ratified, it has superior authority over any French legislation (Articles 54 and 55 of the 1958 Constitution). See, for instance, *Cour de Cassation, Chambre Criminelle*, 11 March 1997.
3 Article 226, Penal Code. Regulation No. 58-1298, 23 December 1958. See, André Vitu, 'Outrage envers un dépositaire de l'autorité publique', *Juris-Classeurs pénal*, 2 (1994), art. 433-5, p. 5.
4 Formerly Articles 222–223 and Article 226, respectively. Both Articles fall in a specific chapter on infringements of the action of justice (*des atteintes à l'action de la justice*), in a section entirely devoted to contempt of court (*des atteintes à l'autorité de la justice*).
5 This and all subsequent citations from French sources have been translated by the author.
6 See, Vitu, 'Outrage', *op. cit.*, p. 4.
7 See below, p. 119.
8 The Court of Cassation decides appeals on points of law and procedures, either upholding the judgment or setting it aside and remitting the matter to a court of appeal for retrial.
9 For a comprehensive list, see André Vitu, 'Outrage à magistrat', *Juris-Classeur pénal*, 2 (1994), art. 434-24, p. 3, and *Code Pénal*, Litec (1997–98), p. 275.
10 Note that the general notion of contemptuous act (*outrage*) applicable to agents of the public authority is principally covered by Article 433-5 of the new Penal Code. Article

434-24, indeed, provides no more than a specific application of the principle declared in Article 433-5 to the particular case of judges.

11 See, Vitu, 'Outrage à magistrat', *op. cit.*, p. 4.

12 Ibid., pp. 4–5.

13 Ibid., p. 5.

14 P. Malibert, 'Dénonciation d'une infraction imaginaire', *Juris-Classeur pénal*, cited in *Code Pénal*, (Litec, 1997–98), p. 277.

15 On the distinction between a contemptuous gesture and an act of violence, see *Cour de Cassation, Chambre Criminelle, Rabouin*, 19 June 1985.

16 *Cour de Cassation, Chambre Criminelle*, 16 February 1994, *Renard Marc* (Pourvoi c/CA Reims, 29 October 1992), *Droit Pénal* (1994), commentary 130, note M. Véron.

17 Ibid., *E . . .*, 27 April 1994.

18 Provisions of the Law of 29 July 1881 would nevertheless be applicable.

19 The actual location of the victim is irrelevant, provided it can be related to the performance of the duties. Also it does not matter whether or not the judge wore the robe.

20 See Vitu, 'Outrage à magistrat', *op. cit.*, pp. 6–7.

21 Article 121-3 of the new Penal Code.

22 Article 434-24 speaks of 'acts . . . tending to reflect upon'.

23 See Vitu, 'Outrage à magistrat', *op. cit.*, p. 7.

24 For instance, the contention by the defendant that the judge was lying. See Vitu, 'Outrage à magistrat', *op. cit.*, pp. 8–9.

25 *Cour de Cassation, Chambre Criminelle, B . . .*, 22 October 1996 (Article 41 does not apply to contemptuous acts taking place outside a hearing). See, generally, J. Sauvel, 'Les immunités judiciaires, étude sur l'immunité de la parole et de l'écriture en justice', *Revue de Science Criminelle et de Droit Pénal Comparé* (1950), p. 557.

26 This statement was made with regard to Article 226 of the old Penal Code. See Barend Van Nierkerk, *The Cloistered Virtue*, (London: Praeger, 1986), p. 81.

27 See below, p. 119.

28 *Cour de Cassation, Chambre Criminelle, B . . .*, 15 November 1983 (offence committed under Article 226 by means of posters). See, generally, André Vitu, 'Discrédit sur une décision juridictionelle', *Juris-classeur pénal*, 5 (1994), Art. 434-25, p. 3.

29 In cases where the offence is committed by the press or media, the criminal responsibility of the authors of the offence is to be determined by the particular provisions applicable to the press – that is, the Act of 29 July 1881 on the freedom of the press.

30 See, Vitu, 'Discrédit sur une décision juridictionnelle', *op. cit.*, p. 6.

31 Ibid., p. 7.

32 *The Concise Oxford Dictionary of Current English*, (Oxford: Clarendon Press).

33 *Cour de Cassation, Chambre Criminelle*, 11 March 1997, *Droit pénal* (1997), commentary 106, note M. Véron.

34 In this regard, article 434-25, Penal Code, is similar to article 30, 1881 Act, which protects courts, tribunals and any organs exercising a judicial function against defamation.

35 *Cour de Cassation, Chambre Criminelle*, 15 May 1961 and *Tribunal Correctionnel de Pointe-à-Pitre*, 1 December 1971, cited in Vitu, 'Discrédit sur une décision jurisdictionnelle', *op. cit.*, pp. 4–5.

36 Paragraph 2.

37 *Cour de Cassation, Chambre Criminelle Forni*, 7 March 1988, ibid., *V . . .*, 14 March 1989, ibid., 9 December 1993 and, *Cour de Cassation, Chambre Criminelle, Le syndicat des avocats de France et autres*, 16 October 1997: a union of judges may not introduce criminal proceedings under Article 434-25 of the new Penal Code since the main purpose of this article is to protect the public interest. See, in particular, the observations by

W. Jeandidier, below the *Forni* case, in *La Semaine Juridique*, Jurisprudence (1988), No. 21133.

38 Paragraph 4. This rather short time limit may only be suspended through steps taken in criminal proceedings – that is, an investigative measure – and may not be so by interlocutory procedural steps (*Cass. crim, V. . .*, 30 April 1996).

39 *Cour de Cassation, Chambre Criminelle, R.*, 10 February 1987; *B . . . et autres*.

40 In this last case, the decision shall also be posted in public or distribution to the public.

41 Paragraph 1. The term 'defamation' comes from the Latin word *diffamare* which means to 'spread evil report' (*The Concise Oxford Dictionary of Current English*, (Oxford: Clarendon Press)). On the constitutive elements of the offence of defamation, see *Cour de Cassation, Chambre Criminelle*, 10 February 1987, and *Cour d'appel de Paris*, 18 May 1988, *F. . . et autres*.

42 Article 33, paragraph 2.

43 *Cour de Cassation, Chambre Criminelle*, 1 December 1987.

44 See the commentaries below Article 23 of the Act of 29 July 1881 in, *Code Pénal*, Litec (1997/98), p. 1492.

45 *Cour d'Appel de Paris, F. . . et autres*, 18 May 1988, *La Semaine Juridique*, Tableaux de Jurisprudence (1989), p. 6.

46 Paragraph 3.

47 That is, Articles 222-227. See Vitu, 'Outrage envers un dépositaire', *op. cit.*, pp. 18–19.

48 That is, Articles 434-24/25.

49 Note, however, that contemptuous acts committed during a hearing or committed by an *avocat* are subject to special procedures. See Vitu, 'Outrage à magistrat', *op. cit.*, pp. 9–10.

50 *Revue de science criminelle et de droit pénal comparé* (1976), observations Vitu, p. 101 and (1956), observations Hugueney, p. 540. When no such connection exists, the offence does not fall under Article 31 but may instead be covered by Article 32 of the 1881 Act. See, for instance, *Cour de Cassation, Chambre Criminelle, D . . .*, 27 March 1990.

51 Formerly Article 222.

52 That is, Article 222 *et seq.* under the old Penal Code, but no longer under Article 434-24.

53 See Vitu, 'Outrage envers un dépositaire', *op. cit.*, p. 20.

54 See Vitu, 'Discredit sur une décision jurisdictionnelle', *op. cit.*, p. 4.

55 Ibid., pp. 4–5.

56 In 1994 there were around 6000 judges in France, in contrast with only 945 full-time judges in the United Kingdom. See M. Delmas-Marty, *Procédures pénales d'Europe* (Thémis: PUF, 1995), p. 427.

57 Cited in A. Giresse and P. Bernert, *Seule la vérité blessé* (Paris: Plon, 1987), p. 431.

58 Ibid., p. 424.

59 Ibid., p. 11.

8 Criticizing Judges in Denmark

Marianne Holdgaard, Jørgen Albaek Jensen and Rasmus Møller Madsen

Introduction

Freedom of expression has enjoyed constitutional protection since the Constitution of 1849. Article 77 of the present Constitution which provides that:

> Any person shall be at liberty to publish his ideas in print, in writing, and in speech, subject to his being held responsible in a court of law. Censorship and other preventive measures shall never again be introduced.

The ideal and doctrinal scope of this provision protects against all forms of prior restraint, and thus censorship or other preceding steps to hamper disclosure of statements[1] are not in conformity with the Constitution. Notwithstanding the explicit wording of Article 77, Danish constitutional theory has, albeit reluctantly, accepted certain existing limitations to the protection of freedom of expression in a formal sense.[2] The rationale behind these limitations has been that Article 77 never meant to protect unlawful expressions. Thus, such expressions – for example, clear defamation – may, under very strict conditions,[3] be subject to injunctions to prevent criminal and damaging expressions from being published.[4]

Article 77 of the Danish Constitution is now interpreted in the light of Article 10 of the European Convention on Human Rights,[5] which protects freedom of expression both formally and substantively,[6] but the constitutional provision does not directly offer protection against civil or criminal liability. Although actions against expressions may be imposed only by the courts, theoretically there are no limits whatsoever in Article 77 to the legislature's power to enact specific laws incriminating the expression of opinions or thoughts on certain matters.[7] However, it is obvious that the value of constitutional protection of freedom of expression in the formal sense is almost worthless if the exercise of this right can be sanctioned by, for example, criminal liability. In practice the parliament has, to a large extent, resisted the temptation to penalize expressions in order not to hamper a free debate, but in certain areas the balancing between freedom of expression and the need for protection against injurious statements has motivated legislative actions – for example, the laws concerning professional secrecy, defamation, protection of privacy and so on.[8]

These laws are, however, not seen as derogating from Article 77. On the contrary, the courts have, on several occasions, stressed that, in applying these laws in concrete cases, consideration must be given to the protection of freedom of speech in Article 77.[9] Thus the courts, alongside Danish constitutional theory, acknowledge that, although not explicitly mentioned in Article 77, some constitutional protection of freedom of expression in a substantive sense can be derived from this provision. It is, however, difficult on the basis of the existing case law to identify areas or subjects where full substantive protection can be said to exist since the case law seems to be rather specific in its assessments.[10] Projected to the criticism of judges, this means that there may be constitutional limits to legislative initiatives prohibiting criticism of certain groups – for example, judges. This chapter assesses the compatibility of the relevant statutes concerning criticism of judges with the constitutional demands laid down in Article 77.

The Provisions of the Penal Code

The Penal Code contains provisions penalizing libel, in order to protect both a person's self-esteem and reputation. According to s.267, para. 1, both accusations and offensive words or conduct, capable of insulting the honour or respect of others, are criminal offences. An accusation is characterized by an allegation concerning a person's moral conduct or characteristics, which can be verified objectively. Offensive words or conduct cover terms of abuse or other ways of insulting other persons.[11] Whereas such contemptuous statements, by definition, fall outside the sphere of permitted expressions, accusations can, in principle, be either verified or disproved, and accusations are only offences insofar as they are false.

According to s.269 of the Danish Penal Code, an accusation is exempt from punishment if the statement issued can be proven correct or if the person has acted in good faith and has been under an obligation to speak or has acted in justified protection of obvious public interest or of the personal interest of himself or of others. This difference between accusations and contemptuous statements is therefore important. Whereas society has no general interest in protecting people calling others all sorts of names, the importance of free and critical debate demands that grave and unpleasant accusations be protected so long as they are truthful.[12]

Under Danish criminal law the general rule is that the police and prosecution authorities *ex officio* press charges if they find a basis for doing so. However, the provisions on libel are subject to private prosecution, meaning that legal actions are only carried out on the initiative or request of the victims of the offence.[13] In other words, the Penal Code acknowledges the need to have remedies against insulting statements, but does not consider it a public responsibility to investigate, proceed against or punish such statements unless the addressee of the statements feels a need to do so.

The protection of libel applies to everybody, but certain groups enjoy better protection than others. According to ss.119 and 121 of the Danish Penal Code,[14] persons required to act by virtue of a public office or function enjoy protection against being attacked by insults, abusive language or other offensive words or gestures while executing their office or function.[15] The group of persons covered by this provision encompasses public officials, including judges, police officers and so on. The statements covered by s.121 are more limited than those falling under the general libel provision in s.267 mentioned above: s.121 supplements s.267, para. 2, which makes it an aggravating circumstance to commit offences covered by s.267, para. 1 as regards the group of persons protected by s.121. The difference between s.121 and s.267, para. 2 is that the main purpose of s.121 is to protect public officials in a situation where a person is addressed directly, while s.267, para. 2 covers a situation where a person is commented upon.[16]

The enhanced protection for public officials under s.121 can be seen as an extension of the need to protect public officials against violent attacks or assaults as in s.119. But whereas it seems logical to grant persons representing public authorities a relatively high protection against physical attacks while carrying out their tasks as is done in s.119, it does not necessarily follow that the same considerations need to be given in relation to protection against defamation, as regards accusations which, if true, would be important to discover and disclose.[17]

The Penal Code does not contain any special provisions regarding criticism of judges in general, but does give judges better protection in one specific situation. According to s.119, para. 2 it is a criminal offence to threaten to accuse a judge of a criminal act or of dishonourable conduct. The same applies to other persons exercising judicial authority – for example, lay judges, jurors and so on – with regard to accusations of a defamatory nature. However, s.119, para. 2 is limited in its sphere of application to situations where the threat is made in respect of the execution of the office or function. Thus, the judge is protected under s.119, para. 2 only when performing his duty as judge. The difference between s.119, para. 2 and ss.121 and 267 is that, whereas the latter are only consummated when the statements have been made, s.119, para. 2 makes the mere threat of making an accusation a criminal offence. The justification for this distinction is that the fear of, even untrue, threats of allegations or information concerning the judge might influence his decisions unduly. In practice, however, s.119, para. 2 is very rarely used.

A crucial question when applying the provisions in the Penal Code is how the courts interpret and apply the vague wording of the provisions, such as whether a statement is likely to disparage the person in question in the estimation of his fellow citizens (cf. s.267, para. 1). The yardstick for measuring which statements are too harsh changes with the general opinion on what is considered insulting, but the provisions cover all statements on, for instance, personal, ethical and professional matters.

However, expressions may be assessed differently depending on where, in which context, and to whom they are expressed. For example, politicians must tolerate rather harsh criticism and accusations from which other groups, such as judges, may be protected.[18] Although – apart from the rarely used s.119, para. 2 – there are no special provisions in the Penal Code addressing criticism of judges, they are still public officials who are covered by both ss.267 and 121. There have been only very few cases concerning libel against judges,[19] but the most notorious of these in recent memory is the *Barfod* case.

Following a judgment in a tax case from the Greenlandic High Court, Mr Barfod (who was not a party to the case) published an article in a local newspaper criticizing the participating judges. The Bench was composed of one professional judge and two lay judges, the latter both employed in the public sector by the local government. Besides criticizing the principle of using lay judges, Mr Barfod accused the two lay judges in this specific case of having ruled in favour of their employer, the defendant in the case – the Greenlandic authorities. The article included the following passage:

> Most of the Local Government's members could . . . afford the time to watch that the two Greenland lay judges, who are by the way both employed directly by the Local Government, . . . did their duty, and this they did. The vote was two to one in favour of the Local Government, and with such a bench of judges it does not require much imagination to guess who voted how.[20]

Subsequently Mr Barfod was charged and convicted of defamation[21] both in the district court and the High Court. In its ruling the High Court held:

> The Court agrees with the prosecution that the wording of the article . . . represents a serious accusation which is likely to lower [the two lay judges] in public esteem. Proof of the accusations has not been adduced, something which, moreover, would not have been possible since it cannot be excluded that they would have reached the same result had they not been employed by the Local Government.[22]

Although Mr Barfod could criticize the composition of the court (objective criticism), the European Court of Human Rights did not grant him protection of his right to criticize the persons involved for not being impartial (subjective criticism) unless he could actually prove his allegations. The precedential value of the case, both on a national and on an international level, seems questionable.

Criticism of judges – at least other than in the most simple form of contemptuous statements – is not only an issue under Article 10 of the European Convention on Human Rights, but also an issue under Article 6 of the Convention if the criticism (as in the *Barfod* case) has to do with the impartiality of the court or the judges. The European Court of Human Rights has, in its application of Article 6, frequently stressed the importance of impartiality both from a subjective and objective point of view.[23] In other words, justice must not only be done but must also be seen to be done.[24] Thus, neither the accused nor others must have any reasonable doubt as to the impartiality of the judges in a case. In order to give this principle effect it seems natural and necessary to allow accusations of partiality to be put forward even if these accusations imply that the judge has manifestly misused his position.[25]

It is, however, noteworthy that the national High Court in the *Barfod* case acknowledged that the two lay judges should not have been acting as judges in a case against their own employer. In other words, the two lay judges did not pass the objective test used by the European Court of Human Rights. Mr Barfod's conviction was aimed at ensuring respect for the judiciary in the eyes of the public. It is, however, questionable whether restrictions on freedom of expression imposed by the organ being criticized in general will contribute to the respectability of that body.

The Provisions in the Administration of Justice Act

In addition to the provisions in the Penal Code which provide general remedies against defamatory and insulting remarks, there are rules concerning behaviour *in* court that should be mentioned – namely the judge's powers to call to order persons misbehaving in the courtroom and the professional liability of lawyers. According to s.150 of the Administration of Justice Act, the procedure in court is led by the chairman of the court – that is, (one of) the judge(s). As part of this leading role he may, according to s.151, correct parties, witnesses and others when making unseemly remarks or improper personal accusations. If, after a warning, the behaviour continues, the chairman may order the person in question to be removed from the courtroom and may also sentence him to a fine.[26]

S.151 primarily aims at the *way* in which things are said or done, rather than imposing a limit on which issues can be brought before the court. Thus, s.151 primarily deals with statements equivalent to contemptuous statements, but the threshold for what is considered improper may very well be lower in s.151 than in the Penal Code provisions mentioned above.[27] Whereas it is difficult to ascertain how often s.151, para. 1 is used,[28] there are only a few cases in which the chairman has felt it necessary to impose a fine under its provisions, and even fewer of these cases concern defamation of the judge[29] in the process.

Practising lawyers in Denmark must be members of the Danish Bar.[30] The Bar, as a quasi-judicial organ, adjudicates on disputes relating to ethical standards of the Law Society. It also has the competence to decide cases of professional misconduct on the part of its members.[31] In grave cases a lawyer may be deprived of his right to practise as a lawyer.[32] In terms of defamation these rules could become relevant if the lawyer for one of the parties insults the judge.[33] However, an important point to mention in this connection is, of course, that a lawyer as part of his representation in a case may claim that the judge is biased, and is therefore not suitable to have on the Bench. According to ss.60–62 of the Administration of Justice Act, a judge may not participate in cases where he has a personal interest, is related to one of the parties, has previously been involved in the case and so on. These provisions may be invoked as part of a party's argumentation without violating any rules.[34] However, the rules in ss.60–62 deal only with *objective* grounds of partiality.

The question, therefore, is whether, for example, one of the lawyers in the tax case relating to the *Barfod* case could have made the same accusations in court as did Mr Barfod in the press. Such *subjective* grounds for partiality – if they are untrue – seem to fall under s.267 of the Penal Code as mentioned above. However, according to s.269, accusations are not criminal offences if they are made in justified protection of obvious public interest or the personal interest of oneself or of others. This includes lawyers' work for clients. In other words, the lawyer is free to take in all circumstances supporting his case.[35]

Conclusion

The statutory regulation on this subject shows that criticism of judges is considered a criminal offence rather than a civil law subject. There is a special rule relating only to judges in s.119, para. 2 of the Penal Code but, as this provision is hardly ever used in practice, the reality is that, besides the general rules of defamation which apply to everybody, judges are only protected through their status as public officials. However, case law may treat judges with greater respect, leaving a more narrow possibility for accusations against them.

Nevertheless, criticism of judges in Denmark is, in fact, a very common phenomenon; inside, as well as outside, the courtrooms the behaviour of the judges and the accuracy of their rulings is the object of discussion and criticism both from an academic and political point of view and in the press.[36] With respect to criticizing the individual judge it is important to stress that it is perfectly legitimate to claim that a judge is unsuitable to rule in a concrete case due to objective legal incapacity – for example, a close connection with one of the parties. What is probably still inadmissible is an insinuation of deliberate favouring of certain interests in complete conflict with the interests of fairness.

However, for several reasons, cases of defamation of judges are raised very rarely. First, it is probably fair to say that most people – and certainly professionals such as lawyers – do, in fact, respect and trust the authority of the Danish judiciary, so it is probably rare to find parties who believe the judge to be corrupt. There have never been any serious scandals involving Danish judges, and the training and ethical standards of the judges are believed to be very high. Similarly, if or when judges are defamed, they are unlikely to bother to make a case out of it, since such statements often speak for themselves. Moreover, defamation proceedings involving judges are very rare: most of the reported cases are old and it seems as if the average judge does not need an official decision to refute allegations or accusations. Whether this is because notions as 'honour' and 'reputation' are less important in Danish culture, or whether the means of refutation are more informal is hard to say.

Against such a background it is somehow paradoxical that one of these rather rare cases – the *Barfod* case – progressed to the European Court of Human Rights. Although Denmark won the case it is certainly possible that developments in Danish case law would result in a different outcome of a similar case today. Since the *Jersild* case it seems as if the balance – when a choice between protection of the freedom of expression versus other considerations is inevitable – has swung towards a greater protection of the former at least as long as the statements in question contain more than just simple insults in the form of contemptuous statements. The *Barfod* case may not, after all, be representative of the state of law in Denmark any longer.

Notes

1   The wording 'in print, in writing, and in speech' has, through a teleological interpretation, been extended to cover expressions communicated through other means – for example, pictures, sculptures etc. Cf. J. Albaek Jensen and M. Hansen Jensen, *Danmarks Riges Grundlov – med kommentarer* (The Danish Constitution – Annotated Edition) (Copenhagen: DJOEF Publishing, 1999), p. 428.

2 H. Zahle, *Dansk Forfatningsret* (Danish Constitutional Law), vol. 3, 2nd edn (Copenhagen: Christian Ejlers' Publishing, 1997), pp. 32–33.

3 See the Administration of Justice Act, Chapter 57.

4 In practice the possibility of using injunctions is very narrow, and great consideration is given to the importance of Article 77. See for example, *Ugeskrift for Retsvaesen* (Weekly Law Review) (hereafter *UfR*) (1980), p. 1037, Supreme Court decision, where a request to stop the distribution of a poster allegedly jeopardizing severe export interests was denied by the Supreme Court.

5 The European Convention on Human Rights was incorporated into Danish law in 1992. Due to the dualistic system, ratification did not in itself make the Convention applicable in Danish courts. Since the coming into force of the incorporating act, the protection of human rights has thus achieved a more solid foundation. The hierarchy of norms means that the Convention, in principle, is just a regular statute which can be changed or abolished by new statutes. In practice it is clear that the Convention prevails over other statutes, and it is likely that even the Constitution will be interpreted in light of the Convention.

6 However, the protection of substantive freedom of expression is not absolute since Article 10, para. 2 lists quite a few exceptions to Article 10, para. 1.

7 Albaek Jensen and Hansen Jensen, *op. cit.*, p. 439.

8 Ibid., p. 434.

9 In the Danish Supreme Court's ruling in the case later known as the *Jersild* case, the question before the court was whether a journalist, by broadcasting an interview with a group of people expressing racist statements, had aided or abetted in violating Section 266(b) of the Penal Code concerning racist and degrading statements. After having stated that the acts carried out by the journalist from an objective point of view did violate the Penal Code the majority of the judges continued: '[We] do not find that an acquittal of [the journalist] could be justified on the ground of freedom of expression in matters of public interest as opposed to the interest in the protection against racial discrimination.' In other words, a balance between, on the one hand, the content of the Penal Code and, on the other hand, the principle of freedom of expression *was* achieved but the Supreme Court did not, contrary to the European Court of Human Rights, find that the public interest in bringing the concrete statements overruled the interest in the protection against racist statements.

10 Albaek Jensen and Hansen Jensen, *op. cit.*, p. 448–49. It has been argued that, since the Constitution is founded on democratic ideas and provides for democratic elections, a right to campaign before elections inherently enjoys constitutional protection. The range of this argument is, however, discussed in ibid., p. 441.

11 K. Waaben, *Strafferettens specielle del* (Criminal Law – The Specific Crimes) 5th edn, (Copenhagen: Thomsen Publishers, 1999), pp. 219 and 223.

12 Certain limitations to this principle exist. According to s.270, the way in which an accusation is stated may be so improper that criminal liability may come into question notwithstanding that the statement is true.

13 Cf. Article 275. See, further, V. Greve *et al.*, *Kommenteret straffelov. Speciel del* (Annotated Edition on the Penal Code – The Specific Crimes) 6th edn (Copenhagen: DJOEF Publishing, 1997), p. 261f.

14 S.119.

15 From the wording of s.121 it seems as if it covers only contemptuous statements. Practice has, however, interpreted s.121 as also covering accusations. See Greve, *Kommenteret straffelov, op. cit.*, p. 48.

16 Cf. ibid., p. 342.

17 Again, a distinction between contemptuous statements with the sole purpose of offending

people and accusations that may, or may not, have that purpose, has to be drawn. Some margin for even untrue accusations must be given, whereas the need to protect comtemptuous statements seems very little.

18   Waaben, *Strafferettens specielle del, op. cit.*, pp. 216–17.

19   *UfR* (1935), p. 418, High Court decision: seven people were convicted for violating s.267 for accusing a judge, without any evidence, of having committed rape in the past. See also *UfR* (1935), p. 657, High Court decision: a person had during a public political meeting stated that 'our judicial system is corrupt and rotten' and was sentenced to 30 days' imprisonment; cf. s.267. It is very likely that the case is no longer representative of the standard for when political opinions become defamation.

20   The translation as it appears in the judgment of the European Court of Human Rights: see para. 7ff.

21   The initiative to press charges was taken by the professional, not the lay, judges of the case.

22   Mr Barfod then filed a complaint to the European Commission on Human Rights claiming, amongst other things, a violation of his freedom of expression; cf. Article 10. Whereas the Commission found the conviction in breach of Article 10, the Court took the opposite view:

> . . . the Court is satisfied that the interference with his freedom of expression did not aim at restricting his rights under the Convention to criticize publicly the composition of the High Court . . . . Indeed, his right to voice his opinion on this issue was expressly recognized by the High Court in its judgment . . . . It was quite possible to question the composition of the High Court without at the same time attacking the two lay judges personally. In addition, no evidence has been submitted to the effect that the applicant was justified in believing that the two elements of criticism raised by him were so closely connected as to make the statement relating to the two lay judges legitimate. The High Court's finding that there was no proof of the accusations against the lay judges remains unchallenged; the applicant must accordingly be considered to have based his accusations on the mere fact that the lay judges were employed by the Local Government . . . . Although this fact may give rise to a difference in opinion as to whether the court was properly composed, it was certainly not proof of actual bias and the applicant cannot reasonably have been unaware of that. The State's legitimate interest in protecting the reputation of the two lay judges was accordingly not in conflict with the applicant's interest in being able to participate in free public debate on the question of the structural impartiality of the High Court . . . . The impugned statement was not a criticism of the reasoning in the judgment . . . but rather . . . a defamatory accusation against the lay judges personally, which was likely to lower them in public esteem and was put forward without any supporting evidence.

23   *Hauschildt* v. *Denmark* (1989) ECHR, Series A.154 para. 46ff. in which the court talks about an objective and subjective test that has to be passed. See also D.J. Harris, M. O'Boyle and C. Warbrick, *Law of the European Convention on Human Rights* (London: Butterworths, 1995), p. 234f.

24   Harris *et al.*, *Law of the ECHR, op. cit.*, p. 235.

25   Under s.146 of the Danish Penal Code judges who make manifestly unfair judgments are committing a criminal offence. In other words, *if* Mr Barfod had been able to prove a deliberate ruling in favour of one of the parties, s.146 *might* have come into play.

26   S.151, para. 2. The possibility of invoking the provisions under the Penal Code is unaffected by such fining, cf. s.151, para. 3.

27   At least under s.151, para. 1 the chairman is vested with a considerable margin of appreciation to determine whether or not the language used is improper.

28   The exercise of the power given under s.151, para. 1 does not require a formal decision from the chairman and cannot be subject to acts of appeal (contra fines under s.151, para. 2).

29   Presumably the chairman in most cases chooses simply to have the person in question removed from the room so that the hearing may continue.

30   S.143 of the Administration of Justice Act.

31   Chapters 15a and 15b of the Administration of Justice Act.

32   S.147c.

33   The situation seems very hypothetical since the ethical standard and behaviour of lawyers in general is above defamatory remarks. There seems to be no case law on the situation.

34   In wake of the *Hauschildt* case several cases concerning the impartiality of judges have been tried. See, for example, *UfR* (1990), pp. 13 and 181, (1994), p. 536, and (1996), p. 234, Supreme Court decisions.

35   Whereas the content – the accusation – may be protected by s.269, the form in which it is expressed may, of course, in itself be so rude that it constitutes a contemptuous statement – for example, terms of abuse, nicknames and so on.

36   At present there is much discussion about whether judges, in the future, may hold other jobs while being a judge. There is a considerable backlog of cases waiting to be settled and, in these cases, judges have agreed to act as private arbitrators, to gain extra income. This has attracted some criticism. At the same time it has been argued that judges, by engaging in arbitration, may jeopardize their impartiality and independence since they are being paid by companies or other bodies to conduct the arbitration, and these companies may later become parties to disputes in the courts.

9   Criticizing Judges in Iceland

Agust Karlsson

Introduction

The judiciary plays an important role in the daily affairs of Iceland. The relationship between the judiciary and other organs of government, as well as with other public and private institutions, is based on gradually evolving practice through case law and legislation. It is true to say that the effectiveness of the Icelandic legal system generally depends on the effectiveness of the judiciary. It is thus natural that the judiciary can be the subject of general discussion, and sometimes criticism, from the public. In this respect, Iceland is no exception. Open discussion regarding the Icelandic courts tends to focus on controversial cases. Losers in litigation sometimes feel the urgent need to put forward their opinion on the judgment. Such complaints are seldom subject to open discussion, mainly because the judges are not expected to express their views in reply once their judgments are delivered.[1] In that a response from judges whose work is criticized is not expected, it is possible to argue that judges are in a somewhat different position from laymen when their work is criticized. The interesting question is whether the legislature has given judges an option protecting them from public criticism in other ways. The aim of this chapter is to describe Icelandic law on this matter, but in conjunction with common rules on the freedom of expression and its limitations.

Freedom of Expression

Before looking at Icelandic laws on the freedom of expression one should look at the legal system in a historical context in order to get a full picture of system. The first Icelandic inhabitants came from Norway around 874 AD. In 930 they established a parliament, *Althing*, whose administration was based on regional leaders and legal order from Norwegian laws. After conflicts between the leaders the *Althing* decided in 1262 to surrender the administration to the Norwegian Crown. In the year 1281 the *Althing* legalized a civil code, the *jonsbok*. From the end of the twelfth century to the eighteenth century there were no formal legislative changes in the country, but during that period the domination of the country moved from Norway to Denmark. At the end of the eighteenth century the Icelandic people began to campaign for independence, the outcome of which was the gaining of sovereignty in 1918 and independence in 1944. The legislative power is in the hands of parliament (*Althing*).

Due to the small population and the historical background the legal system has been closely connected to those of the other Nordic countries, especially of Denmark. Direct translation from Danish law is not uncommon, and Danish legal literature and precedents have substantial influence in the Icelandic courts – for instance, in company law and family law. This has, however, changed somewhat since Iceland joined the European Economic Area in 1993, and now the legislation is largely influenced by European law in a wide sense. Iceland's long-standing membership of the Council of Europe, the OECD and EFTA has also influenced the legal framework.

The right to freedom of expression without interference by the government is recognized in Iceland as one of the fundamental human rights and is protected in the Constitution of the Republic of Iceland, No. 33, from 17 June 1944 and also in the laws on the European Convention on Human Rights, No. 62/1994. The Icelandic state also has legal obligations under the Universal Declaration of Human Rights (1948) and under the United Nations Covenants (1966) (on Civil and Political Rights and also on Economic, Social and Cultural Rights), although Icelandic litigants cannot rely directly on the rights conferred by these treaties before domestic courts. To be useful in the domestic context, treaty provisions have to be made part of the domestic law.

Article 73 of the Icelandic Constitution, as it was last amended by Act no. 97/ 1995, protects freedom of expression by the following words.

> All are free to have opinions and persuasions.
> Every man has the right to express his thoughts, but he may be held responsible for them in court. Censorship or other limitations on the freedom of expression may never be imposed.
> The freedom of expression may only be restricted by laws for the purpose of national order and security, for the protection of health and morals or because of the rights or reputation of others, on the condition that the limitations are necessary and in accordance with democratic tradition.

The explanatory text presented with the legal text which became Act 97/1995, states that the Article 73 is based on an older article which protected the right to express thought in print[2] and also on Article 10 of the European Convention on Human Rights. This has been interpreted by scholars to mean that there are no material differences between Article 73 of the Constitution and Article 10 of the Convention.

This is illustrated by the fact that there are three conditions for interference according to the Constitution. The interference may only be restricted by formal laws, it must have a legitimate aim – that is, the protection of morals and so on – and it must be necessary and in accordance with democratic traditions. The similarity with the conditions in Article 10 of the Convention is obvious.

It is indisputable that the above general rules also apply to the persons who criticize judges, in one way or another. It is just as clear that judges are protected, like others, by the exception from the general rule. *Althing* has, over the years, enacted rules which affect the freedom of expression and the most important of these will be examined below, paying close attention to how they affect the work of judges. The discussion of these rules are divided into two parts: first, those rules which apply in courts and, second, those rules which apply outside the courthouse.

Criticism in Court[3]

According to the Icelandic judicial system the judge first and foremost has to resolve the dispute between two or more parties, which has been allocated to him by a certain formal procedure. A typical case starts with the issuing of a writ and, on a named day, the case is forwarded to a court. The parties or their legal representatives then meet with the judge and make procedural decisions. Finally, after the trial, the judge delivers his judgment. It is safe to say that the relationship between the judges and the parties or their representatives is generally very good, but occasionally people feel that their case does not get fair attention or that the judge is biased. An aggrieved person may well feel a pressing need to express his or her opinion on the matter in words which may be considered out of line, and the question is how the judge can respond under Icelandic laws.

The law on procedural sanctions are to be found in Article 135 of the Act on the Civil Case Procedure at lower court No. 91/1991. According to Article 135(1)(e) a judge can fine a party for unjustified written or verbal expression addressed to the judge in court. Para. (1)(f) adds to the above provision in that the judge can also impose a fine for any other act performed by the party, which offends the judge. These two provisions apply only to the parties but, according to para. 2-4 of Article 135 the judge has the authority to apply the same punishment to the parties' agents – that is, his or her advocate,[4] or any other person situated in court during the process.

The main rule is that the punishment against a litigant or his agent is written in the finding of the judgment or, if no judgment is delivered, in a special adjudication from the judge. This is in accordance with Article 136 of the above law on civil procedure. Consequently, the judge has no immediate punishment available, and this gives the party and his agent substantial protection since they can proceed with the case and put forward all their arguments. The importance of this may be illustrated by an example of a case in which one of the parties accuses the judge of bias. If the judge disagrees with this accusation, he may feel that the party's argument to be defamatory, and might misuse penal sanctions in order to frustrate legal debate. This is not possible according to Icelandic law. On the other hand, when the unjustified expression is made by any other than the party or its agent, the sanctions are decided immediately.

The Icelandic legal system is not rich in cases where procedural fines have been used, and there are even fewer cases in which an unjustifiable act is addressed to the judge. The following examples can, however, be found in the case law from the Supreme Court of Iceland. In the case *Jon Gislason* v. *Kristjani Asgrimssyni*[5] an advocate claimed that the opposing advocate was deliberately lying. The Supreme Court said that this statement was unjustified and fined the advocate. There are, similarly, a few cases in which written observations have been the subject of civil fines under Icelandic law. An example of such a case is *Gudmundur Jonasson* v. *Minister of Finance and Advocate Bjorn Thordarson*[6] in which one of the parties wrote, in a document, that the authorities were criminals. The Supreme Court not only imposed a fine on the party but decreed also that the comment should be struck off the record. The same sanction – that is, nullification – was also imposed in *Fiskur & Is* v. *Hojgaard & Schultz A/S*,[7] in which an advocate's comment on a certain witness was annulled.

Practically the only direct punishments available under Icelandic law for criticizing judges are fines, sometimes followed by the annulment of the unjustified comment. The fines are based on the above articles in Act 91/1991 on Civil Procedure and it should be mentioned that the laws on procedures in criminal cases have no provision on this matter, except only from the general rule that, when some matter is not addressed in that law, one should refer to the civil law procedure when appropriate. The annulment of the unjust expression is based on Article 241 of the General Penal Code No. 19, from 19 February 1940, a rule which will be discussed in more detail below. There are, however, some questions regarding the use of these provisions as in the case *Hordur Valdimarsson* v. *Minister of Communications and Minister of Finance*[8] in which the judge at the lower court stated that it was not possible to annul a comment in the case documents because the other party did not demand such reaction under the procedure. The judge continued by stating that the comment was not subject to a fine, but then rebuked the advocate for the comment. Rebuke, as the mildest penalty available to the judge, has been used in a few cases in different situations – for example, in *Akæruvaldid* v. *Gudmanni Krisjanssyni*[9] in which a defendant's advocate was rebuked by the Supreme Court for an unnecessary appeal.

In all of the above cases the injured person was someone other than the judge himself. A thorough search for cases where the judge's wounded feelings were the main issue proved fruitless and, even though one or two such cases might exist, they seem to be of little importance and not accessible to general discussion.[10] This barrenness in the case law is interesting, particularly as other countries seem to differ in this respect. Although there might be several reasons for this situation, a principal factor might be that Icelandic judges are competent and respected for their work. This means that advocates and others generally have no reason to complain about their handling of cases. Another factor might be the small size of the legal community, which means that people are more in touch with each other and build personal relationships, which is more difficult in larger countries.

Criticism Outside the Courts

A judge offended outside the courthouse has no power under the legal provisions to bring the offender into his chamber, and can thus not apply the above sanctions. What he can do is force the offender to meet in court by issuing a writ, but in these circumstances the judge will have to present his case like any other citizen. The general rules which apply to defamatory expression are discussed below.

It was mentioned above that the general rules on the freedom of expression in the Constitution and the Conventions on Human Rights provide that this freedom can be restricted under certain circumstances – for example, for the protection of the morals and the rights of others. The legislature has issued general rules regarding defamatory expression in the Act on the General Penal Code, mentioned above. The main provisions are in Chapter 25, where the general rules are set forth and in Chapter 12 which has a special provision regarding public officers.

The most important provision in Chapter 25 are those in Articles 234 and 235 which concern defamatory expression. The rules state as follows:

Article 234: Whoever, [which] set forth insulting allegations against another person, in words or by actions, and whoever, [which] vituperates such, shall be fined or detained for up to one year.
Article 235: If anyone alleged that another person has performed anything, which could defame him, or vituperates such, shall be fined or detained for up to one year.

The difference between these two articles lies in the strength of the offence: Article 234 refers to insulting allegations, whereas Article 235 deals with defamatory allegations. 'Defamatory' has, in this context, been defined as an allegation of criminal offence, such as murder, theft or similar crime, but also as an allegation of immoral actions.[11] Insulting allegations referred to in Article 234, on the other hand, are defined as negative comments which may affect person's self-respect or lower his reputation.[12] It is not easy to see the difference between those rules in praxis, and most cases are based on breach of both of the rules.[13] Alleged defamation or insult has been the issue in several cases in the Supreme Court of Iceland, and in a few of them judges or a similar authority have been among the parties. In the case *Sveinn Arnason* v. *Gudmundi Hannessyni*[14] the facts were that S wrote a letter to the administration and complained about how G, a judge, had dealt with his case against a third person. In the letter S said that it was his assumption that G had not read the writ issued in the case and thus grossly neglected his duties and should therefore be rebuked. S continued by asking the authorities to respond to his claim and show the judge that he ought to read his cases thoroughly. The judge was unhappy about this letter and claimed, in a defamatory case, that S's expression violated the laws on defamation. The Supreme Court stated that, taking into account the facts of the case, S's writings were unjustified; they were humiliating and insulting to G. S was therefore penalized and his remarks deemed null and void.[15]

The power to declare some words null and void is grounded in Article 241 of the General Penal Code.[16] The purpose of nullification is to give the damaged person some kind of official purification;[17] it is an indication that the remarks are untrue or unjustifiable. A demand for nullification is usually one of the main features of defamatory cases and it is not uncommon, in such cases, for a few remarks to be declared null and void, but no penalties imposed on the alleged offender.[18] One of the reasons for this is that the legal grounds for nullification are not as limited as sanctions under Articles 234 and 235. It is, for example, possible to declare remarks null and void in circumstances where it is not possible to punish the offender with a fine or detention. Another difference is that, according to Article 29 of the Penal Code, a damaged person must initiate a legal action for himself, within six months of the offence.[19] This six-month rule does not apply to the nullification claim. This provision on nullification has been subject to criticism recently, and scholars have argued that the Article 241 is incompatible with Article 10 of the European Convention on Human Rights.[20] The reasoning is that the article is not neutral against the alleged wrongdoer, as it may be very difficult for him to prove that every word expressed was true. It is impossible for the alleged wrongdoer to prove ideas and feelings and, when the judge annuls his words, the public get the impression that he has been telling untrue stories. This is especially true of cases involving the press and directly results in restricted discussion and thus limitation on the freedom of expression.

Special Rules on Official Employees

In Chapter 12 of the Penal Code there are special rules regarding alleged breach against official employees – for example, judges. This provision has been the subject of dispute, as it is not clear why officials should have more protection than others. The main difference for the officials is that the prosecutor acts under Chapter 12, which is not the case in defamatory cases. Chapter 12 had a special defamatory provision until 1995, which stated the following:

> Art. 108. Whoever vituperates or otherwise insults a civil servant in words or actions or makes defamatory allegations against or about him when he is discharging his duty, or about him when he is discharging his duty, or on account of the discharge of his duty, shall be fined, detained or imprisoned for up to three years. An allegation, even if proven, may warrant a fine if made in an impudent manner.

With Act 17/1995, the above article was abolished, and the reason for the amendment was a judgment from the European Court of Human Rights, in the case *Thorgeir Thorgeirsson* v. *Iceland*.[21] The facts of this case were that T wrote two articles about police brutality. He was charged and subsequently convicted for defamatory allegations. T appealed the case to the Supreme Court which confirmed the conviction. T then petitioned the Strasbourg institutions where he at last found justice, as the European Court found that the state of Iceland had breached Article 10 of the Convention on Human Rights. The outcome of this case came as a big surprise to Icelandic authorities which believed that human rights were sufficiently secured in Iceland, compared with other countries. The judgment demonstrated that this was not the case and the government reacted by re-evaluating its human rights policy. Among the changes made were the amendment of the human rights chapter in the Constitution, legislation of the European Convention on Human Rights, and the amendment of Article 108 of the Penal Code.

The Advocates' Profession

Judges and advocates work in a close relationship and it is thus natural that sometimes advocates feel the urge to criticize judges' work or behaviour. Advocates have generally the same rights as others to express their opinion on judges, but there are, however, a few factors that they must consider. The Icelandic Bar Association enacted a code in 1960 for practising advocates (Codex Ethicus) which defines, *inter alia*, acceptable working standards and methods. The code has a special chapter on the duties of advocates to the courts. The main rule is in Article 18, which states that an advocate shall, in his duties, show full respect to the courts and only criticize on professional and objective grounds. According to Article 40 of the Codex, the Board of the Bar Association has the duty to ensure that advocates comply with the rules. On the basis of those rules a judge can complain to the Bar Association and demand that an advocate be rebuked.[22]

Criticism from the Press

Freedom of expression is especially important for the press. It is generally recognized in Iceland that the press should be given extra freedom in the interests of both democracy and the public. This has been established in the case law of the Supreme Court,[23] but it is, however, sometimes questionable how effective this protection is in practice. Anyone, including a judge, who claims that the press have written an unjust article can address his opinion to a special body of the Journalists' Association, the Ethics Commission. This Commission analyses how the article was prepared and whether the journalist used standard procedure in investigating the matter before publishing it. The decisions of the Commission are not binding in any way but have a certain impact on the further proceeding of such a case.

Actual Cases

The case law on criticism on judges in Iceland is not very rich, but there does exist a recent case in which all possible aspects were at stake. The facts were that the weekly newspaper P, published an article where the handling of a certain estate under official proceedings by M, a judge, was criticized,[24] and among other things claimed that an heir had lost his rights in the estate as a result of M's mistakes. The article referred to words from the advocate, S, who was the heir's legal representative in the estate proceedings. M claimed that this article contained unjustifiable and defamatory remarks and took swift action. He started with a complaint against S to the Icelandic Bar Association. His next step was to charge the author of the article and the editor of the paper to the Ethics Commission of the Journalists' Association. Then he sent a letter to the Icelandic Judges' Association requesting their opinion on the matter. Finally, he sued the editor of the newspaper in the courts for defamation

The request to the Judges' Association was the first to bear fruits. The secretary of the Board investigated the case and returned with a reasoned opinion to the effect that M had not made any mistake in his management of the estate and there was thus no ground for the paper to write the article. The Board then voted to adopt the Secretary's report. One of the Board's members refused to participate in the proceedings, arguing that the Association should not have an opinion on a judge's performance in an individual case.[25]

The Ethics Commission of the Journalists' Association also came to the conclusion that M had been wrongly accused in the article. According to its findings the preparation and presentation of the story were unsatisfactory, and it was noted that the journalist had not presented the story to M or asked him for information before publishing the article. The decision of the Commission was that the article was a serious breach of the journalistic ethics.

A judgment in the case against the editor of P was delivered by the district court of Reykjavik.[26] The court referred, in its findings, to the constitutional freedom of the press, and then continued that any person who expressed his opinions must be ready to be held responsible for the remarks in court. The court then said that the article contained serious defamatory allegations against M. The editor was therefore found guilty, and the defamatory words in the article were thus declared null and void. The case was not appealed.

The fourth and final stage of the case and, in many ways, the most interesting one, was M's complaint to the Bar Association, based on the fact that it related to disciplinary power over advocates. The Board of the Bar Association held that S had breached Article 18 of Codex Ethicus, with his comment to the press and rebuked him. S was unhappy with this solution and appealed to the Supreme Court,[27] which upheld the Board's decision.[28] S's next move was to complain to the European Commission of Human Rights, which declared the case admissible. The Commission then suggested an amicable settlement by which S would be awarded a nominal compensation. Both parties agreed on this solution, and this concluded the case of Judge Mar Petursson.

Do Judges Have More Protection Than Others?

In analysing the legal situation in Iceland, the question arises: do the judges have more protection than others? Before we answer this question it is necessary to distinguish between three categories of criticism: criticism addressed to the judge as a private person, criticism as an official person, and also criticism focused on a judgment.

Judges are human and they can, like other human beings, make controversial decisions in their private life. In Icelandic law criticism of such behaviour, either verbally or in writing, is treated differently from criticism of their official behaviour. There are a few recent cases where a judge's personal decisions have been criticized and where it is generally recognized that such criticism is not addressed to the official function. One such example of such criticism involved a Supreme Court judge who ran for the presidency of Iceland in 1996. After the campaign, in which he came second, he returned to his work at the Supreme Court. It has since been argued that he is more and less partial in all cases, as either of the parties could be a supporter from his presidency campaign. This criticism is only considered to be directed against him as a person as a result of his decision to run for the presidency.

Cases where criticism is addressed to the judge in his official capacity – that is, if claims that the judge has not carried out his duties effectively – are another matter. At first glance, one might think, correctly, that there is nothing in the legislation granting judges more rights than others. This is partly true since the abolition of Article 108 in the Penal Code. On the other hand, deeper investigation reveals other factors which affect judges' protection, and a clear example exists. When the facts in the case *Mar Petursson* v. *Gunnar Smari Egilsson o.fl.*[29] are examined closely, it seems that the editor never had a chance: the judge concerned obtained a favourable opinion from his colleagues and, thereafter, there was no possibility of anyone standing up for the editor. The Judges' Association's handling of this case was questionable, and it is not clear whether other judges can rely on such protection in the future. However, the importance of the case is somewhat diminished by the fact that it was not appealed and also because it was not argued that the judge was partial. It would have been interesting to see the claim of argument addressed to the Human Rights Commission in Strasbourg. It is, however, interesting to compare this case with the *Barfod* case[30] in which B criticized the use of official employees as judges in a case where the state was one of the parties. Here, the European Court of Human Rights emphasized the need to protect the impartial reputation of the judges, and the importance of the judges' reputation seems to be the big issue. This can be compared with the findings against the advocate in the *Petursson* case,[31] in which both the Board of the Bar Association and the Supreme Court focused on the fact that he had given the journalist unclear or inexact information which gave the journalist the chance of misunderstanding them and drawing the wrong conclusions; the words were not unjustifiable but rather the manner in which they were put forward to the reporter. This seems to put a heavy burden on advocates to address journalists only with precise and clear remarks which cannot be misunderstood, when the reputation of judges is at stake.

Finally, there is the question whether a criticism on the findings or the result of a judgment has some special character. First, it should be noted that judges have a duty to solve the case put on their desk, whether they like it or not. Consequently, it is generally recognized in the jurisprudence that this gives judges more freedom to express their opinions.[32] For instance, a judge must decide whether a person is guilty of a crime or not. Even if he convicts this person and this turns out to be wrong he cannot be held responsible. The same applies in civil cases. The question is: does this affect people's right to criticize the judgment and has such criticism anything to do with the judge himself? In Iceland you can always expect to hear or see open discussion on the result of one case or another in the press or in the legal literature. Nor is it uncommon for either lawyers or others to give their contrasting opinion on a judgment, especially if they are on the losing side. Generally, such remarks would not be subject to any reaction at all – at least if the remarks concern only the judgment itself. However, if the criticism is, in one way or another, addressed to the judge himself, it may be considered that the line has been overstepped – and it is sometimes a thin line between a criticism of the judgment and an allegation that the judge has not done his duty.

Conclusions

This chapter has attempted to give the reader a broad overview of the Icelandic rules on the freedom of expression and defamatory expression, with a special focus on judges. Over the last few years there have been open discussions on the judiciary among lawyers. In that discussion several issues have been noted. Only recently it was suggested that it was difficult to win a case against the state, especially if the case had something to do with taxes. Members of the press have also complained that the judiciary denies them their rightful share of freedom of expression. They feel that the provisions of Chapter 25 of the Penal Code gives individuals too much protection at the cost of the freedom of the press. This is usually illustrated by reference to recent case law in which the aggrieved person seems to have the upper hand in almost every instance. Such victories have not necessarily been big – maybe the nullification of couple of words – but they are victories nevertheless. There are, however, signs that this is about to change and that the court will, in future, give the press and others more freedom. This goes hand-in-hand with the increasing influence of the European Court of Human Rights on the Icelandic legal system.

   With respect to criticism on the judges it is possible to discern a trend towards protecting their official reputation. However, the strength of this trend is open to question and it is interesting to take a look at the Greenlandic *Barfod* case which took place in a legal system closely related to the Icelandic one. One might think that a person would be unlikely to be penalized for defamatory allegations by, for instance, saying that a certain judge was partial and that his judgment reflected this, but at the same time it is clear that the ways of defamatory cases are unpredictable, especially when the protection of the judiciary is at stake.

Notes

1   See, for example, Thor Vilhjalmsson, 'Svör dómara við opinberri gagnrýni' ('A judge's reply to open criticism'), *Tímarit lögfræðinga*, 1 (1992), pp. 15–19.

2   This rule, Article 72, applied only to printed material, according to the text. It was generally recognized that any other method of expression was, in fact, protected by this rule by analogy. This was based on scholars' opinions and several judgments on the issue.

3   The concept of 'Contempt of Court' is not known in Icelandic legislation and is therefore not used in this chapter.

4   The term 'advocate' is used here for the Icelandic lawyer who has the right to try a case in court. The profession bears the title *Logmenn*, and is divided into those who have permission to try a case in the Supreme Court and the others.

5   *Hæstarettardomar* 1938, p. 64.

6   *Hæstarettardomar* 1938, p. 113.

7   *Hæstarettardomar* 1951, p. 90.

8   *Hæstarettardomar* 1981, p. 1183.

9   *Hæstarettardomar* 1994, p. 461.

10 It has to be mentioned that the cases from the lower courts are not published officially, so it is impossible to know whether such cases have been concluded at lower court and not appealed at the Supreme Court where it would be subject to an open discussion in the press or within the legal profession.

11 See Gunnar Thoroddson, *Fjolmæli*, (Reykjavik, 1967) p. 136.

12 Ibid., p. 141.

13 The argument has been put forward that Article 234 does not comply with the case law from the organs of the European Convention of Human Rights. The reasoning is that Article 234 prohibits 'insulting' another person but the TT judgments allow words that offend, shock or disturb. The argument is that what one person considers insulting could be just the way in which another person expresses his or her opinion, regardless of whether this opinion shocks or disturbs (that is, insults) the other person. See, for example, *Thorgeir Thorgeirsson* v. *Iceland*, Eur. Ct. HR, Series A.239; 18 (1994) EHRR, p. 843, 25 June 1992. If this is true under Icelandic law how can someone be punished for insulting another person, as stated in Article 234, if you have the right to have an opinion which others might feel insulting.

14 *Hæstarrettardomar*, I, 1923:527.

15 There are a few other old cases concerning courts and judges. In an old case from National Superior Court no. 1/157 the defendant had written an article in which he claimed that all the Icelandic judges were biased towards the Governor which could force them to resign if he disliked their behaviour. This was considered untrue and the defendant was penalized. Those old cases, before 1900, have little precedent because the regime has changed considerably.

16 This special provision in defamation cases to deem remarks null and void (mortification) is only known in Nordic laws, but a similar concept, *Ehrenerklarung*, is known in German law, according to Thoroddsen, *Fjolmæli, op. cit.*, p. 289. In his book Thoroddsen refers to Jon Skeie, *Om ærekrænkelser efter norsk ret* (Kristiania, 1910). According to Skeie this provision is rooted in old laws where the damaged person issued two cases, one where he claimed punishment over the wrongdoer and another where he had to prove that he was not guilty of the alleged act. The result of such cases were thus a sanction on the offender and some purification from the alleged act by declaring the remark null and void. See Thoroddsen, *Fjolmæli, op. cit.*, p. 289 and Skie, *Om aerekraenkelser, op. cit.*, pp. 111–12.

17 See Thoroddsen, *Fjolmæli, op. cit.*, p. 289.

18 There are examples of cases where this has got out of hand – where the demands concern one or two pages, and it becomes the judge's responsibility to select a few remarks out of the whole. As could be expected, such a method is controversial and the result in such cases seems to be based on the judge's mood when he writes the judgment.
19 Those cases fall under the category of private criminal cases (*i. einkarefsimal*).
20 See Páll Thorhallsson, *Tjaningarfrelsid og Æruvernd*, (Reykjavik: Thorhallsson, 1995), p. 88. He also remarks that similar discussions have taken place in Denmark and Norway.
21 Eur. Ct. HR, Series A.239, 18 (1994) EHRR, 843.
22 See Article 40, para. 5 of the Codex. This was one of the issues in the case *Sigurdur Georgsson hrl.* v. *Ma Peturssyni, Judge at Lower Court and the Board of the Bar Association, Hæstarettardomar*, 1995, p. 2335. This case is discussed below.
23 See, for instance, *Hæstarettardomar*, 16 February 1995, case 122/1992, *Kristjan Thorvaldsson o.fl.* v. *Galleri Borg o.fl.*
24 It should be noted that, when this case started, the old system where the administration and judiciary was under the same governmental body was still in force. Under this system one person acted at each regional government office, as both judge and administrator. Official proceedings concerning the estate of deceased persons was thus in the hands of administrator but, if arguments arose, he changed clothes and became judge in the same matter. Those rules were changed in 1 July 1992, after this system had been criticized by the European Commission of Human Rights in the case *Jon Kristinsson* v. *Iceland.* The case ended in an amicable settlement.
25 See Sigurdur Mar Jonsson, 'Rikid greidir miskabætur an thess ad vidurkenna sok', *Bladamadurinn, Felagstidindi Bladamannafelags Islands*, September 1997, vol. 2, year 19. This Mr Jonsson worked at the weekly paper P, when the article was written. In his article Jonsson commented on several issues regarding the case. He claimed, for example, that the proceedings of the Judges' Association had in fact disqualified every judge in the country from the case, as it was very unlikely that any judge could, in his findings, come to a conclusion other than the one presented in his professional association. The opinion of the Association did thus have a decisive effect on the outcome of the case in its different stages. Apart from this, Jonsson noticed that the secretary who did the investigation had worked with M earlier and was a personal friend. The secretary never contacted anyone from the newspaper to get their side of the story, according to Jonsson. Finally there were no precedents of such a formal opinion from the Judges' Association, and the judiciary did not provide for such an opinion at any stage.
26 *Mar Petursson* v. *Gunnari Smara Egilssyni o.fl.*, case no E-10674, 19 March 1994.
27 At this time one could appeal the decision of the Board of the Bar Association to the Supreme Court. This rule has now been abolished.
28 *Hæstarettardomar* 1992, 2335, *Sigurdur Georgsson* v. *Ma Peturssynni, Judge at Lower Court and Icelandic Bar Association*, 17 December 1992.
29 Case E-10674/1992.
30 *Barfod* v. *Denmark*, Eur Ct HR, Series A.149; 13 (1991) EHRR, p. 493 (22 February 1989).
31 *Hæstarettardomar* 1992, 2335, *Sigurdur Georgsson* v. *Ma Peturssynni, Judge at Lower Court and Icelandic Bar Association*, 17 December 1992.
32 See Thoroddson, *Fjolmæli, op. cit.*, 1967, p. 226.

PART IV
THE INFLUENCE OF
CULTURE AND HISTORY

10 Criticizing Judges in the Netherlands

Leny E. de Groot-van Leeuwen

Introduction: The Dutch Consensus Culture

In the normal discussions relating to the criticism of judges one would expect visions of conflicting ideals, often couched in controversial language. For example, it is not unusual for the subject to be assessed in the context of the need to shield the judges from criticism on the one hand and the constitutional right of free speech on another. It is argued in the first section of this chapter that the conflict perspective is inappropriate to describe the Dutch situation. The other sections each explore a recent theme of critical discussion and the responses of the judiciary.

Dutch culture is a culture of bridging contradictions. Many institutions have historically grown in the successful appeasement of tensions between Protestantism and Catholicism, and between capital and labour. The mechanisms of encapsulating conflict and drawing extremes into the mainstream are not conducive to the blossoming of great art and philosophy but, on the whole, the culture of consensus has an uncontested status in society, and has even gained international recognition under the name of the 'polder model' of organizing socioeconomic relationships.

In Dutch culture, outspoken criticism tends to be frowned upon, especially if voiced in public. The expression of too outspoken public opinions prevents adversaries from returning into consensus arrangements, and these arrangements – hence not the quality of arguments – are what is really valued. Such arrangements are sought within and between the economic, cultural, political and legal elites, behind closed doors. Free speech, then, is recognized as an important principle for communication from the public to the elites, but certainly not a right to be exercised by the elites in public! You wash your dirty linen inside, and put it outside only after that.

Legal culture is no exception to this rule. Dissenting opinions between judges, for instance, are never published in court decisions. The public nature of court sessions and verdicts complies with the European rules, of course,[1] but that is where openness ends. Requests for access to court files are always rejected, 'for reasons of privacy', for instance. In the Dutch rules of evidence, the key criterion to the acceptance and weighing of evidence is the inner conviction of the judge; the judge's decision-making is therefore essentially withdrawn from the public eye. Within the legal elite, criticizing judges has been a very strict taboo, described as 'chilling' by Van Niekerk.[2] One example cited by Van Niekerk is that, in 1963, an advocate took the unheard-of liberty to write that 'the judgement of a judge is after all a simple human judgement'. This induced another advocate to write that this '. . . filled me with a profound sense of shock'. The taboo has certainly relaxed in recent years, as we will see in the next section. Overall, however, the norm that intra-elite criticism should be kept away from the public eye still stands.

The relationship between the judges and the public cannot be regulated by such simple means. The press, for instance, has been progressively shedding its self-imposed censorship on criticizing the elite still prevalent a decennium ago.[3] In fact, a wave is going through the Netherlands to clean society from the general silence concerning the darker sides of intra-elite dealings. In 1998 the front-page of a newspaper was dominated by two headlines: 'Minister of Finance forced to lie in parliament on the Philips deal' and 'Ministry of Agriculture involved in meat fraud'.[4] The judiciary is not exempt from this new openness. As we will see in the following sections, recent criticisms have concerned the judges' sideline jobs, the institution of the 'honorary judge' and some aspects of legal judgments. As we will also see, however, judges have not responded in a defensive manner, by belittling their adversaries or by employing other 'conflict-style' strategies but have, rather, tended to quietly redress the criticized points. This style of response may have contributed to the ease with which the Dutch judiciary survived the general 'crisis of trust' of the 1960s and kept its high standing on the ladder of the most prestigious professions in the Netherlands.[5]

In all this, obviously, there is little to be seen of tensions between the practical need to shield the judiciary from criticism versus the constitutional right of free speech. Within the elite, free speech is willingly sacrificed on the block of social harmony. Between the judiciary and the public, no shield is felt to be necessary.[6] Both ways, there is no conflict. The stories in the next sections, therefore, although they are stories about criticism of the judiciary, are not stories of legal struggles. They are social stories of an elite group coping with criticism from below.

Sideline Functions of Judges

In 1986 the president of the court at Almelo gave a controversial ruling. Against general expectations he prohibited a strike in a number of Almelo's industrial firms. This led to protests that grew even stronger when it was revealed that the president of the court had a sideline job as a director of one of the firms hit by the strike. This triggered a debate in parliament with the Minister of Justice concerning the sideline functions of judges, without a concrete result. In 1988, however, the Dutch Association of Judges designed and adopted a voluntary ruling that all sideline functions of judges, paid and unpaid, should be registered in a file accessible to the public at every court. This typically Dutch solution ('spontaneous' action of the professional organization without public criticism from the polity) has functioned well since then, after an initial period of complaints about a rather chaotic and halfhearted implementation.[7]

One final controversy erupted in 1991, when a firm of which a judge in Amsterdam was a director was accused of real estate misconduct in the USA. Although the debate did not involve decisions by the judge in question, commercial sideline jobs are informally discouraged by the Association and the court presidents, and are probably decreasing in number. From 1997 onwards, the sideline functions lists have been open to the public, by law.

It is remarkable, and also typically Dutch, that all this came about without using the legal instrument of challenging judges. The grounds on which judges can be challenged were broadened in 1990,[8] but challenging runs counter to the principle of avoiding public intra-elite criticism, and is in fact used with some enthusiasm only by a few 'American-style' criminal advocates.

Honorary Judges

A more or less analogous issue concerned 'honorary judges' comprising selected advocates, civil servants and university professors. In return for a (modest) payment, these honorary judges help the courts out in a limited number of cases, sitting as judge, on average, eight times per year. The institution of the honorary judge began to attract attention when, in 1992, judges in Roermond dissented about whether or not the mayor of a village within their jurisdiction should be accepted as honorary judge in their court organization. A few legal scientists joined in the discussion but the matter ignited only when, in 1994, a group of critical citizens began to point out the risk of conflict of interest. Their chief bone of contention here was the case of an honorary judge in Arnhem who had decided in favour of an insurance company – the same company with which he had many friendly connections in his main job as an attorney.

After an initial period of resistance and irritation, in which the group of critical citizens were accused of 'insinuations' and denied access to certain files of uncertain public nature, the issue was accommodated by the judiciary. As stated by the Dutch Association of Judges in 1996,

> The public attention on the honorary judge, whatever one may feel about it, is in any case proof that the Dutch citizenry has a sharp eye for the importance of judiciary impartiality and independence.[9]

This newly found attitude was accompanied by several symposia, a study commissioned by the Association and many articles in the news and professional papers. The general opinion was that, especially with respect to the advocates, the risk of conflict of interest was serious enough to take action. In 1997 the Minister of Justice and the court presidents jointly announced that honorary judges who were advocates in the same district would be removed from the honorary judges' list.

Local Variations in Penalty Levels

In 1992 a simmering debate about unacceptable regional variations in the level of punitive sanctions was stoked up by Berghuis who found that, in some districts, sanctions for comparable cases were 2.5 times higher than in others.[10] This resulted in such newspaper headings as 'Judges in The Hague hand out the stiffest penalties' and 'Judges surprised about weakhearted collegues', and television followed suit. A special issue of the bulletin of the research institute of the Ministry of Justice was devoted to the subject later in 1992.

Proposed solutions were quick in the making, all of them comprising a certain degree of unification of the legal system. One alternative, for instance, was to establish a unified list of 'first bids' for commonly occurring punishable acts, which should indicate the penalty level reflecting only the seriousness of the act, without taking into account the circumstances of the act or the person of the perpetrator.[11] In this vein, many guidelines for penalty levels have been designed by the courts since 1992. Nationwide unification has been a slow process, however. The most recent and official proposal to date, therefore, concerns the establishment of a national Judiciary Council, one of the tasks of which will be to coordinate a cooperative effort by the courts to arrive at a national set of guidelines.[12]

The Pikmeer Rulings

The Pikmeer rulings of the Dutch Supreme Court concern the criminal immunity of government activities. Is government allowed to do things that citizens would be criminally prosecuted for? Contrary to these citizens' sense of justice, the Dutch answer has always been that this is indeed the case. The official reason is that criminal judges should not become involved in political matters, and that there are many other, more appropriate, ways to redress government actions. In the unspoken background we may also suspect the Dutch attitude that chasing each other with criminal sanctions is something you just don't do within the elite. The debate on this 'doctrine of immunity', which had always had an uneasy position in legal theory,[13] was revived in connection with the environmental (mis)management activities of lower government units, one of the cases being the dredging of toxic sludge and its subsequent illegal dumping in the Pikmeer lake. In a ruling concerning the Pikmeer case in 1996, the Supreme Court reinforced the immunity principle, forcing to a halt many other ongoing procedures against environmental misbehaviour on the part of municipalities and other agencies.

Protests came from the prosecution offices, the environmental movement, the press and the universities. In parliament, preparations were made to change the law. The principal criticism was that many activities of lower government units are, in fact, not real acts of government but activities that other actors could do as well. Why should a firm dumping toxic waste be liable to punishment, but not a municipality dumping toxic waste? The Supreme Court referred the issue back to a lower court, and the lower court convicted the municipality, arguing that the dumping was not part of the municipality's 'public office'. This conviction was appealed and the matter returned before the Supreme Court, thus offering the opportunity to redress something of its former ruling. Early in 1998 the new ruling was that immunity was restricted to activities that 'can be done by no other than the government unit'. This is generally regarded as a breakthrough, although the interpretation is as yet unclear.

'Dubious Cases': Criticism of the Rules of Evidence

With their book *Dubieuze Zaken* ('Dubious Cases'), social scientists Crombag *et al.* successfully put the quality of criminal verdicts on the public agenda.[14] The authors conducted a detailed study of 35 criminal cases of which the verdicts were identified as 'dubious' by advocates – for example, because the advocate was still convinced that the convicted could well be not guilty, or because a guilty verdict had in fact been reversed by a higher court. The book details the time pressures on judges, the deficient preparation of cases by investigative judges, the failure to hear witnesses in person, and so on. Generally, Dutch judges appear to work from a presumption of guilt and tend to lend more credibility to evidence confirming this presumption than to evidence of the reverse. The story of the prosecution, the personality of the suspect and the context in which the crime is placed often lures judges into neglecting the weakness of evidence. The prosecution's evidence tends to be accepted even if legal and logical rules of evidence may have been broken by the police or the prosecution. Evidence brought forward by the defence is sometimes completely ignored for no reason.

The book was a bestseller and provoked a great deal of irritation in the legal elite. A major criticism against the book was that it was obviously not written by jurists but by social scientists, who could not properly appreciate the judge's work. And, indeed, the authors did make some criminal law blunders – for example, they were unaware that witnesses do not have to take the oath in front of the investigating judge.[15] Another criticism against the book was that many of the problems diagnosed in the book were in fact already known and had been solved. 'Rest assured that the judge knows that he should be careful with witness statements', writes Frijda. According to this judge:

> The critique of Crombag et al. on identifications by eyewitnesses . . . concerns cases from the past. During those days much less attention was given to the conditions of valid confrontations . . . . Moreover, they do not take into account that the judge, doubt about the method notwithstanding, may reach a verdict on the basis of other evidence.[16]

Others, such as Schuyt and Vermeulen, wrote that Crombag *et al.* themselves made the same mistakes as the judges they criticize; their research starts from a strong suspicion, and the only evidence taken seriously is evidence confirming the suspicion.[17]

As may be surmised already from the tone of these quotations, the 'Dubious Cases' issue is the only one which, to my knowledge, has not resulted in a significant responsive action of the judiciary; there has been no re-research, no commission to look at the way in which the material could be incorporated into judiciary education, no systematic review of possible remedial actions such as improved rules of evidence, or any such possible follow-up. One of the reasons here may be found in the adage of the book, a quote from a US paper: 'Justice is supposed to be blind, of course, but must it be stupid too?' Many of the cases discussed in the book, indeed, have this implication, and being exposed as absurd by social scientists (as opposed to sometimes being exposed as legally wrong by fellow-lawyers) may have been just too hard to admit and react to, in public.

Conclusions

In the foregoing I hope to have illustrated the argument of this chapter's introduction, – that is, in regard to criticism on the judiciary, the Netherlands is a nation of moderation and 'reasonableness'. Although less than some decades ago, the *burgermansfatsoen* described by Van Niekerk is still the dominant cultural trait.[18] The advantage of this style is that it allows the target of the criticism to respond in the same vein. The cultural pressure is to find solutions rather than escalating the argument. The only case in which the judiciary did not respond with a relatively simple action of redress was that of the 'Dubious Cases' book – possibly because it broke the cultural code. In almost all cases, the public and the press played an important role in activating the discussions. The logic of this is that, in Dutch consensus culture, open criticism is not rewarded within the elites.

Notes

1 See, for example, Article 6 of the European Convention on the Protection of Human Rights.
2 Barend van Niekerk, *The Cloistered Virtue. Free Speech and the Administration of Justice in the Western World* (London: Praeger, 1987), p. 80.
3 Ibid., p. 79
4 *NRC-Handelsblad*, 14 March 1998.
5 Leny E. de Groot-van Leeuwen, *De rechterlijke macht in Nederland. Samenstelling en denkbeelden van de zittende en staande magistratuur* (Arnhem: Gouda Quint, 1991); Leny E. de Groot-van Leeuwen, 'The Equilibrium Elite: Composition and Position of the Dutch Judiciary', *The Netherlands' Journal of Social Sciences*, **28** (1992).
6 An obvious 'shield provision' has been Article 137a of the Penal Code, reading that 'Whosoever expresses himself intentionally and publicly – whether orally, in writing or in image – in an insulting manner as regards public authority [*openbaar gezag*] or a public body or institution, shall be punished with imprisonment not exceeding two years or a fine': Niekerk, *The Cloistered Virtue, op. cit.*, p. 276. Note, however, that this article is confined to the form, not the content of the criticism. As long as elite manners were maintained, one was free to say anything. Cf. G.E. Langemeijer, 'Bescherming der openbare orde', *Nederlandsch Juristenblad* (1934), pp. 149–58; T.J. Noyon, *Het wetboek van strafrecht verklaard* (Arnhem: Gouda Quint, 1954). The article lay dormant during most of its time, only resulting in 13 convictions in the peak year of 1966. It was quietly dropped in 1978: *Staatsblad van het koninkrijk der Nederlanden* (1978), p. 155.
7 M. de Werd, *De benoeming van rechters, Constitutionele aspecten van de toegang tot ht rechtersambt in Nederland en in de Amerikaanse deelstaat New York* (Arnhem: Gouda Quint, 1994).
8 Trudie van Niejenhuis, 'De regter blijft toch altijd mensch', *Ars Aequi*, **46** (1997).
9 A.P.C.T. Aarts and W.H.J. Stemker Köster, 'Verslag van het NVvR/SSR symposium: De onafhankelijkheid van de rechtspraak en de inzet van de rechter-plaatsvervanger', *Trema*, **9** (1996), pp. 305–9.
10 A.C. Berghuis, 'De harde en de zachte hand – een statistische analyse van verschillen in sanctiebeleid', *Trema*, **15**(3) (1992), pp. 84–93.
11 B.C. Punt, 'Een lichtvoetig alternatief', *Trema*, **15** (1992), pp. 266–68.
12 'Adviescommissie toerusting en organisatie zittende magistratuur (Comissie Leenhuis)', *Rechtspraak in de tijd*, January 1998.
13 A.M. Fransen, 'Crimineel overheidsgedrag in de doofpot', *Nederlands Jursitenblad*, **1**(3) (January 1997), pp. 69–74.
14 H.F.M. Crombag, P.J. van Koppen and W.A. Wagenaar, *Dubieuze zaken. De psychologie van het strafrechtelijk bewijs* (Amsterdam: Contact, 1992). The English version has been

published under the title *Unsafe Justice: The Psychology of Criminal Evidence* (London: Harvester Wheatsheaf, 1993).

15   H. de Doelder, 'Stupid Justice?', *Trema*, **15** (May 1992), pp. 175–82.

16   L. Frijda, 'Over dubieuze zaken en oppervlakkige domme rechters', *Delikt en Delinkwent*, **22**(7) (1992), pp. 662–72.

17   C.J.M. Schuyt, 'Het juridisch en het sociaal-wetenschappelijke bewijs', *Delikt en Delinkwent*, **7** (1992), pp. 655–61; Frank Vermeulen, 'Vrouwe Justitia is niet blind maar mank', in *NRC Handelsblad*, 2 May 1992.

18   Van Niekerk, *The Cloistered Virtue, op. cit.*, p. 78.

11 Criticizing Judges in Italy

Annamaria di Ioia

Introduction

Looking at the provisions of the Italian Constitution relating to the Italian judiciary, one might conclude that Italian judges are among the most independent in the world. Unlike other Western countries, in which the Members of the Supreme Courts are directly appointed by the Government,[1] the system of appointment by public competition ensures a clear separation from the executive. In addition, the regulation of Italian judges is undertaken by a system of 'self-government' through the National Council of Magistrates, an institution established by the Constitution and made up mostly of judges.[2] This body decides issues of promotion, dismissal and transfer, as well as the discipline of all judges.

The constitutional guarantee of independence has proved to be crucial in recent events in Italy. The inquiries and trials against corruption involving numerous members of the government and powerful politicians could take place only because of the independence of the judges, notwithstanding the strong pressure and the several attempts at obstruction by parties and lobbies.[3] The main instruments used by the Constitution in order to ensure the independence of the magistracy include the principle of the 'natural judge',[4] security of tenure[5] and judicial autonomy.[6] However, the independence which secures Italian judges against abuse by institutional powers of state could also act as a barrier to effective judicial accountability to the public. Judicial independence confers power which may be called upon to restrain criticism by the public and the media in breach of the freedom of expression guaranteed in Article 21[7] of the Constitution. In practice, primacy has so far been accorded to the freedom of expression. Thus, in Italy today, it is possible to criticize judges without undue fear of prosecution. This chapter will assess the nature of criticism usually levelled against the judiciary and the legal consequences of such criticism.

Freedom of Expression and the Magistracy

The limits of Article 21 of the Constitution have been tested recently, most especially in the context of 'public interest' trials involving corrupt public officials. Ironically, these trials in which Italian judges have made their strongest assertions of independence have also had the effect of focusing critical public and media attention on their work. The relationship between magistrates and media has had to change radically, since the pressure exercised by the strong criticism led to frequent press conferences and formal declarations by the magistracy, with the aim of justifying decisions and defending themselves from the numerous attacks by journalists. In 1994 the National Association of Magistrates, in an effort to streamline the relationship between judges and the media, adopted a 'moral code' containing directives on which any formal declaration by judges should be based.[8] Extracts from the most significant articles include:

Article 5. Information on office matters. Prohibition of use by non institutional aims. The magistrate does not use improperly, information on office matters and does not provide or require information on pending proceedings, and does not give recommendations in order to influence their development or their final result.

Article 6. Relationship with media. In having contacts with media, the magistrate does not press for publicity of information concerning his office. When he is not obliged to secrecy or discretion on information on his functions and he believes to have the duty to provide clarifications on his actions with the aim of guaranteeing the correct information of citizens and the exercise of the right to chronicle, he avoids using privileged or reserved channels of information. Notwithstanding the right to full freedom of expression, the judge uses criteria of balance and measure in giving declarations and answering interviews by newspapers or other media.

Article 8. Independence of magistrates. The magistrate guarantees and defends the independent exercise of his office and keeps an image of impartiality and independence. He avoids any involvement with lobbies, political parties or businessmen which could influence the free exercise of these tasks or damage his reputation. He does not accept tasks or activities that could be an obstacle to the full and fair exercise of his functions or which, because of their nature, and modality by which they are conferred, can undermine his independence.

Article 12. Behaviour in his own decisions. . . . In the exercise of his function, the judge listens to opinions of other people, in order to submit his own conviction to a continuous verification, and to take from the dialogue the chance of professional and personal enrichment. In writing the motivation of the collegial sentences, he explains fairly the reasons of the decision, and examines with accuracy facts and arguments presented by both parties . . . . He does not evaluate the professional capacities of other magistrates, or lawyers.

It is also relevant to look at a formal document by the National Council of Magistrates:

> In general, every magistrate has the duty of secrecy in the proceedings he is treating. . . . Eventually, from time to time, when there is a public interest in the knowledge of certain information, the judge can evaluate the opportunity of giving declarations or press communications whose content has previously been discussed with his direct superior. Certainly, there does not exist any obligation for judges to keep contact with journalists in order to give them information. What is more, wrongful interpretation and deformation of declarations given by judges have to be avoided by limiting them only to the cases in which they are absolutely indispensable to confer clarity and transparency, and when there are relevant reasons of public interest.[9]

Criticism by Judges

It is interesting to point out that the Italian magistracy comprises judges coming from the widest range of backgrounds, and that sometimes the strongest criticism against judicial decisions might come from other judges. This chapter will not deal with the disciplinary proceedings brought on judges by superiors and their consequent sanctions, normally imposed for the infringement of personal duties established by law, but more generally with criticism by other judges outside any disciplinary action, and concerning either a particular sentence or the intended role of judges in the system.

The method of exercising the judicial function has totally changed in the last 40 years of the Republic, and judges' roles today are the result of persistent conflict within the magistracy as well as with other public institutions. One of the biggest battles in the name of freedom of expression began in 1968 when the *Magistratura Democratica*, a political association of judges, adopted a document against the punishment of 'opinion crimes' then present in the criminal code since its promulgation during the fascist government.[10] This document was distributed widely and often referred to in trials in which freedom of expression was an issue. The document was read out by some judges during one such trial of the director of a communist newspaper who was accused of complicity in crime because of publications in his magazines, which incited the working class to react to restrictions introduced by their new employment contracts.[11] The fact that a document containing strong criticism of all the judicial decisions concerning opinion crimes was read by magistrates in front of a judging court, constituted a real scandal and caused a number of members' resignations from the *Magistratura Democratica*.[12] This episode has to be seen in the light of the peculiar situation of the late 1960s, in which, on one side, there was a part of the magistracy still linked to a pre-constitutional exercise of the judicial function and, on the other side, those who were attempting an 'alternative application of the judicial office, conceived nearly as a weapon used to break the balances of the popular sovereignty'.[13] Nevertheless, its impact continues to underlie the standards which define freedom of expression in relation to judges. Today, also thanks to all debates generated by the above-mentioned case, these deep conflicts have been overcome in favour of a unitary vision of the judicial function by all the judges, in substance much less influenced by political ideologies and linked more to the application of the rule of law.

In general, the whole climate is less disparate and characterized less by contrasting ideologies among opposite extremes; criticism among judges is now constructive and even encouraged.[14]

Criticism by Journalists and the Media

The main task of the National Council of Magistrates is to safeguard the prestige and credibility of the judiciary, with the aim of protecting those magistrates who are targets not only of criticism, but of defamatory denigration. Acts of magistrates can certainly be criticized and discussed, the solutions adopted can be objected, their hypothesises can be considered groundless, but anyway, outrageous expressions towards a single judge or the whole magistracy cannot be used, on the ground of the freedom to criticize judges.

The above statement is taken from a resolution of a plenary assembly of the National Council of Magistrates in order to clarify what can be considered a legitimate criticism and what constitutes an illegal offence or an illegitimate tort. Some legitimate limits of freedom of expression are defined in the general criminal and civil law.[15]

The Criminal Law

The Italian Criminal Code was published under the fascist regime. It contains two provisions expressly protecting public institutions and public officers such as judges. First, there is Article 290 of the Code which concerns vilification of public institutions and, second, Articles 342 and 343 concerning *oltraggio a pubblico ufficiale*. The article concerning the crime of 'vilification of institutions' has very rarely been applied, since it requires a total contempt of the institution – for example of the judiciary function itself; thus it clearly refers to a concept of crime which is totally different from what may reasonably be termed criticism. Furthermore, the offence has to be expressed in a formal context such as in the face of the institution concerned – for instance, a judging court. In one of the very few examples of criminal proceedings for vilification,[16] the Court of Turin pointed out 'the contradictions of article 290 of the criminal code, in its failure to distinguish between criticism and its modalities as expressions of freedom of speech, and therefore in conflict with the Constitution'.

Different from the hypothesis of vilification is the *oltraggio a pubblico ufficiale*. The aim of this provision is to defend the person and dignity of all public officers, including judges. A good example of a criminal prosecution for this crime is a 1972 case,[17] in which a lawyer was prosecuted because he said, after sentence had been passed and in a very loud voice, that 'the right of the defendant party had been infringed, and the sentence was wrongful in such a way to be an enormous mistake, hasty and out of place'. When the Italian Constitutional Court assessed the compatibility of the crime of *oltraggio* with Article 21 of the Constitution (freedom of expression), it confirmed the constitutionality of the crime.[18] According to the Court the particular objective of the article is the protection of the prestige and special role of the public administration. The Court reached the conclusion that, although Articles 342 and 343 of the Criminal Code are clearly the result of a very conservative climate, the seriousness of the offences therein defined and the relevance of the sanctions – which are more severe than the ones imposed for defamation – are justified by the aim of protecting the honour of the institution's function and not the reputation of the man behind it. As a result, the prestige of the public administration deserves special protection, in order to ensure the best results from the services provided to all citizens.

In his review of the law in this field, one author[19] objects that, in the first place, there is no trace of a specific protection of the prestige of the public administration in the Constitution and, in the second place, safeguarding its prestige does not imply the consequence of its best functioning. Furthermore, to limit criticism by way of criminal sanctions would help 'to wrap up the public administration in an atmosphere of holiness', whereas the best way of ensuring the good functioning of public institutions is to expose them to constant criticism, in order to obtain the best response to the changing requirements of society's needs'.[20]

In relation to the 1972 example referred to above, the author expressed the view that:

> . . . to say that a sentence is wrongful and infringes the right of the defending party is not an offence to the judge, but a simple criticism of his actions. Not only can a criticism, although rough and penetrating, not be confused with an offence, but moreover it cannot be considered offensive (and therefore prosecuted on the ground of defamation) if it is expressed by words which do not constitute an insult to the officer himself.[21]

In this particular case the criminal prosecution of *oltraggio* is arguably an infringement of the right to freedom of expression. It is reassuring that only a minority of cases are brought before courts on the ground of *oltraggio*, since the great majority of them are prosecuted on the ground of criminal defamation.

In the Criminal Code, defamation is not a special crime instituted for the protection of magistrates but, rather, safeguards the reputation of all citizens. It is, however, relevant in this context because it is frequently used by magistrates when their reputations are attacked. Moreover, the associated sanction of prohibition from the exercise of the profession can be applied to journalists if found guilty of defamation.

In order to resolve the conflict between the freedom of expression and the protection of reputation, the Italian legislature created a formal 'cause of justification' by which the crime of defamation may be excused. These include:

1   the *objective interest* in the published facts for the public opinion (*principio di pertinenza*);
2   the *correctness* by which those facts are published (*principio di continenza*);
3   the *correspondence* between what really happened and the facts published (*principio di verita*).[22]

In numerous cases the jurisprudence has adopted these criteria as defences in favour of the free exercise of the right of freedom of expression.[23] There is a general theme in the judgments that 'it is essential in every democracy to have free information on people charged with public functions, like magistrates, and the right to criticize them has also to be exercised as widely and deeply as possible'.[24]

The right to chronicle has to be distinguished from criticism: the former is the objective narration of facts, while the latter is an interpretation of facts, involving a writer's subjective opinion,[25] which certainly includes the right to disagree with a sentence – in which case the object of the criticism is a judge. The legitimate exercise of the right to criticize the judges'discretional choices ceases when sentences are criticized for being influenced by external agents or political strategies since, in this case, there is an attack on reputation which has to be rigorously proved.[26]

In particular, defamation proceedings in which the aggrieved person is a judge are usually peculiar because they represent a conflict between state powers. A recent study of the actions for defamation brought before courts by magistrates shows how often they use this avenue to defend their reputation.[27] The most important result shown by the research is a significant inversion of tendency: while, on the one hand, only 10 per cent of the normal actions for defamation end with a prosecution of the defendant, the percentage of criminal prosecutions is significantly higher (90 per cent) when the offended person is a judge.[28]

This is probably due to the fact that the numerous trials against politicians focused the media's attention on the magistracy, and consequently to unprecedentedly heavy criticism, which can be considered the reason for its vulnerability. Furthermore, even the penalties are higher; fines are of a relevant amount and, in some cases, journalists have been sentenced to imprisonment.[29] In addition, prohibition from exercising the profession of journalist has been recently considered as a legitimate accessory penalty for defamation on the ground that defaming a reputation can constitute a violation of the profession's duties.[30] Exclusion from a profession can be provided as an accessory penalty to any crime, as established by Article 30 of the Criminal Code, if the profession itself is abused or improperly used in order to commit a crime. Although the application of Article 30 to defamation is still controversial, there are some examples of cases in which it has been held as applicable.[31]

The Supreme Court has, however, held that it is not sufficient to use one single violation of the duty of adherence to the truth to convict a journalist[32] but there must be numerous and relevant violations of the professional ethics enumerated by the legislature. The jurisprudential tendency is not only restrictive in relation to defamation, but is made worse by the additional possibility of applying the accessory sanction to the press. Together, this represents a considerable danger for the free exercise of the right to chronicle, especially in view of the fact that in other European countries, such as France, the application of the penalty of exclusion is forbidden by law in all kinds of 'press crime'. In Italy, exclusion is still considered as one of the best means of preventing abuses of the profession of journalism. This power of penalizing journalists is not covered by any kind of legislation concerning defamation in particular, but is entirely left to the discretion of the judging courts.

The Civil Law

In addition to the criminal law, the civil law, especially the tort of defamation, may also be available to judges who are falsely criticized. The grounds on which it is possible to bring an action for defamation as a tort are much wider than those relating to defamation as a crime. First, there is a subjective requirement of fault and, second, the notion of reputation in tort law is much wider, since not only the moral, but also the political, economic and professional reputation is considered as a ground for the action before the civil court. Moreover, the concept of reputation varies according to the social position of the subject involved. The grounds of justification are the same as in criminal law (the truth of the facts, the public interest and the correctness of the exposition). Also in tort law, the liability is shared between the author and the publisher, but compensation is due for both economic and non-economic loss.

When defamation concerns the reputation of a judge, the evaluation of the amount of the compensation has to take into account a variety of elements, and among those particularly relevant are 'the offence to the professional prestige, the negative influence in family and social environment, the diffusion of the defamatory article, the pain suffered'.[33] The tribunal of Naples considered as one of the criteria of evaluating compensation of an offence to the reputation of a judge 'the plurality of the participants to the offence, who contributed with the same aim, and the consequential reiteration of the offences themselves'.[34]

Conclusion

As it has already been pointed out, the Italian system is still full of contradictions. The gap between the Constitution, fully guaranteeing the freedom of speech, and the Criminal Code, still punishing 'opinion crimes', still exists. In the absence of adequate action from the legislature, it is still left to the magistracy to protect the right to freedom of expression and all its corollaries in the practical exercise of the judicial function.

The rather rigid structure of division of powers still makes the Italian magistracy one of the most independent of Europe, in order to protect it from interference from other state powers. But this strong independence is balanced by strong criticism from the media, jurists and also lawyers. It has been said that 'Italian lawyers avail themselves with impunity of declarations that in Germany, at least, would entail the imposition of ethical sanctions and would be unthinkable in Holland'.[35] Also, in the most recent history of the Republic, criticism from the media has become stronger than ever and, as a consequence, the reaction of the magistracy has caused a stricter relationship between judges and journalists, with the resultant danger of compromising the correct exercise of the judicial function.

Ironically, the standards for criticizing judges arose from judges' own criticism in the 1960s when they stood firmly against some of their colleagues' decisions against opinion crimes. Despite this, judges continue to rely heavily on the protection afforded by the ordinary law when the criticism comes from the public and the media. The situation is compounded by the fact that public prosecutors tend to pursue a stricter policy on prosecutions against offenders who criticize judges.[36] In Italy, abuses of freedom of expression are judged more severely when they concern criticism of judges but, undoubtedly, this can be interpreted as a direct consequence of the exasperating climate of recent years which has threatened the balance between state powers.

Notes

1 In the UK judges of the superior courts are appointed by the Queen on the advice of the Prime Minister and the Lord Chancellor. In the USA, judges of the Supreme Court are nominated by the president and confirmed by Congress.

2 All the provisions regarding the appointment, removal, the career and the sanctions of judges are of exclusive competence the Council, whose members belong mostly to the magistracy. Two-thirds of them are appointed by magistrates among themselves, and one-third by the parliament out of the most prestigious jurists.

3 *Mani pulite* (clean hands) is the name of one of the biggest inquiries in the recent history of the Republic. A summary of the attempts of delegitimation of the inquiry and the magistrates conducting it can be found in Gian Carlo Caselli, 'La normalita' come progetto', *Micromega*, (1) (1996) and also in M. Travaglio, 'Cinque anni vissuti vergognosamente', *Micromega*, (4) (1997).

4 Article 25 of the Constitution.

5 Article 103 of the Constitution.

6 Article 102 of the Constitution.

7 Article 21 states: 'Everybody has the right to freely express his thoughts by talking, writing or any other means of diffusion. The press cannot be subject to authorizations or censorship. . . .'

8 The moral code was approved and transmitted by the Association to the National Council of Magistrates on 19 May 1994. Although the code does not have the value of law, but contains only principles, its importance lies in the fact that it establishes criteria on which the relations of the judiciary with media have to be safeguarded in order to guarantee the correct exercise of both freedom of expression and judicial function.

9 Resolution adopted by the Council in the assembly of 18 April 1990.

10 For a complete analysis of this matter see L. Ferrajoli, 'Referendum sui reati politici di opinione', *Quale Giustizia* (5–6) (1970); L. Ferrajoli, 'Il caso 7 aprile: lineamenti sul processo inquisitorio', *Dei delitti e delle pene* (1983); E. Bruti Liberati, *Il governo dei giudici* (Milan: Feltrinelli, 1985), pp. 65–71; E. Ferri, 'Appunti per tentare insieme la definizione di un rapporto difficile', *Legalita' e giustizia* (Viareggio, 1985), p. 121; and G. Caliendo, 'Diritti di liberta' e processo penale', *Giustizia e Costituzione* (5) (Ancona, 1995).

11 For a complete analysis on this matter, see S. Pappalardo, *Gli iconoclasti*, ed. Franco Angeli (Milan: Legalitè e Giustizia, Vareggio, 1987). Of a different opinion is R. Bertoni, 'Fuori la politica dalla giustizia', *Questione Giustizia* (5) (1996).

12 A severe punishment was imposed to the journalist prosecuted. He was condemned to one year and five months' imprisonment. The motivation behind the sentence included a strong reprobation of the content of the article on the ground that in the Italian democracy 'there is no room at all for violence. A free dissenting opinion is admitted, even if radical and polemic, provided that it is expressed in a civil way and in the absolute respect of the law'. For the complete text of the sentence, see *Quale Giustizia* (1) (1970), p. 30.

13 R. Bertoni, 'Fuori la politica dalla giustizia', *op. cit.*

14 *Questione Giustizia, Quale Giustizia* and *Micromega* are only a few examples of magazines edited and published by specialized operators of the sector.

15 A study of the relationship between magistrates and media is given in L. Magliaro, 'Informazione televisiva e magistratura', *Questione Giustizia* (4) (1994), p. 855; G. Palombarini, 'Giustizia e mass media', *Documenti Giustizia* (1–2) (1997), p. 30; and in C.A. Marletti, 'Media, magistratura ed opinione pubblica', *Questione Giustizia* (3) (1996).

16   Tribunale di Torino, ord. 18 March 1976, in *Foro Italiano* 1976, II, p. 336. The Court did not find the grounds for prosecution under Article 290 and decided to reshelve the case.
17   Tribunale di Verona, 24 February 1972, in *Giustizia Costituzionale* (1972), p. 775.
18   The most relevant decision on this matter is Corte Costituzionale, 28 November 1972, in *Giurisprudenza Costituzionale*, suppl. (1972), p. 273.
19   G. Pedrazza, 'Il tono dell'espressione verbale: nuovo limite alla liberta' di pensiero?', *Giustizia Costituzionale*, *op. cit.*
20   Ibid., p. 779.
21   Ibid.
22   These principles have constantly been applied by the jurisprudence: see, for instance, Cassazione penale, 14 December 1993, *Massimario cassazione penale 1994*, p. 70.
23   Cassazione penale, 27 April 1992, in *Rivista penale* (1993), p. 828; Cassazione penale, 7 February 1996, n. 982, *Corriere giudiziario* (1996), p. 264.
24   Tribunale di Roma, 3 October 1986, in *Cassazione penale* (1987) p. 662.
25   V. Manzini, *Tratto di diritto penale*, vol. v (Torino, 1962), p. 473.
26   Cassazione penale 24 November 1994, in *Dir. Inf.* (1996), p. 81.
27   See the research in Zeno Zanchovich, 'La reputazione del magistrato', nota a Tribunale di Roma, 19 June 1985, *Il diritto dell'informazione e dell'informatica* (1986), p. 138. A detailed list of cases is provided, although the author specifies that the research does not have any statistical value, being just a study of cases considered relevant because of the public interest in them and because of the proportion of the increase of actions brought by magistrates in recent years.
28   Among all the sentences examined by the law reporter, the most relevant concern famous newspapers and important events of the ten years 1975–1985, the year of the publication of the research in question: see, for instance, Tribunale di Firenze 14 May 1973, *Archivio Penale*, **II**, (1976) p. 160; Tribunale di Roma 29 September 1975, *Archivio Penale*, **II**, (1976), p. 71; Tribunale di Napoli 17 October 1977, *Giurisprudenza di merito* (1979), p. 999; Tribunale di Napoli 23 June 1978, *Giurisprudenza Italiana*, **II**, (1979), p. 41; Tribunale di Orvieto 17 July 1980, not published; Cassazione 1 April 1982, *Rivista Penale* (1982), p. 798; Tribunale di Firenze 29 October 1982, (Magistratura Democratica- Radio Onda Rossa), not published; Tribunale dell'Aquila 17 January 1985 (Vitalone-Golpe Borghese), not published; Tribunale di Perugia 20 May 1985 (marrone- Gazzetta del Mezzogiorno), not published.
29   *Gallucci e Versichelli* v. *Il Manifesto* (two years and eight months detention), *Di Crecchio* v. *La Repubblica* (six months for the journalist, four months for the director) are two of the many examples of this tendency.
30   See nota a Tribunale di Perugia 19 June 1985, *op. cit.*
31   Cassazione section 5, 31 March 1970, *Cassazione penale*, Massimario annuale 1971, 686, n. 962.
32   Law n. 69/73, published in the *Official Gazette* (29) (20 February 1973).
33   Tribunale di Roma 19 June 1985, *Foro Italiano*, **I**, (1986), p. 128.
34   Tribunale di Napoli, 8 April 1995, *Foro Italiano*, **I**, (1995), p. 1009, in Stella, 'Responsabilita' civil', *op. cit.*, p. 134.
35   Van Niekerk, *The Cloistered Virtue*, *op. cit.*
36   Ninety per cent of the cases of criticism against judges are prosecuted compared to 10 per cent in other instances.

12 Criticizing Judges in Greece

Lefteris Ktistakis

Everyone can [criticize] in the context of the well established freedom of discussing the acts of public authorities, since these acts and, particularly, the acts of judicial authorities are the property of all people and thus, subject to public opinion's criticism . . . . (Choidas, Attorney of Arios Pagos (highest court), 1930)

Introduction

In the Greek legal system, legal theory draws a clear distinction between the enactment and the application of law. Judges apply the rules that have been given the force of law by the Greek legislator, as the Constitution provides and requires.[1] This fundamental distinction is common in continental legal systems and has led to the development of three theories.

The first one (almost abandoned today) considers the judge to be '*la bouche qui prononce les paroles de la loi*' (Montesquieu). Thus, the personal evaluations of the judge do not play any role either in taking the decision or in its reasoning.[2] The second theory, a much more radical one (the theory of free judicial decision) takes the view that the application of law is based on the judge's evaluations and, therefore, the law itself can not determine it in advance. In other words, the application of law is necessarily a judicial task.[3]

Lastly, the theory of lawful and rational decision considers that it is the analysis of characteristics of legal ratio, of legal wording and of legal system that plays the most significant role in taking and reasoning a judicial decision.[4] No matter which theory one favours, the judge lies *de facto* in the centre of the debate: he applies the law. The review of law application – that is, the review of the judge's decisions – may take two forms: it can be either prescribed by law (higher courts reconsider the judgments of lower) or it can be non-statutory, such as the criticism by the legislative and administrative authority, the litigants, the legal theory and public opinion.[5]

This chapter deals with the non-statutory. First, the criticism of judges while the judgment is still pending will be examined. Then, the issue of criticism after the delivery of judgment will be discussed. Finally, the third part will deal with the criminal law provision which makes it a criminal offence, under certain circumstances, to criticize the judges and which was in force until 1993.

Criticizing Judges before whom Cases are Pending

Article 87(1) and (2) of the 1975 Constitution reads as follows:

> 1. Justice shall be administered by courts composed of regular judges who shall enjoy functional and personal independence.
> 2. In the discharge of their duties, judges shall be subject only to the Constitution and the laws; in no case whatsoever shall they be obliged to comply with provisions enacted in violation of the Constitution.

The Constitution distinguishes between functional and personal judicial independence.[6] The first concerns the relationship of judicial authority with the other authorities of the state. The basic principle characterizing the judge's independence towards the legislative authority is his obligation not to apply any provision of law which is in contradiction with the Constitution.[7] Article 87(2) is generally accepted to prohibit any interference by Parliament in a trial pending before a Greek court.[8]

The Constitution, also, forbids official interventions of any kind in judicial function from the representatives of administrative authority. Thus, judges are not subject to any control by administrative or political superior. The same is true of any unofficial intervention in the affairs of the judiciary. Consequently, judges are protected from governmental statements and comments made in public.[9]

The personal independence of judges, referred to in Article 87(1) of the Constitution, 'is achieved by setting guarantees related to their employment situation, so that they do not entertain fears of disadvantageous treatment when they fulfil their duties in an impartial and unprejudiced way'.[10] The Constitution, in articles subsequent to Article 87, deals in detail with the issue of judges' personal independence, which will be further developed in the second part of this chapter.

As a matter of principle, it is clear that the legislative or administrative authority should refrain from controversies, control or official or personal criticism of the Greek judge, in relation to cases which are still pending before the judge.[11] This principle of non-intervention is firmly established in Greek legal theory and practice, since the legislature dealt with this issue in the area of criminal law as early as 1938:

While a criminal case is yet undecided and until a final judgment has been delivered, for which appeal is not allowed, it is prohibited to publish estimations or evaluations concerning either the litigants or the alleged act and especially, concerning the guilt of the defendant.[12]

A similar provision is included in Article 3, Law 1730/1987, which prohibits any comments or the transmission of pictures which may distract the process of the trial and influence the judgment of the court.

The Greek Constitution, however, secures the publicity of both the trial and the judgment. Thus, Articles 93(2) and (3a) provide:

2. The sittings of all courts shall be public, except when the court decides that publicity would be detrimental to the good usages or that special reasons call for the protection of the private or family life of the litigants.
3. a) Every court's judgment must be specifically and thoroughly reasoned and must be pronounced in a public hearing.[13]

Professor Tsatsos remarks that these principles of publicity and of pronouncement of judgments in public hearings are closely connected to the gradual alteration of what 'authority of the state' means: the position of the citizen has been strengthened from the time the state authority has been made subject to law; as a consequence, 'the state can no longer demand the *a priori* acceptance of its acts, without the existence of an apparent legal reason that would support them'.[14] The majority of legal theory comes to the same conclusion as well.[15]

The attempt to prescribe, by law, conditions of contact between the judicial authority and public opinion (as reflected to the principle of publicity and of pronouncement of judgment in a public hearing) is part of the continually changing relationship between citizen and state. In addition, those principles have become communal in European legal theory and have been laid down in Article 6(1) of the European Convention on Human Rights:[16]

In the determination of his civil rights and obligations or of any criminal charge against him, everyone is entitled to a fair and public hearing . . . . Judgments shall be pronounced publicly . . . .

The relationship between the citizen and the state is realized through the information disseminated by broadcasting media or the press. This information appears to be necessary as long as it accords with the principle of the respect and protection of the human personality.[17] The prohibition by the Greek state of publication by the press and media should satisfy the preconditions of Article 10(2) of the ECHR, as clarified by the European Court in *Sunday Times* v. *United Kingdom.*[18]

Furthermore, apart from policy reasons which may justify the close connection between judicial authority and Greek citizens, there are other constitutional provisions that in fact foresee such a connection. One of the fundamental provisions of the Greek Constitution is Article 1(3): 'All powers derive from the people and exist for the people.' Thus, the judicial authority derives from the people and is expected to be exercised for their benefit.[19] By this principle, a court cannot disregard public opinion, while, arguably, the judge tries the cases on behalf of the public. Professor Beis refers to Eichenberger[20] and points out the practical significance of this principle in the context of the theory of lawful and rational decision. He argues that (a) where the application of law is a prerequisite to the definition of a vague legal term (for example, an immoral transaction), then this definition is made by reference to public opinion's beliefs, and (b) the judge refers to his personal knowledge only when it comes to obvious facts or to common knowledge beliefs.[21] These observations are in line with the case law of the Greek highest court.[22]

Criticizing Judges after the Judgment has been Delivered

In a civil trial the judgment is not a precedent as far as its reasoning is concerned.[23] The decision is binding, of course, upon the litigants, but this does not extend to its reasonableness or its correctness. It is evident that the decision does not bind the public. The same applies both to the judgments of criminal and administrative courts.[24] The most widespread and often vehement criticism of judges and their judgments is often found in academic writings. The Constitution, in Article 16(1), guarantees this freedom of academic criticism.[25] In practice, legal theory's right to criticism has not so far been challenged. The scant case law concerning this article confirms that no particular problems have arisen.[26]

In the first part of this chapter, we noted the provisions that safeguard the independence of the Greek judge before delivering the judgment. The general framework of this protection which, also, covers the period after the pronouncement of decision is supplemented by constitutional provisions, which regulate:

- the control of judges by their superiors[27]
- their appointment for life[28]
- their remuneration[29]
- their translocation[30]
- their promotion[31]
- their discharge[32]
- the inconsistencies with the judicial profession[33]

- the age limit[34]
- disciplinary action[35]
- the judicial association.[36]

This constitutional framework is necessary in order to secure the personal and functional independence of judges. Justice is one of the three authorities of the state and is certainly independent of the other two – the legislative and administrative. However, while this distinction is self-evident (or at least generally accepted), the relation between the public and judicial authority is not that crystal clear. In accordance with Article 1(3), which provides that all powers derive from the people and exist for the people, Article 26(3) reads as follows: 'The judicial powers shall be exercised by courts of law, the decisions of which shall be executed in the name of the Greek people.'

Thus, people are named as the source of all powers. People are the source and the objective of the powers. It is therefore evident that those powers are not above the people and that their exercise cannot be beyond criticism. Furthermore, each authority should be exercised within the boundaries that public opinion sets, having the Constitution and the law as the principal basis.[37]

Accordingly, public opinion challenges the validity and effectiveness of justice on a daily basis and, through that process, judges gain the necessary social recognition and acceptance for their decisions.[38] The principle of publicity accords with this social necessity. This social demand is further supplemented by the constitutional provisions which require specific and thorough reasoning of judgments,[39] as well as the compulsory publication of the opinion of dissenting judges.[40] This has led to the formation of a triangle of constitutional provisions[41] aimed at 'guaranteeing and indeed strengthening the criticism in public of judgments and raising the standard and sense of judges' responsibility'.[42]

The individual's entitlement to freedom of information is relevant and significant in this context. This particular right has been encoded in Article 14 of the Greek Constitution and also in Article 10 of the European Convention on Human Rights. The European Court has elaborated on this provision in a number of cases, including *Handyside* v. *United Kingdom*,[43] *Sunday Times* v. *United Kingdom No. 1*,[44] *Observer and Guardian* v. *United Kingdom*[45] and *Sunday Times* v. *United Kingdom No. 2*[46] and has widened its scope so as to include the area of justice as well.[47]

This freedom is based on the pressing demand for control of the authorities' actions and decisions on behalf of citizens. At the same time, care has been taken so that this social control does not permit intervention and pressure on judges' duties.[48] Constitutional and European provisions safeguard judges and their work from criticism by aggrieved litigants, academics and public opinion.

Insult of Judicial Authority: The Adventure of a Criminal Provision

In the context of the present issue, it is of great significance to follow the adventure of Article 181 of Greek criminal law which deals with insulting authorities, including the judiciary. This provision had been in force since the promulgation of the current Penal Code (1950).[49] In 1987 it was amended by Law 1738/1987 to restrict the scope of the 1950 provisions but, insulting the judicial authorities expressly remained as a criminal offence.[50] Finally, Article 33 of Law 2172/1993 abolished it.[51]

The criticism of Article 181 of the Penal Code over the years is not surprising.[52] The main issue was whether this provision was in accordance with the Constitution.[53] Academic opinion regarded it vague in respect of the protected subject as well as of the legal description of the prohibited acts and, therefore, incompatible with Article 7(1) of the Constitution.[54] Moreover, Article 181 had been argued to have contradicted a predominant provision – that is, Article 6(1) of the European Convention on Human Rights[55] (which secures a fair trial), since cases concerning the insult of judicial authority are in fact tried by the 'victims' colleagues.[56] In addition, the application of the provision should, in any case, have been limited by Article 14 of the Constitution that safeguards the freedom of speech.[57]

However, the application of Article 181 had caused even more problems: what was protected under it – the judicial authority itself or its personnel?[58] The courts vacillated between the two views – protection of the authority[59] and protection of its representatives[60] – and, finally, they favoured a view in-between.[61] After a review by the legal theory of several requirements for the fulfilment of the preconditions in Article 181,[62] it denounced the provision as dangerous, especially in relation to the prosecutions for insulting the authority as such.[63]

There was a similar discussion about the insult of public officials. Particular attention focused on the content, as well as the interpretation, of 'insult'. Before the amendment of 1987, academic discussion and the case law had tried to harmonize this offence with the constitutional provision permitting the challenge of authorities' acts.[64] They had attempted to keep the criticism of acts of authorities, and particularly of judicial authorities, out of the scope of the criminal provision of Article 181. This was not successful because it was argued that unfavourable criticism *de facto* lowers the prestige of judicial authority and thus has always been considered an 'insult to authority'.[65] The enactment of Law 1738/1987 solved this problem by expressly excluding criticism from the scope of the article: 'Criticism in itself shall not constitute an insult of authority.'

Thus, criticism of judges or justice was no longer clearly a criminal offence, unless debasing or defamatory acts took place.[66] Provisions in Law

1738/1987 also excluded from its application the depreciation of the prestige of judicial authorities. In relation to the interpretation of 'defamatory act', the new law relied on Articles 362 and 236 of the Penal Code,[67] and academic opinion agrees that degrading acts and attitude fulfil the conditions of the article.[68]

In interpreting the amended Article 181, another problem emerged – namely, the requirement that the insult should have been made 'publicly'. It could have been regarded as already solved, since both the case law and theory have accepted that 'someone acts publicly, when his act may become perceivable from a large number of people, who do not have personal or other relation with him'.[69] However, the courts held that the submission of pleadings or the mail of a sealed letter fulfilled the requirement of 'public act'.[70]

Fraudulent and malicious intent was not required; it was sufficient to have knowledge that the acts or the expressions might constitute 'insult of authorities' and that a large number of people might take notice of it.[71] Moreover, it was suggested (and rather accepted) that the criticized act of the authority ought to be typically legal; otherwise, any criticism should be allowed.[72]

In addition to all these, Professor Manoledakis, in concluding his research on the insult of judicial authorities (before the provision was abolished), made two significant observations about the Greek case law:

- Courts have expressed a greater sensibility when the insult concerned judicial authorities than in the case of other authorities protected under Article 181.
- Most cases were unanimous when the insult of judicial authorities was concerned (even those of Arios Pagos, in plenary session), while there was a rather strong minority dissenting when insult of other authorities was at issue.[73]

The abolition of this criminal provision in 1993 put an end to these problems and controversies, to the relief of both the legal theory and judges.

Conclusion

It seems that, at the end of this study, one cannot but refer to the opinion of Arios Pagos' Attorney Choidas, as laid down at the beginning of this chapter. Judgments are subject to the public's critique. The doctrine of the supremacy of judicial decisions has long been abandoned by modern Greek society. There were not only problems of application, but also objections in principle. The abolition of the provision, which made the criticism of judicial authorities a criminal offence, was an expression of this new dominant theory.[74]

Notes

1   See, *inter alia*, D. Tsatsos, *Constitutional Law – Organisation and Function of State*, Volume B, (Athens-Komotini: Ant. N. Sakkoulas Publishers, 1993), p. 456.

2   For example, see the doctrine of legal positivism (K. Bergdohm) and of the analytical jurisprudence of the nineteenth century (J. Austin).

3   See the work of F. Gény and of J. Frank (in the Common Law context).

4   See the work of A. Arnio, R. Alexy or N. MacCormick. In the context of Greek law, see the work of Professor K. Beis and the jurisprudence of Arios Pagos (highest court – for example, Decision 7/1944).

5   It is worth mentioning that N.I. Saripolos, in his *Essay on Constitutional Law*, (1851), points four possible sources of influence on a judge: the legislative and administrative authority, the litigants, the social institutions and lastly, the *forum internum* of the judge. This position is also adopted by Tsatsos, *Constitutional Law, op. cit.*, p. 554. However, for the purposes of this essay, a different distinction is followed.

6   Basic analysis by P. Pararas in *Constitution and European Convention on Human Rights* (Athens-Komotini: Ant. N. Sakkoulas Publishers, 1996), pp. 252–5.

7   Articles 87(2) and 93(4) of the 1975 Constitution. Article 93(4) provides, *inter alia*, that 'the courts shall be bound not to apply a statute whose content is contrary to the Constitution'.

8   See Tsatsos, *Constitutional Law, op. cit.*, p. 555. Also, see the European Court of Human Rights' decisions: *Greek Refineries and Stran Andreadis* v. *Greece*, Eur. Ct. HR, Series A.301-V; 19 (1995) EHRR, 293 and *Papageorgiou* v. *Greece* (22 October 1997). In both cases, the Court unanimously found violation of Article 6(1) of the ECHR.

9   Tsatsos, *Constitutional Law, op. cit.*

10   E. Spiliotopoulos, *Handbook of Administrative Law*, (Athens-Komotini: Ant. N. Sakkoulas Publishers, 1993), p. 384.

11   K. Beis, 'The Permanent Lawful Judge and Public Opinion' in *Essays in Honor of J. Rammos* (Athens: Ant. N. Sakkoulas Publishers, 1979), p. 13.

12   Article 39(1) Law 1092/1938, as amended by Article 27(1), Decree 2493/1953.

13   See, also, Article 113(1) of the Code of Civil Procedure and Article 329(1) of the Code of Criminal Procedure.

14   Tsatsos, *Constitutional Law, op.cit.*, p. 483. Also, D. Tsatsos, 'The Authority of the Judge', *Yperaspisi*, (1991), p. 361.

15   E. Kroustalakis, 'The Media and the Administration of Justice: An Unsolved Problem?', *Armenopoulos*, **51** (1997), p. 321; I. Manoledakis, *Insult of the Judicial Authority* (Athens-Komotini: Ant. N. Sakkoulas Publishers, 1992), pp. 33–39.

16   Greece ratified the European Convention in 1974 (Decree no. 53/1974). The Convention is part of the Greek law and prevails over any contradicting provision of other laws. For a detailed discussion, see A. Fatouros, 'International Law in the New Greek Constitution', *American Journal of International Law*, **70** (1976), pp. 492–507.

17   Article 2(1) of the Constitution: 'Respect and protection of the value of the human being constitute the primary obligations of the State.' See also Articles 57 *et seq.* of the Civil Code.

18   Eur. Ct. HR, Series A.30 (1979) 2 EHRR, p. 245.

19   The second part of this chapter will deal in detail with this principle.

20   *Die richterliche Unabhangigkeit als staatsrechtliches Problem* (Bern: Verlag Stämpfli, 1960) para. 5 II, pp. 103–4.

21   Beis, 'The Permanent Lawful Judge', *op. cit.*, p. 13.

22   Arios Pagos (highest court) 7/1944, noted in *Themis*, **55**, p. 43.

23 Beis, 'The Permanent Lawful Judge', *op. cit.*, pp. 14–15.
24 Beis, *The Concept, the Function and the Nature of Judicial Decision* (Athens: Ant. N. Sakkoulas, 1972), p. 122.
25 Academic freedom is safeguarded in Constitution by Article 16(1): 'Art and science, research and teaching shall be free and their development and promotion shall be an obligation of the State. Academic freedom and freedom of teaching shall not exempt anyone from his duty of allegiance to the Constitution.' According to principles of constitutional law, both the personal freedom of researching and the communication of scientific knowledge in every way fall within the scope of this article.
26 See, *inter alia*, G. Papadimitriou, 'Constitution and Freedom of Science', *To Syntagma*, (1992), pp. 515–28.
27 Article 87(3).
28 Article 88(1) and (3).
29 Article 88(2).
30 Article 88(6).
31 Article 90.
32 Article 88(4).
33 Article 89(1–4).
34 Article 88(5).
35 Article 91.
36 Article 89(5).
37 See, especially, E. Kroustalakis, 'Judicial Authority, its Independence and Public Opinion', *Elliniki Dikaiosyni*, **27** (1986), p. 39.
38 E. Kroustalakis, 'The Media and the Administration of Justice: An Unsolved Problem?', *Armenopoulos*, **51** (1997), p. 321. See also P. Gilles, 'Improper Behaviour of Persons who Take Part in Trial and of Witnesses', *Armenopoulos*, (1985), p. 629.
39 Article 93(3a): 'Every court judgment must be specifically and thoroughly reasoned . . . .'
40 Article 93(3b): 'Publication of the dissenting opinion shall be compulsory.'
41 Articles 93(2) and (3a, b).
42 Tsatsos, *Constitutional Law, op. cit.*, p. 483.
43 Eur. Ct. HR, Series A.24 (1976).
44 Ibid.
45 Eur. Ct. HR, Series A.216 (1991).
46 Eur. Ct. HR, Series A.217 (1991).
47 Other cases to be noted in this context are *Lingens* v. *Austria*, Eur. Ct. HR, Series A.103 (1986), *Castells* v. *Spain*, Eur. Ct. HR, Series A.236 (1992), *Jersild* v. *Denmark*, Eur. Ct. HR, Series A.298 (1994) and *Vogt* v. *Germany*, Eur. Ct. HR, Series A.323 (1995).
48 It should be noted that Greek legal theory and Greek judges have agreed on the need for criticism of judicial decisions in the context previously referred. The discussion on independence of justice which is published in *Elliniki Dikaiosyni*, **27** (1986), pp. 46–71 is indicative.
49 Article 181 of the Penal Code read as follows: '1. One who publicly insults a public, municipal or community authority or a national party leader recognized under the Rules of Parliament shall be punished by imprisonment for not more than three years . . . .'
50 Article 181 as amended: '1. Any person shall be punished with imprisonment for up to two years who: a) publicly insults the Prime Minister of the State, the Government, the Greek Parliament, the Chairman of Parliament, the leaders of political parties recognized by the Rules of Parliament and the judicial authorities . . . 2. Criticism in itself shall not constitute an insult of an authority.'
51 In fact, Article 181 was not wholly abolished – only the provision which made the criticism

of authorities a criminal offence. Article 181, as it stands today, deals with the insult of emblems of the state.

52   *Inter alia,* A. Kostaras, *In Memory of N. Chorafa, H. Gafou, K. Gardika,* Vol. I (Athens: Ant. N. Sakkoulas Publishers, 1986), p. 101; I. Manoledakis, 'The Criminal Offence of Insulting Authorities should be Abolished', in the newspaper *Ta Nea* of 3 April 1986.

53   A. Manesis, *Citizens' Individual Rights,* 3rd edn (Athens: Ant. N. Sakkoulas Publishers, 1981), pp. 197–98; D. Spinellis, 'Issues from the 1975 Constitution's Effect on Criminal Law', in *Five Years' Application of the 1975 Constitution* (Athens: Ant. N. Sukkoulas Publishers, 1981).

54   Article 7(1): 'There shall be no crime, nor shall punishment be inflicted unless specified by law in force prior to the perpetration of the act, defining the constitutive elements of the act. In no case shall punishment more severe than that specified at the time of the perpetration of the act be inflicted.'

55   See above, note 16.

56   Manoledakis, *Insults of Judicial Authority, op. cit.,* p. 38.

57   G.-A. Magakis, 'On the Meaning of the Offence of Insulting Authorities and Art.181 Penal Code', *Poinika Chronika,* (1962), p. 323.

58   See, *inter alia,* N. Androulakis, *The Authority of Power and the Offence of Insulting Authorities* (Athens: Ant. N. Sakkoulas Publishers, 1978), No. B. 49.

59   Arios Pagos (highest court) 155/64, (1965) Poinika Chronika 368; Ef. Dod. (appeal court) 8/79, (1979) Poinika Chronika 509.

60   Arios Pagos (highest court) 94/63, (1963) Poinika Chronika 227; Arios Pagos (highest court) 1004/74, (1975) Poinika Chronika 293.

61   Arios Pagos (highest court) 1405/83, (1984) Poinika Chronika 373; Arios Pagos (highest court) 691/85, (1985) Poinika Chronika 915; Arios Pagos (highest court) 1572/88, (1989) Poinika Chronika 391.

62   Manoledakis, *Insults of Judicial Authority, op. cit.,* pp. 43–49.

63   Ibid., p. 40.

64   Androulakis, *The Authority of Power, op. cit.,* pp. 10–11; Magakis, 'On the Meaning of the Offence', *op. cit.,* p. 323.

65   Arios Pagos (highest court) 1405/83, (1984) Poinika Chronika 373; Arios Pagos (highest court) 787/1985, (1985) Poinika Chronika 985.

66   Manoledakis, *Insults of Judicial Authority, op. cit.,* p. 53.

67   Article 362 reads as follows: 'One who by any means asserts or disseminates information before a third party concerning another which may damage his character or reputation shall be punished by imprisonment for not more than two years or by pecuniary penalty. The pecuniary penalty may be imposed in adition to imprisonment.'
Article 363 reads as follows: 'If in case under Article 362, the information is false and the offender was aware of the falsity thereof, he shall be punished by imprisonment for not less than three months and, in addition, a pecuniary penalty may be imposed and deprivation of civil rights under Article 63 may be decreed.'

68   Manoledakis, *Insults of Judicial Authority, op. cit.,* p. 59.

69   H. Gafos, *Criminal Law, Specific Provisions,* Vol. I (Athens: Ant. N. Sakkoulas Publishers, 1957), p. 136. For a detailed analysis of the issue, see I. Manoledakis, 'The Execution of an Act "Publicly" as Element of the Crime', *Armenopoulos,* (1989), p. 1.

70   Arios Pagos (highest court) 82/1992, noted in (1992) Yperaspisi 577 and Tr.Ef.Thess. (appeal court) 85/1991, respectively. Also, the submission of a report has been held to fulfill the precondition: Arios Pagos (highest court) 1572/1988.

71   Arios Pagos (highest court) 226/1911; Arios Pagos (highest court in plenary) 1283/1992, noted in (1992) Poinika Chronika 922. The theory agreed on that: Gafos, *Criminal Law,*

op. cit., p. 130.

72 I. Manoledakis, 'The Legality of the Acts of Authority as Precondition for its Protection', *Poinika Chronika*, (1976), p. 780.

73 Manoledakis, *Insults of Judicial Authority, op. cit.*, p. 98.

74 The same applies for the similar provision of the Military Penal Code (Article 74). Quite recently, in *Gregoriades* v. *Greece* (25 November 1997), the European Court of Human Rights held that the application of Article 74 in the *Gregoriades* case violates the right to free speech and Article 10 of the ECHR.

PART V
LEGAL SYSTEMS IN TRANSITION

13 Criticizing Judges in Russia

Bill Bowring

Introduction[1]

Judges in Russia today are not immune from criticism. Indeed, a polemical article in the human rights weekly, *Express Chronicle*, states:

> Of all the branches of power, the judicial is the most hardy. Our own 'perestroika' has petered out, the authority, finances and economic connections between enterprises have crashed, the countries flag, and state and social system have been changed, but somehow the leaders of the Russian judges have for the most part contrived to hold on to their former seats. This is quite understandable: while the leaders of the other branches of power have scorched their wings in the fire of social life, judges have managed to lie low in their lairs (or, if you like, in their ivory towers), carving out for their cast of 'untouchables' still more subsidies, more independence, and, naturally, more rights to impunity.[2]

This chapter analyses and evaluates the criticism of judges in Russia. As is so often the case when considering the extraordinary dynamism and unpredictability of recent Russian history, analysis is difficult and prognosis unwise. According to Gorbachev in 1988,[3] Russia was to become a state under the rule of law, in which universal human values would prevail. For many observers, this meant the acceptance of the dominant discourse prevailing in Western Europe. What is now, ten years later, becoming increasingly clear is that Russia will not follow any existing model of development. New trails are being blazed, not least in the role of the judiciary in consolidating the new and fragile democracy. This chapter endeavours at least to set the stage, by analysing the historical context, and showing how the judges have arrived at their present position.

First, there is an account of the development of the judiciary in Russia – as a Russian commentator asks, is it even now the 'third power' or the 'fifth wheel'? To what extent are Russian judges still merely state functionaries, *'chinovniki'*? Third, there is an overview of the more recent legislation on the status of judges and the new criminal provisions which seek to protect their dignity. Fourth, there is an account of relations between the Russian mass media and the Russian judiciary. This is perhaps the most controversial and crucial area in which the freedom to criticize judges is now being tested in Russia.

The History of the Russian Judges

Russia's legal evolution has been quite different from that of Western Europe. There was never a conception of government under law. Instead, the principle of autocracy became a national symbol, differentiating Russia from the rest of the world, a mark of superiority. Thus, the first courts appeared only in the late fifteenth and early sixteenth centuries as administrative bodies, responsible for enforcing the tsar's policies, and resolving disputes between subjects.[4] By the mid-nineteenth century, there was a proliferation of courts, with complex appeal procedures and endless delays.

The abolition of serfdom permitted a radical reappraisal of the system. In 1861 Tsar Alexander II instructed the Imperial Secretary, Butkov, to prepare a report of judicial reform, guided by 'those fundamental principles, the undoubted merit of which is at present recognised by the science and experience of Europe'.[5] The Commission set up for this purpose included M.I. Zarudny who made a thorough comparative study of the various European systems. This Commission worked speedily, and produced its Basic Principles in 1862. These were approved by the tsar in September of that year. Detailed statutes were prepared in 1863 and, after extensive discussion, were approved in November 1864.

As implemented in 1865–66, these included the establishment of a basic regional court (*okruzhny sud*), one in each province, for civil and criminal cases; above them, a Chamber of Justice (*sudebnaya palata*), of which there were ten in Russia; and at the top two 'cassation' departments, civil and criminal, which could also meet jointly.[6] Some special courts, notably ecclesiastical and military courts, remained outside this general system which, moreover, did not hear cases concerning peasants – comprising some 80 per cent of the population – who went to separate *volost* courts. A system of justices of the peace dealt with cases punishable by a rebuke or reprimand, a fine of not more than 300 roubles, or a prison term of three months to a year. These justices were elected for three years by the *uezd zemstvos*, and heard all local cases in both towns and villages.[7] The most radical and important change, however, concerned the judiciary. Judges, although appointed by the Ministry of Justice, were required to have clearly defined legal qualifications, were paid good salaries, and had life tenure. They were effectively irremovable. Moreover, all criminal cases were to be tried in public by a judge and jury.

Judges began to demonstrate an unprecedented independence. In 1878, in an exemplary case, the revolutionary Vera Zasulich, was charged with the attempted murder, in front of several witnesses, of the Governor of St Petersburg, General Trepov. When the Minister of Justice, Count Palen, asked A.F. Koni,[8] the judge in the case, whether he could guarantee a guilty verdict, saying, 'In this damned case the government has the right to expect special services from the court', the judge replied, 'Your Excellency, the court gives verdicts, not services.'[9] Zasulich was acquitted.[10]

These reforms were, in the main, successful, and, with the establishment of an independent Bar (of which both Lenin – briefly – and his arch-opponent Kerensky were members), went a long way, according to Hosking, 'towards erecting the framework for a civil society'.[11] However, as Seton-Watson points out, 'the conception of the rule of law, the notion that there must be clearly defined laws and rules, binding on all alike, against which the actions of all citizens must be measured, was never accepted'.[12] Thus, it was easy for the revolutionary authorities, after 1917, to remove the entire edifice of reform – as easy as it would have been for a more authoritarian tsarism. The rule of law had not put down roots.

Judges in the Soviet Period

Following their successful uprising, the Bolsheviks moved swiftly to eliminate this reformed judicial system. On 22 November (5 December) 1917 the Council of People's Commissars issued the Decree 'On the Court'.[13] This provided, in Article 1, for 'The abolition of all existing general judicial institutions'. By Article 2, the activities of justices of the peace were to be suspended and replaced by local courts composed of a permanent local judge, elected by direct democratic vote, and two rotating assessors. There was to be no appeal – that is, appeal by way of rehearing – from the decisions of these courts, but cassation (a review to vacate a decision purely for errors of law) by a court of cassational review composed of local judges. By Article 3, judges were to try cases according to the laws of the overthrown government only insofar as such laws had not been abrogated by the Revolution and did not contradict revolutionary conscience (*sovest*) or revolutionary legal consciousness (*pravosoznaniye*). According to P.I. Stuchka, writing in 1918, the laws abrogated by this decree were 'all that contradicts the minimum programme of the Social Democratic and Social Revolutionary Parties i.e. the parties that were victorious in the present revolution'.[14]

This new system was consolidated and formalized in the Statute of October 21, 1920, 'On the RSFSR[15] Peoples Court',[16] which provided in Article 1 that

'There shall be within the boundaries of the RSFSR a unitary people's court composed of permanent people's judges and rotating judges – people's assessors'. A Decree of March 10, 1921, 'On Supreme Judicial Control',[17] provided that, in order to ensure the correct and uniform application of the laws of the RSFSR and 'their harmonisation with the general trends in the policies of the workers' and peasants' government', the People's Commissariat of Justice would be entrusted with the general supervision and training of judges and with the power to decide whether court cases should be reopened by reason of newly discovered evidence. There were the following grounds for invalidating judicial decisions:

1   a clear violation of or failure to apply the laws of the Soviet government;
2   the acceptance of jurisdiction by the judicial bodies over cases not subject to court proceedings (disputes concerning land and questions of official acts of the Soviet government); and
3   a clear conflict between the judgment or decision and the guiding principles of the workers' and peasants' government.

During the immediate post-revolutionary period and the Civil War, justice was administered by untrained but politically reliable workers and peasants. The 'New Economic Policy', which restored a large measure of free market economic relations, made legal and judicial reform essential. The Supreme Court of the RSFSR was created by the Decree of November 11, 1922, 'On the Judicial System of the RSFSR'.[18] This decree was itself an essential component of the complementary legal reforms which saw the adoption, in 1922, of new Civil[19] and Criminal Codes, themselves largely based on German and Swiss models. The decree provided that 'in order to safeguard the conquests of the proletarian revolution and to protect the interests of the state and the rights of the labouring masses and their organizations' a unified system would be established. This would consist of:

• people's courts, consisting of a permanent judge
• people's courts consisting of a permanent people's judge and two people's assessors
• provincial courts
• the Supreme Court of the RSFSR and its divisions.

People's judges were to be elected by the provincial executive committees, on the recommendation of the provincial court, or the People's Commissariat of Justice, for a term of one year, with eligibility for re-election. They could be dismissed by decision of the provincial executive committee which elected them. Since these committees were firmly under the control of the Party, the judges, almost all Party members, were at all times subject to actual or threatened interference. This was the origin of the notorious 'telephone justice'.

On paper, however, it was the Supreme Court which was to deal with supervision of all courts of the RSFSR. It was to do this through cassational[20] review of decisions of the provincial courts, and supervision of all cases heard by any of the courts of the RSFSR. It was also to hear trials of special state importance, as a court of first instance.

Even in the eyes of Soviet commentators, the quality and standing of judges did not change much. Commenting in 1926 on the social composition of the Soviet judiciary,[21] Ia. Brandenburgskii wrote that there were then 1642 people's judges, of whom 26 per cent were workers, 50 per cent peasants and 24 per cent members of the intelligentsia; 60 per cent were members of the Russian Communist Party. In view of the fact that some 76 per cent of people's judges were workers and peasants, he did not find it surprising that 72.5 per cent had only received a primary education, 17.5 per cent a secondary education, and only 10 per cent higher education. Of these, only 140 – or 8.5 per cent of the total – had graduated from university law faculties. A similar situation prevailed in provincial courts, where 70 per cent were workers and peasants. In these circumstances, it was 'more than a critical necessity that they gradually go through a systematic course on our Soviet law'.

Another commentator, E.I. Kelman, noted in 1925 that:

> . . . novel legal relations necessitated by the new economic policy are creating a complicated situation and making thorough preliminary training for legal workers a truly urgent matter. It is impossible by class consciousness and revolutionary fervour alone to untangle the juridical problems that arise in applying the Civil and Criminal Codes . . . it has been cogently stated that, in the wake of the adoption of the . . .Codes, both substantive and procedural, a higher level of education is required of our proletarian judges, and henceforth references solely to socialist legal consciousness will surely be insufficient to support judicial decisions and judgments.[22]

That is probably as far as criticism of judges could go, given the fact that their role in the new order was largely symbolic. There could be no judicial power in a state in which the Party was supreme.

The 1936 (Stalin) Constitution was considered by one of its draftsmen, Nikolai Bukharin, to be a serious document which would make it impossible for the people any longer to be pushed aside.[23] It proclaimed the end of class anatagonisms and contained a number of serious rights – for example, a guarantee of freedom from arbitrary arrest (Article 127), inviolability of the home and secrecy of correspondence (Article 128) and freedom of the press, of meetings and of demonstrations (Article 125). None of these provisions saved Bukharin, who was arrested and tried in 1937. His trial, before a court which knew exactly what it had to do, proved the point that an independent judiciary, able to protect fundamental rights, was an impossibility in the Soviet system.

On paper at least, however, the Stalin Constitution raised to the level of constitutional provisions a number of features of the judicial system, particularly the principles of election of judges and participation of people's assessors. On 16 August 1938 the USSR Supreme Soviet adopted a Law on Court Organization to replace the USSR's Fundamental Principles of Court Organization of 1924, which were in similar terms to the RSFSR's legislation.[24]

Judges after Stalin

This law remained in place until replaced by the all-union Fundamental Principles of Legislation of the USSR and the Union Republics on the Judicial System of the USSR of 25 December 1958.[25] These principles themselves continued in force, slightly modified by the 1977–78 USSR and constituent republic (Brezhnev) Constitutions, until the collapse of the USSR itself in December 1991. There was thus remarkable continuity within the Soviet system.

The statistical picture in the early years of Gorbachev's rule as Party General Secretary was remarkably similar to today's. By 1987 there were 15 500 judges in the whole USSR, elected for five-year terms by the Soviet at the corresponding territorial level. In June 1987, 12 122 people's judges were elected (29 per cent of judges were elected for the first time), as well as 850 344 people's assessors, who were themselves elected for a two-and-a-half-year term. Of the judges, just over 50 per cent had higher legal education (in 1941 only 6.4 per cent of all judges had this qualification!), and 55.5 per cent were men. The high proportion of women as judges reflected the comparatively low status of the job.[26] In 1986 some 76 judges were dismissed, and 837 subjected to disciplinary measures for incompetence. There were only 3000 judges serving in union republic Supreme Courts and other courts superior to people's courts.[27]

However, the position of judges in society was very much as it had been since the Revolution. Judges were firmly under the control of the local Party organization which could appoint or remove them at will. Their role was to reinforce the legitimacy of the regime and its ideology. The Fundamental Principles provided that:

> . . . through all its activity the court shall educate citizens of the USSR in the spirit of devotion to the Motherland and the cause of communism, in the spirit of strict and undeviating observance of the Constitution of the USSR and Soviet laws, solicitous attitude to socialist property, observance of labour discipline, honest

attitude to the state and social duty, respect for the rights, honour and dignity of citizens, and the rules of socialist community life.[28]

Official commentators such as V.I. Terebilov, writing as late as 1986, when he was president of the USSR Supreme Court, stressed the educational role of the court system in Soviet life. Explaining the public nature of trials in the USSR, Terebilov stressed that 'publicity in court is needed primarily for the purpose of increasing the educational effect of judicial examination and judgments among the population'.[29] For the same reasons, 'the Soviet style of press coverage primarily pursues an educational purpose, serving to foster in its readers intolerance of crimes, respect for the law, the court and the rules of socialist community life'.[30] In so doing, he made it plain why public criticism of judges was inconceivable. Judges were not intended to perform an independent judicial role. How could they then be criticized for failure to do something which was outside their remit? If they failed, it would be in relation to their duty to the Party. The press was equally under Party control, and had a very similar educative role.

There were valiant attempts to present the judicial system, particularly for Western observers, as a properly functioning and independent branch of state power. For example, judges, on paper at least, were obliged to report back to the electorate or to the legislative organs which had elected them. According to Terebilov, this was 'natural and conducive to the improvement of judicial work'. He recognized that the reader might raise a question: did this not contradict judges' independence? His answer was that 'the long-standing practice of the Soviet courts has shown that these apprehensions are unfounded'. He flatly denied the possibility of Party interference:

... [a]ny interference in the adjudication of cases on the part of officials, government, Party or any other organs is totally impermissible ... Party directives ban any intervention by Party bodies in the administration of justice.[31]

Contrary to Terebilov's assertions, one of the most notorious features of Soviet justice was the so-called 'telephone justice'. As Professor V. Savitskii, former presidential representative at the Russian Constitutional Court, put it in 1993:

... until just recently, communists comprised 85 to 90 percent of all district judges and 100 percent of judges at higher level courts. On the basis of their party membership, they were subject to party discipline and were guided not so much by the law as by the instructions of party committees and individual communist functionaries. It was the system of *nomenklatura*[32] that nourished the method of influencing judges known as 'telephone law'. It was the system of *nomenklatura* that created the faceless, subjugated judicial system that was completely dependent on the party apparatus.[33]

Judicial dependence on the Party only ended with President Yeltsin's Decree of 20 July 1991, 'On ending the activity of the organisational structures of political parties and mass social movements in state organs, institutions and organisations of the RSFSR'.[34] Promulgation of the decree was one of the events which precipitated the notorious attempted *putsch* of August 1991.

A New Status for Judges

Judges began to acquire an enhanced status during Gorbachev's *perestroika*, as part of his new emphasis on constructing a 'socialist rule of law state'. One of the first, and highly significant, indications of a new attitude to judges was the law of the USSR of 2 November 1989, 'On Disrespect for the Court'.[35] This provided as follows:

1. Exertion of any influence on judges or people's assessors in order to impede a thorough, complete and objective examination of any matter before the court or to obtain an illegal judicial decision – shall be punished by correctional labour for a term of up to one year or by a fine from 300 to 1,000 rubles.

2. The same actions committed by taking advantage of one's official position – shall be punished by deprivation of freedom for a term up to three years or by correctional labour for a term from one year to two years.

3. Insulting a judge or a people's assessor regarding his actions in the administration of justice – shall be punished by correctional labour for a term up to one year or by a fine up to 300 rubles.

4. Intentional non-compliance with a judicial decision, judgment, determination, or decree, or interference with its execution, by an official – shall be punished by a fine from 300 to 1,000 rubles.

5. Disrespect for the court, manifested in a malicious refusal by a witness, victim, plaintiff, or defendant to appear in court, or in a failure by the said persons or other citizens to obey the directives of the presiding judge, or in a violation of the order in court, or in other actions of any kind that clearly evidence contempt for the court and for the rules of judicial decorum – shall entail an administrative penalty in the form of administrative arrest for a term up to 15 days or a fine up to 100 rubles.

On 11 December 1989 the chairman of the RSFSR Supreme Soviet added, by decree, a new Article 176 to the 1960 Criminal Code, making the insulting of judges or people's assessors in connection with their judicial activities punishable by corrective labour for up to one year or a fine of up to three times the monthly minimum wage.[36]

Reform of the status of judges was a longer process. The USSR law, 'On the Status of Judges in the USSR' of 4 August 1989,[37] extended judicial tenure from five years to ten years, and limited the possibilities of dismissal ('recall') of judges to instances of specific misconduct – conviction in a criminal case, violations of 'socialist legality', or other unworthy behaviour. In October 1991 the First All-Russian Congress of Judges (the first-ever congress of Russian judiciary) proposed a series of reforms, including a return to the jury system,[38] and life tenure for judges.[39] However, it was only after the dissolution of the USSR in December 1991 that there was a significant change in the status of judges.[40]

The law 'On the Status of Judges in the Russian Federation' of 26 June 1992[41] was the most important step in transforming the Russian judiciary. Article 3 prohibited judges from holding membership of political parties and movements. Any possibility of 'telephone justice' was ended by Article 4, which provided that judges 'are not accountable to anyone', and were henceforth to be appointed for life. In the provincial and higher courts they were to be elected by the Supreme Soviet of the Russian Federation on the recommendation of the president of the Supreme Court of the Russian Federation. Judges were obliged to have an academic degree in law (higher legal education). For the very first time in Russian history, there was provision for the irremovability of judges (Article 12). The inviolability of the person, home, property, correspondence and documents of judges was guaranteed (Article 16); their material support was raised (Article 19); and measures for the social protection of judges and their families were established (Article 20). According to Savitskii, 'all of this taken together makes judicial work prestigious and removes the administration of justice from the degraded humble position that it occupied since the time of the October Revolution'.[42]

Chapter 7 of the new Constitution of the Russian Federation, adopted by referendum on 12 December 1993, contains constitutional provisions on the judiciary, embodying many of these reforms. Justice in the Russian Federation shall be administered only by law courts (Article 118). Citizens of the Russian Federation aged 25 or over, who hold a law degree and who have worked in the legal profession for at least five years may become judges.[43] Judges shall be independent and shall obey only the Russian Constitution and federal law and, once a court of law has established the illegality of any act of government or other body, shall rule in accordance with law (Article 120). Judges may not be replaced, and may not have their powers terminated or suspended except under procedures and on grounds established by federal law (Article 121). They possess immunity, and may only be prosecuted for criminal offences according to federal law (Article 122). Judges of the Federal Constitutional Court, the Federal Supreme Court, and the Federal Supreme Arbitration Court shall be appointed by the Federation Council following nomination by the President, while the President shall appoint judges of other federal courts (Article 128).

The new Criminal Code, which came into force on 1 January 1997,[44] contains two provisions of note. The first, in Article 297, concerns 'Disrespect to the Court'. Insulting behaviour to judges, jurors or others concerned with the administration of justice is to be punished by a fine of 200 to 500 times the minimum wage, or two to five months income, or corrective labour from one to two years, or arrest for a period from four to six months. The second, in Article 298, prohibits 'Defamation of Judges, Jurors, Prokurors, Witnesses, and Bailiffs'. Defamation of judges is to be punished by a similar fine, or corrective labour for one to two years, or arrest from three to six months, or imprisonment for up to two years. There are no statistics as to prosecutions under these sections. It is unlikely that there have been any. As I show below, judges have turned to other means of inhibiting criticism.

Criticizing Judges in Russia

It might be thought that the position of judges in Russia is now secure, and that their prestige is worth defending from criticism. The new Russian Constitution of December 1993 consolidates the judicial branch as one of the real powers of the new state. The Supreme Court, at the pinnacle of the system of courts of general jurisdiction, the Higher Arbitration Court (the commercial court), with its own system, and the Federal Constitutional Court, are given equal status. There are now about 15 000 judges of general jurisdiction in Russia, plus a little more than 2000 arbitration judges. The profession of judge has become more attractive. In the first half of 1997 there were 695 applications for judicial appointment (200 of them for arbitration positions), and 80 and 26 persons respectively were appointed. Nevertheless, Russia possesses only two-thirds of the full complement of arbitration judges, while there is continual shortage of about 1000 judges of general jurisdiction.

Yet there are many voices of scepticism. For example, the commentator Leonid Nikitinskii asks whether the judiciary should be described as the 'third power' or rather as the 'fifth wheel'.[45] He notes that levels of pay are very low, and cites the fact that a court registrar in an ordinary Moscow district court is paid only 200 000 rubles (around £21) a month.[46] This might, he says, even be rather a large salary compared with salaries outside Moscow.

Evidence is provided by a rather extraordinary case.[47] The newspaper *Sankt-Peterburgskiye Vedomosti* published, on 11 October 1996, an article about the difficult material circumstances of St Petersburg judges. It claimed that judge Ye. Ye. Lyubomirskaya of the Kuibishevskii District Federal Court, who has five children, was receiving only 100 000 rubles (£10.50) per month salary. Following a complaint by the judge as to the impermissibility of publication of details of a citizen's private life, the newspaper published a further article containing the judge's remarks. Nevertheless, the judge issued proceedings in the St Petersburg city court claiming against the editor and journalist, under Articles 43 and 44 of the Federal Law 'On the Mass Media',[48] protection of her honour, dignity and professional reputation, as well as damages. However, it would appear that she has not contested the information as to her earnings.[49]

Indeed, according to Alexei Simonov, president of the leading human rights NGO *Fond Zashchiti Glasnosti* (Glasnost Defence Foundation), defamation claims ('claims for the defence of honour and dignity') have now become a leading instrument of pressure on the mass media.[50] He contends that, ten years on from *perestroika*, there has been a huge rise in non-payment of salaries, coalminers' strikes, the numbers of homeless, refugees, contract killings – and in defamation claims against the mass media. Thus, there were 1140 such claims before the courts in 1990, 1793 in 1994, 3500 in 1995, and an equivalent rise in 1996.

Claims Brought by the Judges Themselves

A significant and rising number of these claims have been brought by judges. This is a development which, to my knowledge, has no counterpart in Western – at least common law – jurisdictions. The US courts, for example, are less sensitive. Barendt points out that, in federal cases, 'the relevant statute has been narrowly construed so as to confine contempt to misbehaviour in or physically near to the court-room'.[51] The press and lawyers, too, are able to speak their minds. In a recent article, Professor Freedman argues that 'criticism of judges by lawyers is both constitutionally protected and desirable in a democracy'.[52] He relies on the dissenting opinion, later upheld by the Supreme Court,[53] in which Frankfurter J said that judges are not 'anointed priests' entitled to special protection from the public clamour of democratic society. The law gives judges and the institutional reputation of the courts 'no greater immunity from criticism than other persons or institutions'.[54]

Freedman cites a number of cases of judicial criticism by lawyers, in which no disciplinary action was taken, or, if taken, was reversed on appeal. These include: the judge's opinion is 'irrational' and 'cannot be taken seriously'; 'this judge sitting on the bench is a danger to the people of this city'; 'I have had more than enough of judicial opinions that . . . falsify the facts of the cases that have been argued, . . . that make disingenuous use or omission of material authorities, . . . that cover up these things . . .'; the state's appellate judges are 'whores who became madams . . . I would like to [be a judge] . . . But the only way you can get it is to be in politics or buy it – and I don't even know the going price.'; the judges decision is 'overt racism', and the defendants 'have no more chance of a fair hearing in front of [the judge] than they would being judged by the Klu Klux Klan'; the judge is 'dishonest', 'ignorant', a 'buffoon', a 'bully', 'drunk on the bench', and shows 'evidence of anti-Semitism'.[55] All of these were published in the press, against which no action was taken either.

Russia is different. It is hard to say whether this is because of the new-found status of judges or whether it reflects the insecurity of judges who still occupy such a low place in the public esteem. I have not so far been able to locate statistics on the use of civil and criminal proceedings against the Russian mass media, but I set out below some exemplary cases from the late 1990s. Alexei Simonov and the Glasnost Defence Foundation are now carrying out a thorough research project on the question of the relationship between judges and the mass media.

Some Recent Cases

There have been a number of civil cases in which judges have taken action against the mass media, and some examples follow. The first two concern the same newspaper: in Bryansk the Council of Judges of the Bryansk *oblast* claimed against the editors of the newspaper *Dobri Den* (Good Day) and against A. Kostrikin, an expert of the President's representation in Bryansk for alleged defamation in an article published on 4 October 1996, entitled 'Mafia in Judicial Gown'. The Council sought an order requiring the newspaper and Mr Kostrikin to publish an apology to the judges of the *oblast* and forbidding further publication of repetitions or commentaries on the said article.[56] This case was lost by the opposition newspaper *Dobri Den* which, partly as a result, was forced to close in 1998. All newspapers in the region have come under strong pressure from the *oblast* administration.[57]

On 28 March 1997, in the Sovetskii District Court of the city of Bryansk, Judge L.V. Stepinaya, a judge of the Bryansk Arbitration Court, brought an action against the editors of *Dobri Den* and its journalist, V.A. Vladikin, claiming 50 million rubles (£5300) damages for alleged defamation in an article entitled 'How Truth was Disengaged from the Judicial Gown', published on 18 March 1997. According to the plaintiff, the article alleged that she had soiled the gown of a judge, and had sullied the positive evaluation of her professional quality.[58] This case was also lost, with similar effect to the *Dobri Den* case.[59]

In an unusual case in June 1997, Galina Vlasevskaya, a judge of the

Volgograd *oblast* Court, brought an action against journalist Irina Chernova seeking damages of 300 million rubles (£31 500) for alleged defamation in an article entitled 'Bitovukha' ('Domestic Fish-Soup'), published in the fourth issue of the newspaper *Press-Klub*, about the activities of a judge of the Dzerzhinsky district court, Tatiana Kremevaya, who happens to be Judge Vlasevskaya's daughter.[60]

I am only aware of one criminal case. On 10 March 1997 the *prokuror*[61] of the town of Nyagani (in the Khanti-Mansiiski Autonomous *Okrug*) stopped the criminal prosecution of Sergei Arkhangelskii, the editor of the newspaper *Vestnik Priobya*. The editor was prosecuted under Article 130 (3) of the Criminal Code of the RSFSR, 'Defamation',[62] which prohibited 'the deliberate spreading of defamatory falsehoods', and was punishable by corrective labour for up to two years, or a fine up to 20 times the monthly minimum, together with the possibility of loss of the right to practise journalism.

The prosecution was stopped on grounds of 'absence of the substance of a crime'. It had been instituted by Vorsanof Yarondaikin, a judge of the Nyagani town court on 26 November 1996 in connection with the publication of an article by S. Arsentiev entitled '*Khalati byeli, ruki gryazni*' ('White doctor's coats, filthy hands'), which told of abuse of their positions on the part of the head doctor of a hospital, and a candidate for deputy of the Town Duma, Vladimir Gontsov, and the latters' civil claim against the editor for defamation. On 10 January 1997 the criminal case was accepted by the Nyagani town procuracy. However, V. Gontsov had earlier been prosecuted on the basis of the facts contained in the article.[63]

Conclusion

The status of Russian judges has now been substantially enhanced. On 1 January 1997 a new Federal Constitutional Law 'On the Judicial System of the Russian Federation' came into force[64] and was implemented during 1998. This provides, for the first time, for complete independence of the judiciary from legislative and executive powers. The judicial system has been removed from the control of the Ministry of Justice, and a new Judicial Department has been established, under the auspices of the Russian Federation Supreme Court, which now has full control over the administration and government of the system of courts of general jurisdiction.[65] According to the distinguished Moscow judge, Sergei Pashin, this new law, which he helped to draft, is based on the norms of world justice.[66] Article 5, on the independence of courts and judges, provides that they are independent of any power whatsoever, and subordinate only to the Constitution of the Russian Federation and to the law. The new Department is financed from the federal budget, in which it has a separate slot.

In a highly critical review of the draft Criminal Procedural Code, Pashin writes[67] that the most important achievements of judicial reform in Russia to date are:

- the strengthening of the independence of the courts corresponding to the legislation on the status of judges
- the creation of mechanisms permitting the direct effect in the hearing of criminal cases not only of the provisions of the Russian Constitution, but also of international legal human rights instruments
- the establishment of judicial control over the lawfulness of detention and the extension by *prokurors* of the period of detention, as well as over other procedural matters such as the search of dwelling houses and interception of telephone conversations
- the introduction in nine subjects of the Russian Federation of jury trials.[68]

However, this progress is seriously threatened. Pashin identifies the following urgent problems for criminal justice (in particular):

- the grave inadequacy of financial resources in the federal budget
- the great overloading with cases of judges and prosecutors, and the low qualification of both
- the fact that conditions of persons in detention, accused and under suspicion, is tantamount to torture
- the low quality of legal assistance available to the poor
- the slowness of the hearing of cases
- the prevalence of procedural oversimplification and the existing refusal to follow the demands of the appropriate legal procedures.

These are circumstances which bode ill for public confidence in the standing and independence of judges. Public confidence in the administration of justice will be further undermined if judges seek to employ the civil and criminal law in order to prevent public criticism. One question which will inevitably arise is whether their fellow judges can possibly decide such cases fairly.

Notes

1   I wish to express my gratitude to Alexei Simonov, of the Glasnost Defence Foundation in Moscow, who made his extensive collection of data available to me. He heads an exemplary human rights NGO.

2   Z. Konstantinov, 'Presse dozvolyat pochistit sudeiskiye konyushi' ('The press is being permitted to clean out the judicial stables'), *Ekspress Khronika*, 28 November 1997.

3   See, for example, M.S. Gorbachev, *On Progress in Implementing the Decisions of the 27th CPSU Congress and the Tasks of Promoting Perestroika* (Moscow: Novosti, 1988).

4   Gordon B. Smith, *Reforming the Russian Legal System* (Cambridge: Cambridge University Press, 1996), p. 129.

5   Geoffrey Hosking, *Russia: People and Empire (1552-1917)* (London: Harper Collins, 1997), p. 334.

6   H. Seton-Watson, *The Russian Empire 1801-1917* (Oxford: Oxford University Press, 1990), p. 355

7   Justices of the Peace (*mirovoi sudyei*) have now been reintroduced.

8   Anatolii Fedorovich Koni lived from 1844 to 1927, and worked as a *prokuror* in Kharkov, Kazan and St Petersburg before becoming president of the St Petersburg District Court from 1878 to 1881, holding on to his position despite the tsar's efforts to have him removed. He worked within the law as a liberal, holding high positions until 1917, and remaining a university professor after the Revolution. His article on 'Juries', first published in 1914, appears at pp. 28–91 in S.M. Kazantsev, *Sud Prisyazhnikh* v. *Rossii: Gromkiye Ugolovniye Protsessi* (Trial by Jury in Russia: Great Criminal Trials) (Leningrad: Leniizdat, 1991).

9   Samuel Kucherov, *Courts, Lawyers and Trials under the Last Three Tsars* (New York: F.A. Praeger, 1953), p. 215; cited in Hosking, *Russia, op. cit.*, p. 335.

10 Koni's summing up to the jury is to be found in Kazantsev, *Sud Prisyazhnikh* v. *Rossii, op. cit.*, pp. 306–16.

11 Hosking, *Russia, op. cit.*, p. 337.

12 Seton-Watson, *The Russian Empire, op. cit.*, pp. 356–7.

13 Decree of the Council of People's Commissars, 22 November (5 December) 1917, *SU* 1917–1918, no. 4, item 50; translated in Zigurds L. Zile, *Ideas and Forces in Soviet Legal History* (New York: Oxford University Press, 1990) p. 95 *et seq.*

14 P.I. Stuchka, 'Staryi i novyi sud' ('The old and new courts') in P.I. Stuchka, *Izbrannye proizvodenii po markistkovo-leninskoi teorii prava* (Selected Works on the Marxist–Leninist Theory of Law) (Riga, 1964), pp. 227, 231–35, in Zile, *Ideas and Forces, op. cit.*, p. 97.

15 Russian Soviet Federative Socialist Republic.

16 Statute of the All-Russian Central Executive Committee, 21 October 1920, *SU RSFSR* 1920, no. 83, item 407; Zile, *Ideas and Forces, op. cit.*, pp. 98-100.

17 Decree of the All-Russian Central Executive Committee and the Council of People's Commissars, *SU RSFSR* 1921, no. 15, item 97.

18 Decree of the All-Russian Central Executive Committee, November 11, 1922 *SU RSFSR* 1922, no. 69, item 92; Zile, *Ideas and Forces, op. cit.*, pp. 158–59.

19 Civil Code of the RSFSR of 1922, *SU RSFSR* 1922, no. 71, item 904; Zile, *Ideas and Forces, op. cit.*, p. 173. Article 1 provided that 'Civil-law rights shall be protected by law, except in those instances when they are exercised in contradiction to their socio-economic purpose', and Article 2 provided that 'Disputes concerning civil-law rights shall be decided in a judicial proceeding. Waiver of the right of recourse to the court is void.'

20 As opposed to appeal by way of rehearing – that is, a review only of procedural, formal correctness.

21 Ia. Brandenburgskii, 'O sotsialnom sostave sovetskovo suda' (On the Social Composition of the Soviet Judiciary), *Yezhedelnik sovetskoi iustitsii (Annual of Soviet Justice)* 1926 n. 24, pp. 553–54; Zile, *Ideas and Forces, op. cit.*, pp. 169–70.

22 E.I. Kelman, *O sisteme iuridicheskovo obrazovanii* (On the system of judicial education) (Kiev, 1925), pp. 5–6, 28–29; Zile, *Ideas and Forces, op. cit.*, pp. 170–71.

23   R. Conquest, *The Great Terror* (Harmondsworth: Penguin, 1971), p. 134.
24   W. Butler, *Soviet Law*, 2nd edn (London: Butterworths, 1988), p. 100.
25   *Vedomosti SSSR 1959*, no. 1, item 12. There is an English translation at pp. 175–86 of
     V.I. Terebilov, *The Soviet Court* (Moscow: Progress, 1986).
26   Although Gordon B. Smith is of the view that women were heavily represented on the
     bench 'as in other careers involving socialization of societal norms', judges were not only
     expected to determine innocence or guilt 'but also to educate the accused and all present
     in the courtroom'. See Gordon B. Smith, *Reforming the Russian Legal System* (Cambridge:
     Cambridge University Press, 1996), p. 140.
27   Butler, *Soviet Law, op. cit.*, pp. 101–2.
28   Article 3, 'The Tasks of the Court': Terebilov, *The Soviet Court, op. cit.*, p. 176.
29   Ibid., p. 51.
30   Ibid., p. 53.
31   Ibid., pp. 49, 50.
32   The only people who could have state careers under the Soviet system were the so-called
     nomenklatura, a list of names which had various levels and embraced more than 20 000
     positions, including all judicial positions.
33   Valery Savitsky, 'Will there be a New Judicial Power in the new Russia?', *Review of
     Central and East European Law*, **19** (1993), pp. 639, 646.
34   See *Izvestiya*, 22 July 1991, p. 2.
35   Law of the USSR, November 2 1989, *Vedomosti SSSR 1989*, no. 22, item 418; Zile, *Ideas
     and Forces, op. cit.*, p. 526.
36   *Vedemosti VS RSFSR 1989*, no. 50, item 1477. This was incorporated in the RSFSR Law
     of 20 October 1992, *Vedomosti VS RSFSR 1992*, no. 47, item 2664.
37   Law of 4 August 1989 'O statuse sudei SSSR', *Vedomosti SSSR 1989*, no. 9, item 223.
38   A federal law on jury trials came into effect in 1993, and the first jury trial took place in
     the city of Saratov in December 1993. There is a right to trial by jury only in the most
     serious cases – involving punishment of more than 10 years' imprisonment or the death
     penalty. The right applies only in certain regions: initially in Moscow, Stavropol,
     Ivanovo, Ryazan and Saratov *oblasts*, and from early 1994 in Altai, Simbirsk, Krasnodar
     and Rostov-on-Don. See Smith, *Reforming the Russian Legal System, op. cit.*, pp. 147–
     48. See also L.B. Alekseyeva, S.E. Vitsin, E.F. Kutsova, I.B. Mikhailovskaya, *Sud
     Prisyazhnikh: Posobiye dlya Sudei* (Jury Trial: Handbook for Judges) (Moscow: Ivan,
     1994).
39   Savitsky, 'Will There be a New Judicial Power?', *op. cit.*, p. 643.
40   F.J.M. Feldbrugge, *Russian Law: The End of the Soviet System and the Role of Law*
     (Dordrecht: M. Nijhoff, 1993) p. 200.
41   Law of 26 June 1992 'O statuse sudei Rossiiskoi Federatsii', *Vedomosti siezda narodnikh
     deputatov Rossiiskoi Federatsii I Verkhovnovo Sovieta Rossisskoi Federatsii 1992*, no.
     30, item 1792; See also Feldbrugge, *Russian Law, op. cit.*, p. 200 and, for a detailed
     commentary, Savitsky, 'Will There be a New Judicial Power?', *op. cit.*
42   Savitsky, 'Will There be a New Judicial Power?', *op. cit.*, p. 649.
43   Article 83(f) provides that the President of the Russian Federation shall submit to the
     Federation Council candidates for appointment to the office of judges of the Constitutional
     Court, the Supreme Court, and the Supreme Arbitration Court, and shall appoint the judges
     of other federal courts.
44   Adopted by the State Duma on 24 May 1996.
45   Leonid Nikitinskii, ' "Tretya" vlast ili "pyatoye koleso" ?' ('Third' Power or 'Fifth Wheel'?),
     Moskovskii Novosti, (48) 30 November–7 December 1997.
46   The price of articles in shops and markets in Moscow now approaches ordinary Western

levels, and it is said that the average wage is at least £120 per month – accommodation and transport costs are still very much lower than in the West.

47 Information from the database of the *Fond Zashchiti Glasnosti* (Glasnost Defence Foundation), identification code no. 164/79297, date of information 14 May 1997.

48 She also claims under Article 21 (right to dignity of the person) and 23 (right to privacy) of the Constitution, and Articles 150–152 of the Civil Code.

49 At the time of writing, the case has not been decided.

50 Aleksei Simonov, 'Iski o zashchite chesti i dostoinstvo kak instrument davleniya na SMI' ('Claims for the Protection of Honour and Dignity as an Instrument of Pressure on the Mass Media'), unpublished paper, Russian version in the possession of the author.

51 Eric Barendt, *Freedom of Speech* (Oxford: Clarendon Press, 1985), p. 222; *Nye v. US*, 313, US 33 (1940).

52 Monroe H. Freedman, 'The Threat to Judicial Independence by Criticism of Judges – A Proposed Solution to a Real Problem', *Hofstra Law Review*, **25** (1997), p. 729. See also, for a case study, Ronald J. Bacigal, 'The Theory and Practice of Defending Judges Against Unjust Criticism', *Connecticut Law Review*, **23** (1990), p. 99.

53 *Landmark Communications Inc.* v. *Virginia*, 435 US (1978), 829, 838–39, 842

54 *Bridges* v. *California*, 314 US (1941), 252, 292.

55 Freedman, 'The Threat to Judicial Independence', *op. cit.*, p. 731.

56 Identification code 122/33297, date of information 8 February 1997.

57 *Sbornik Dokladov Regionalnikh Organiziatsii o Polozhenii s Pravami Cheloveka v Subyektakh Rossiiskoi Federatsii* (Collection of Reports of Regional Organizations on the Situation with Human Rights in Subjects of the Russian Federation), Vol. 1 (Moscow: Helsinki Group, 1999), p. 108.

58 Identification code 67/33297, date of information 28 March 1997.

59 *Sbornik Dokladov Regionalnikh*, *op. cit.*

60 Identification code 314/35297, date of information 20 June 1997.

61 The Russian Procuracy combines the functions of criminal investigation and prosecution, with wide ombudsman-like review duties to ensure the lawfulness of all governmental actions and decisions, including judicial decisions. This is, of course, a form of institutional schizophrenia.

62 This is the 'old' Criminal Code of 1960, replaced by that which came into force on 1 January 1997. Article 129 of the new Code contains a similar provision, with a punishment of a fine of between 100 to 200 times the minimum wage or one to two months' wages, or obligatory work for 180 to 240 hours, or corrective labour from one to two years, or arrest from three to six months.

63 Identification code 444/87297, date of information 30 July 1997.

64 *Sobraniye Zakonodatelstva Rossiiskoi Federatsii 1977*, no. 1 item 1.

65 An English translation of the Federal Law of the Russian Federation *On the Russian Federation Supreme Court Judicial Department* is in the possession of the author.

66 Valeriya Pantyukhina, 'Sudya Mosgorsuda o sudebnoi sisteme' ('A Judge of the Moscow City Court on the Judicial System'), *Ekspress Khronika*, 14 December 1997.

67 S.A. Pashin, *Review of the Draft Criminal Procedural Code of the Russian Federation*, 2 June 1997; to be found at the Russian Human Rights Online website at: http://www.glasnet.ru/~hronline/ngo/mcprinf/ccomment.htm. The new Criminal Procedural Code has not yet been enacted, although acting President Putin gave it priority in his recent statement to the State Duma. See B. Bowring, 'Politics versus the Rule of Law in the Work of the Russian Constitutional Court', in J. Priban and J. Young (eds), *The Rule of Law in Central Europe: The Reconstruction of Legality, Constitutionalism and Civil Society*

in the Post-Communist Countries (Aldershot: Dartmouth, 1999) and idem, 'Politics, the Rule of Law, and the Judiciary', in N. Robinson (ed.), *Institutions and Change in Russian Politics* (London: Macmillan, 2000).

68   See note 49 above.

14 Criticizing Public Officials in Hungary

Ga'bor Halmai

Introduction

The right to free speech, including criticizing public officials, like judges, is the right that enables the citizen to form and express opinions – to participate in political communication. This right is especially important in those ex-Socialist countries, such as Hungary, which are trying to establish, step-by-step, a state governed by the rule of law and at the same time a democratic public sphere, as well. One of the peculiarities of the Hungarian transition that has been unfolding since 1989 is that there was no revolution in Hungary which would have swept away the Constitution of the ancient regime. At most, we can talk about 'refolution', using the accurate expression of Timothy Garton Ash, the British observer and expert on Central and East European transitional developments. The reforms of this 'refolution' that are of revolutionary importance have cut short the legitimacy of the previous regime by, for example, declaring that Hungary is a republic and guaranteeing a state that operates under the rule of law. Political transformation, though, has stayed within legal bounds throughout.[1] This is also reflected in the fact that judges, after the transition, are the same as in the old system. The final law on lustration,[2] approved by the parliament in 1996, and requiring background checks on a list of influential persons especially as to whether they served as spies of the former secret police, does not include judges, except the president of the Supreme Court and the members of the Constitutional Court. The law specifies that only those public officials who are elected by the parliament are to be subjected to the lustration process. Ordinary court judges are still appointed by the President of the Republic.[3]

Unsurprisingly, the comprehensive constitutional amendments, which came into force on 23 October 1989 and which legitimized the transformation process, dealt with the freedom of expression. The novelty in this text compared to the previous wording is the absence of any reference to socialism and to the interests of the workers, as conditions of exercising these fundamental freedoms.

The Constitutional Court's Interpretation of Freedom of Expression

In the Central and East European countries, the Hungarian Constitutional Court seemed to have been most active in the field of the free speech. This is evidently, but only partly, connected to the above-mentioned fact that, in Hungary, in the absence of a new Constitution, the Constitutional Court has to play a considerably greater role in the interpretation of the Constitution. A similarly important factor is that this Constitutional Court was the first, after the Polish one, to begin its judicial functioning in this region. The Hungarian Court began its work immediately following the political transformation on 1 January 1990. Of course, even this relatively long period of constitutional court activity has been unable to produce a large number of rulings on the freedom of expression, but significant decisions have nevertheless already been made concerning certain components of it.

In these decisions the judges articulated a special interpretation of freedom of expression. In the course of the 1992 constitutional review of legal provisions on the prosecution of incitement to racial hatred – that is, in connection with the freedom of expression – the court stated:

> The substantive fundamental right to the freedom of expression on the one hand, and the state's obligation to guarantee the conditions of a democratic public opinion and to safeguard the maintenance of its functioning on the other hand, can be deduced from Article 61 of the Constitution.[4]

It was perhaps the Hungarian Constitutional Court that went the furthest in stating the privileged nature of the freedom of expression. The explanation of the above-mentioned decision stated, for the first time, that freedom of expression enjoyed a privileged position amongst basic constitutional rights and, in a certain sense, was a 'maternal right' of the so-called 'communication-related basic rights'. In another decision[5] issued a few days later, which ruled that the government supervision of the Hungarian Radio and Hungarian Television was unconstitutional, the maternal nature of the right to the freedom of expression was again confirmed.

The limitations on freedom of expression can be classified on the basis of interests and rights which call for such limitations. There are several interest groups which should have legitimate protection in the various jurisdictions. One of these is state interests, including the protection of constitutional law and order, external and internal state security, state symbols and public officers, such as judges. In protecting the state and its institutions the possibility of imposing limitations on freedom of opinion must be examined very carefully, due to the requirement that the power of criticism should be allowed.

The practice of the Hungarian Constitutional Court has greatly contributed to the fact that the possibility of limiting the freedom of expression is constitutionally restricted by the interest of disputability of public affairs. This has meant that the Constitutional Court has been obliged to remove the earlier taboos, according to which the ruling power could not be challenged and its representatives enjoyed immunity. The judges of the Constitutional Court started this process with a ruling issued in 1991,[6] in which it firmly stated that it was up to the legislators' judgement whether or not the protection offered on the basis of criminal law to the President was extended to the honour and good reputation of the President. However, in case the legislator decides to offer increased protection for the honour and good reputation of the President, the Constitutional Court pointed out that such protection might not limit the essential content of the constitutional right to the freedom of expression. This is so because even if it is a significant interest that the top leaders of the country and through their personality, their functions, should be respected and honoured, there are even more significant arguments in favour of the fact that people fulfilling political functions should be the subject of public criticism at all times.

'Offence Against an Official Person'

In 1994 the Hungarian Constitutional Court reviewed whether Article 232 of the Penal Code on 'offence against an authority or an official person' violates the freedom of expression guaranteed in Article 61 of the Constitution. Article 232 of the Penal Code contained the following provisions:

(1) The person who in the presence of another person states or spreads a rumour about a fact or uses an expression directly referring to such a fact which is capable of offending the honour of an official person or for offending the honour of an authority through an offence against an official person representing an authority, commits a misdemeanour, and shall be punishable with imprisonment of up to two years, public labour or fine.
(2) The person is to be punished according to subsection (1) who uses in connection with the operation of an authority or of an official person an expression or commits an act which is capable of offending the honour of an official person or of offending the honour of an authority through an offence against an official person representing an authority.
(3) The person who commits the crime defined in subsections (1) and (2) in the

presence of a large number of the public, shall be punishable for a crime with imprisonment of up to two to three years.

(4) The perpetrator shall not be punished if the stated fact is proven true. Verification of truth is in order if the public interest or the legitimate interest of anybody justified stating or rumouring the fact or the using of an expression referring to the fact.

(5) Criminal proceedings brought because of an offence against an authority or an official person are in order only on the basis of information laid by an organ or person defined by legal regulation.

According to Article 137 of the Penal Code, Article 34 (1) of Law XVII of 1993, in effect since 13 May, 1993, in the application of the Penal Code:

Official persons are:
a) Members of Parliament;
b) the President of the Republic;
c) the Prime Minister;
d) members of the Government, political state secretaries;
e) constitutional court judges, judges, prosecutors;
f) ombudsmen of citizens' rights and national and ethnic minority rights;
g) members of local government bodies;
h) notaries public;
i) persons serving at the constitutional court, the courts, prosecutors' offices, state administration organs, local government organs, the State Audit Office, the Office of the President of the Republic, the Office of Parliament, whose activity forms part of the proper functioning of the organ;
j) persons exercising public authority, performing state administrative tasks in organs, as well as in bodies authorised by legal provisions for performing public authority, state administrative tasks.

As we can see, according to this regulation, judges enjoyed the same protection as politicians, like members of parliament or of the government. The petitions to the Constitutional Court were motivated by the fact that, in 1993, on the basis of Article 232 Hungarian ordinary courts condemned politicians and social scientists who criticized ministers. But these concrete cases could not be challenged before the Constitutional Court, because it only has the competence to review the constitutionality of abstract norms and not concrete court decisions. That is why the petitioners had to ask for a review of Article 232 and also means that the conflict of that provision with the fundamental right of free speech was not raised on the basis of cases related to criticizing judges.

The Constitutional Court, in its decision,[7] annulled Article 232 as unconstitutional, because it punished defamation and slander committed against persons exercising public authority as against other persons to an equal extent and this obviously conflicted with the principles developed in the permanent practice of the European Court of Human Rights.[8] According to the reasoning of the decision, the annulled provision punished the expression of value judgements in public matters which constituted an unnecessary and disproportionate restriction on the constitutional fundamental right. The Court also stated that, as for communication of facts, Article 232 did not differentiate between true and false statements and, within this, between consciously false statements and those that are false due to carelessness arising from the violation of professional or occupational rules, when only in case of the latter could the freedom of expression be restricted constitutionally by means of the criminal law.

On the other hand, the Court ruled that the protection granted by the criminal law to the honour or reputation of authorities and official persons is not in contradiction with the Constitution. The constitutionally unpunishable sphere of expression protected by the right to freedom of expression is, however, broader in relation to public officials and politicians than as regards other persons. Upon the nullification of Article 232, the protection of the honour of authorities and official persons was taken over by the general criminal law protection against the violation of honour and reputation, as personality rights, provided by Articles 179 and 180 of the Penal Code on defamation, slander and impiety. The position which the Constitutional Court held with respect to these clauses was that, because of the high constitutional value of freedom of expression in public matters, the protection of the honour of public offices, public officials and other actors of public life is less restrictive of the freedom of expression than the protection of the honour of private persons.

The other guideline prepared by the Constitutional Court for the courts applying the law forbids punishment for opinions which express value judgements, regardless of the extent to which such opinion may hurt the honour or reputation of the criticized official. Punishment for statements that wound a person's honour can only be regarded as constitutional if the person uttering such statements was aware that his or her statement was essentially untrue, or the person (for example, a journalist) was not aware that such statements were false because he or she has neglected to exercise the due diligence which is normally expected in connection with his or her profession.

The Constitutional Court also argued that judging crimes against official persons and those against non-official persons differently – that is, maintaining public criminal prosecution – is not to be contested constitutionally. According to the decision, the nullification of Article 232 of the Penal Code did not require a separate criminal procedure regulation since, in the case of defamation or slander, a private prosecution is instituted only if the perpetrator can be prosecuted upon a private criminal action.

After the resolution of the Constitutional Court, the parliament did not regulate the defamation and slander of public officials separately; this also means that these official persons are only protected in terms of their own private actions. In the praxis of the ordinary courts the number of criminal cases initiated by public officials against journalists after the decision of the Constitutional Court are decreasing, while civil law actions are increasing; in many of these actions, the courts are declaring that politicians' personal rights have been violated and are sentencing journals and journalists to pay compensation for both damages and mental anguish.

I would like to mention some specific ordinary decisions in which – in accordance with the resolution of the Constitutional Court – courts ruled that public figures have to tolerate more than ordinary citizens. In one of the cases, the court acquitted a defendant charged with defamation because of his claim, made in a daily newspaper, that the editor-in-chief of a weekly newspaper was not credible; he was a liar. The court argued that the incriminating sentence was not a statement of a fact (it was an expression of a value judgement) and that the victim, as the editor of a newspaper, was a public figure who had to face the possibility of encountering critical opinions.[9] Similarly, the court of second instance acquitted a person charged with libel, who – in a political debate carried out on the pages of the local newspaper – said that the victim was an alcoholic. In its judgment the court pointed out that if someone enters the world of political combat he or she has to prepare to face criticism which is sometimes unfounded.[10] A well known writer's complaint about a scornful critic was also turned down by the court which claimed that the writer was a public figure who might, as such, be subjected to criticism and irony that may violate his inherent rights but not in a manner that has to be dealt with by penal law.

Under Article 179 of the Penal Code the person who rumours a fact which may be to the detriment of another's honour, or uses an expression directly referring to such a fact, also commits a misdemeanour. This means that the press cannot escape liability for disseminating defamatory information by claiming that the information came from somebody else. If the journalist knows that the fact may harm someone's honourable reputation he or she commits the offence irrespective of what he or she thinks about the truth content of the information.[11] However, if the information comes from the authorities – and the journalist draws no further conclusions from it – the journalist may not be held liable for its defamatory nature.

According to another court decision, criticism and value judgement may not be restricted by penal law if it falls within the limits of acceptability. These limits are not dependent on the personal sensitivity of the victim – the 'general judgement' shall be the guideline in such cases.[12] The court acquitted the editors of a daily newspaper who were sued by the writer of an infamous book on account of their claim that the book was anti-Semitic on the grounds that the statement did not exceed the limits of criticism.[13] The court also granted impunity to the genre of satire, holding that such literary devices – like jokes and caricatures – should not be dealt with by penal law.

This system works very well for politicians who are the subjects of public debates. However, the situation of judges is different in that judges and their decisions need more respect than politicians. That is why judges, unlike politicians, are unable to initiate private actions against people who have been sentenced by them. This difference was not taken into consideration by the Hungarian Constitutional Court in treating judges as other public officials.

Some Conclusions

Taking all of the above into consideration, it is obvious that there are different constitutional court practices concerning the freedom of expression in European countries. It is also obvious that, for former socialist countries such as Hungary, it takes time to change from a system of total suppression of political opinion and total protection for the state to a system in which there is freedom of expression, and political opinions are protected, while the interests of the state are only protected in certain justified cases.

In Western Europe Constitutional Courts have already refined the practice so that the freedom to criticize public affairs has resulted in an unlimited freedom of opinion. Of course, there are variations in the practices even of those states which have a longer history as a constitutional state and, in this respect, there is a difference between them and the United States where the freedom of opinion is regarded as an almost absolute right. This is indicated by how the individual countries judge their own constitutional court practices as compared to that in the USA.

Constitutional Courts in Central–Eastern Europe are primarily trying to adopt European standards, despite the fact that, in some cases, rulings used verdicts of the US Supreme Court as an example. Also the reasoning of the Hungarian public officials case bears a ghostly resemblance to the explanation of the US Supreme Court in connection with the verdict in the famous *Sullivan* case[14] in 1964, which provided constitutional protection for lies about public figures made in good faith in order to guarantee the freedom of public debate. Yet the Hungarian Constitutional Court stated that the right to freedom of expression protects opinions regardless of their values or of whether they are true or false. This concept is similar to that of the US judges who stated that expression cannot be limited purely on the basis of an investigation of the contents of the message conveyed.

On the other hand, the constitutional court practices of former socialist states which are becoming parts of the European integration process must move closer to the well known liberal ruling practices of the European Commission and Court on Human Rights, because the citizens of most of those countries have the option of applying to Strasbourg for legal protection against any measures of their respective countries which violate the European Convention on Human Rights. In deciding the public official case the Hungarian Constitutional Court applied the 'test of necessity' developed in *Sunday Times* v. *United Kingdom*,[15] in 1979. That is, the Court examined whether the restriction forming the subject of the complaint was necessary in a democratic society and whether the applied restriction was proportionate for the proper desired goal. According to the permanent practice of the Court, it counts as a disproportionate restriction on the freedom of expression if restriction of the criticism of the government is causeless. The Hungarian judges also referred to several judgments of the European Court of Human Rights,[16] arguing that persons accepting public roles also have to accept that both the press and the wider public follow all their words and acts with attention, and thus have to show greater tolerance of criticism.

Notes

1   On the constitutional and legal aspects of the Hungarian transition, see Gabor Halmai, 'Establishing a State Governed by the Rule of Law', *Review of Central and East European Law*, (4) (1996).
2   Lustration is the process by which public officials, including members of parliament, government officials, judges and officials of the Constitutional Court have to undergo background checks in which their files are scrutinized to see whether they were agents of the secret police under the previous regime.
3   For a more extensive discussion of this point, see Gabor Halmai and Kim Lane Scheppele, 'Living Well is the Best Revenge: The Hungarian Approach to Judging the Past', in A. James McAdams (ed.), *Transitional Justice and the Rule of Law in New Democracies* (Paris: University of Notre Dame, 1997), pp. 155–86.
4   30/1992 (V.26.) AB Resolution. The English language translation has been published in *East European Case Reporter of Constitutional Law*, 1 (1995), 8–26. (Hereafter, the Case Reporter will be abbreviated as *EECRCL*.)
5   37/1992 (VI.10.) AB Resolution. English translation: *EECRCL* 1 (1995), 27–36.
6   48/1991 (IX.26.) AB Resolution. English translation: *EECRCL* 2 (1994), 206–35.
7   36/1994 (VI.24.) AB Resolution. English translation: *EECRCL* 2 (1996), 148–62.
8   See, on this point, *Lingens* v. *Austria*, Eur. Ct.HR, Series A.103; (1986) 8 EHRR, 103; *Castells* v. *Spain*, Eur. Ct.HR, Series A.298; (1992) 14 EHRR, 445; *Oberschlick* v. *Austria*, Eur. Ct.HR, Series A.204; (1991) 19 EHRR, 389; *Thorgeirson* v. *Iceland*, Eur. Ct.HR, Series A.239; (1992) 14 EHRR, 843.
9   Court Decision CD 1995.77.
10   Court Decision CD 1994.356.
11   Court Decision CD 1992.226.
12   Court Decision CD 1995.77.
13   Court Decision CD 1994.300.

14 376 US 254 (1964).
15 Eur. Ct.HR, Series A.30; 2 EHRR, 245.
16 *Lingens* v. *Austria, op. cit.*; *Thorgeirson* v. *Iceland, op. cit.*; *Castells* v. *Spain, op. cit.*; and *Oberschlick* v. *Austria, op. cit.*

PART VI
THE INFLUENCE OF THE
EUROPEAN CONVENTION ON
HUMAN RIGHTS

15 Article 10 of the ECHR and the Criticism of Public Officials

Michael K. Addo

Introduction

Most European countries have joined the Council of Europe and ratified or acceded to the European Convention of Human Rights (the Convention).[1] An assessment of the law and practice of the Convention in the elaboration of standards relating to competing rights in a liberal democratic society will be useful in the appreciation of the issues in the rest of this book. The European Court of Human Rights (the Court)[2] has endorsed the importance of the principle of open debate and the unrestrained exchange of views on matters of public interest[3] in its decisions relating to Article 10 of the European Convention on Human Rights which guarantees freedom of expression.[4] The Court has been particularly unyielding in upholding this freedom and has rejected various attempts to justify restrictions on critical comment about public officials.[5] This chapter assesses the standard of supervision relating to the criticism of public officials generally as a basis to a fuller understanding of the Court's reasoning on the criticism of judges, which is discussed fully in Chapter 16 of this volume.

Criticizing Public Officials

General Principles of Interpretation

In the performance of its supervisory functions the Court is guided by well defined principles of human rights treaty interpretation. Under the recognizable influence of the rules of treaty interpretation as set out in Article 31 of the

Vienna Convention on the Law of Treaties,[6] the Court has approached the interpretation of Article 10 in a European context, bearing in mind the object and purpose of the Convention as seeking to uphold the ideals of democratic society. On this account, the Court has executed its supervisory responsibilities on the basis that the notion of democracy in the European context is not an objective and self-evident one, and is particularly mindful of the fact that the theoretical ideals of liberal democracy may not always coincide with the practice on the ground in the Member States of the Council of Europe. The practice of liberal democracy in Member States, which has invariably been an imperfect version of the ideal, defines the context within which to interpret the Convention and the standard by which to judge the compliance of Contracting States with the Convention. Constitutionally, the Court is not empowered to impose its own standard on Contracting States in instances where there is a consistent practice, and there is no convincing evidence that it functions differently. The importance of interpreting the Convention in the light of the democratic norms defined by the Member States is compatible with the principle of subsidiarity which has been encoded, *inter alia*, in Article 1 of the Convention.[7] According to this principle, the primary responsibility for the protection of the rights guaranteed in the Convention lies with the Contracting States.[8]

In this context, the Court has concluded in relation to freedom of expression that:

> Freedom of expression constitutes one of the essential foundations of such a [democratic] society, one of the basic conditions for its progress and for the development of every man. Subject to paragraph 2 of Article 10, it is applicable not only to 'information' or 'ideas' that are favourably received or regarded as inoffensive or as a matter of indifference, but also to those that offend, shock or disturb the State or any sector of the population. Such are the demands of that pluralism, tolerance and broadmindedness without which there is no 'democratic society'.[9]

Coming from one of the earliest Article 10 cases before the Court, this statement was fair warning to all Contracting States of the Court's bias towards upholding the terms of the first paragraph[10] by insisting on a restrictive interpretation of the second paragraph of Article 10.[11] In the *Sunday Times* v. *United Kingdom No. 1.* case the Court affirmed this approach by indicating, in relation to freedom of expression, that it (the Court) 'is not faced with a choice between two conflicting principles, but with a principle of expression that is subject to a number of exceptions which must be narrowly interpreted'.[12] According to Article 10 and the Court, all restrictions or interferences in freedom of expression must be necessary in a democratic society, where 'necessary' has been interpreted as 'pressing social need',[13] a concept which requires the taking into account of all the theoretical ideals for a democratic society, as well as the peculiar practical circumstances of each case. For any interference to stand a chance of being considered permissible, governments may be called upon to demonstrate the benefits to the wider community as a whole of such an interference in the freedom of expression. This entails a process of balancing of a variety of factors, some of which may contradict each other, in the effort to ensure that the interference is proportionate to the legitimate aim pursued and also that sufficient reasons exist to justify the interference.[14] It is not unfair to suppose that there is, generally, a presumption in the case law of the Court that the interference with the freedom to criticize public officials is not consistent with the ideals of democratic society where the free interaction of ideas and opinions are considered indispensable.[15]

In the litigation involving the criticism of public officials, especially the holders of political office, the Court has held the view that 'the limits of acceptable criticism are accordingly wider as regards a politician as such than as regards a private individual'.[16] The same principle can be said to apply, *mutatis mutandis*, to the limits of criticism of all public officials because the principle is anchored on the suggestion that, in a democratic society, the actions of politicians and other public officials are always of interest to the public,[17] a view endorsed by the Court in its decision in *Thorgeir Thorgeirson* v. *Iceland* involving the criticism of the Icelandic police. The Court concluded that there was 'no warrant in its case-law for distinguishing . . . between political discussion and discussion of other matters of public concern'.[18]

The interpretation of the Convention with regard to issues relating to Article 10 is not always so simple. The interpretative guidelines, created by the Court over the years, and associated primarily with the distinction between issues of public concern or involving the official activities of individuals on the one hand and other, private activities on the other, are themselves a result of complex processes of balancing competing interest. This usually involves the consideration of esoteric and open-ended notions such as proportionality and margin of appreciation,[19] as well as undertaking the near impossible task of defining the role of the press in a democratic society, especially in relation to the publication of matters of fact on the one hand and value judgements on the other. Such a process can often be difficult to explain in terms of a consistent and straightforward policy. By the very nature of the issues, it is impossible to identify a single mechanism of interpretation which can be said to be applicable in every instance. The principle of margin of appreciation, for example, introduces the crucial element of relativity into the uniform interpretation of the Convention which makes the resulting differences in scope and emphasis of the Court's decisions acceptable.[20] Unfortunately, as Judge Macdonald has pointed out, 'being concerned with the appropriate scope of review, the margin [of appreciation] is not susceptible of definition in the abstract, as it is, by its very nature, context-dependent',[21] and:

> It is therefore inevitable that there is a context-dependent spectrum of appropriate intensity, ranging from total deference (amounting to unreviewability at one extreme) through less deferential standards to the most stringent standards of justification on the other.[22]

Hence:

> The margin of appreciation can fail to capture the subtlety of this spectrum if it prevents the articulation of the reasons for deference in any particular case. It would in that case operate as a substitute for a thought-out and principled approach to the ever-present problem of the proper scope of review.[23]

In a majority of cases involving freedom of expression, the breadth of the margin of appreciation accorded to Contracting States in relation to freedom of expression has been at the narrow end of the spectrum, clearly confirming the view that a wide margin of appreciation in matters involving the criticism of public officials may have consequences which are irreconcilable with the ideals of democratic society.

Facts and Value Judgements

In interpreting Article 10 of the Convention, the Court has, where necessary, drawn a distinction between factual statements and value judgements, pointing out that while the existence of facts can be demonstrated, the 'truth' of value judgements is not susceptible to proof.[24] Despite the evident importance of the principle involved in the distinction between facts and value judgements the Court has not so far specifically defined the sort of views that fall under the heading of value judgements. However, on the basis of the Court's case law one may define value judgements as opinions which can be said to derive credibly from a set of facts. In *Lingens* v. *Austria* the Court held that the defamation conviction of Mr Lingens, *inter alia*, for being unable to prove his comment about the Austrian Chancellor's protection of political colleagues who were in the SS during the Second World War constituted an interference with freedom of expression. Mr Lingens had also described the Chancellor's actions as 'basest opportunism', 'immoral' and 'undignified'. The Court concluded that the statements were value judgements which could reasonably be drawn from the facts and circumstances of the case. In the opinion of the Court, the domestic courts erred when they insisted on proof of those statements.[25] Similarly, in *Oberschlick* v. *Austria*, when another journalist was convicted for failing to prove his assertion that a politician's behaviour was guided by National Socialist attitudes, the Court noted that as the journalist had began his publication by reciting factually correct information, 'what followed was an analysis of these statements, on the basis of which the authors of the information concluded that this politician had knowingly expressed ideas that corresponded to those proposed by the Nazis'.[26] The Court concluded by regarding the latter part of the publication as a value judgement, the insistence by the domestic courts on the proof of which was impossible to fulfil and which was itself an infringement of the right to freedom of opinion.[27] The distinction between the effects of factual statements and value judgements in the Court's case law forms a distinct facet of the Court's approach to criticisms as a part of freedom of expression. It enables the Court to tolerate a much wider range of critical opinion – in effect, following its policy of bias towards the first paragraph of Article 10 of the Convention.

The Role of the Press

The Court approaches the meaning of Article 10 by affirming the indispensable role of the press in attaining the Convention's aims in matters relating to Article 10.[28] Although Article 10 does not expressly refer to the press, there is no doubt that corporate bodies, such as the press, are also entitled to enjoy the rights in the provision,[29] especially in the light of Article 34 of the Convention which envisages complaints from non-governmental organizations[30] and also in the reading of Article 10 itself which guarantees freedom of expression to everyone. Any other interpretation of Article 10 in relation to the press will be unsustainable, first because of the inevitable overlaps between individual expression and press expression on occasions when individuals choose to express themselves through the press;[31] and, second, because of the indispensable role that the press is expected to perform in the investigation, analysis and dissemination of information.[32] In the case law of the Court, the issue of whether the press are entitled to rights under Article 10 has never been seriously contested and one doubts if such an objection will ever be tolerated by the Court. In the *Lingens* case, for example, the Court rejected the conclusions of the Austrian courts that the task of the press was to impart information, the interpretation of which had to be left primarily to the reader.[33] The Court has declared in relation to the press that:

> While it must not overstep the bounds set, *inter alia*, in the 'interest of national security', or for 'maintaining the authority of the judiciary', it is nevertheless incumbent on it to impart information and ideas on matters of public interest. Not only does the press have the task of imparting such information and ideas: the public has a right to receive them.[34]

This role of the press affords the public means of discovering and forming an opinion on the ideas and attitudes of public officials.[35] This status of the press as public watchdog[36] has accorded them a higher place in the balancing of competing claims involving the reputation of others, as confirmed by the Court in its declaration in the *Lingens* case, that the limits of acceptable criticism are wider as regards politicians as such than as regards private individuals.[37] While politicians are entitled to the protection of their reputation within the terms of Article 10(2), the requirements of such protection, when weighed against the interest of open discussion of political issues, necessitates a higher and greater degree of tolerance of press criticism of the politicians.[38] Similarly, in the *Oberschlick* case in which the applicant was convicted for reproducing the text of a criminal information which he had laid against a politician, the Court concluded that, although the publication had affected the politician's reputation, it also contributed to a public debate on a political question of general importance; and the press criticism sought to draw public attention to the shocking utterances of a political official. By his utterances, the politician exposed himself to a strong reaction on the part of journalists and the public.[39]

The role of the press as the purveyor of information and public watchdog has not been diminished in relation to the administration of justice and the judiciary. The judiciary, according to the Court in the *Sunday Times* v. *UK No. 1* case, 'serves the interest of the community at large and requires the co-operation of an enlightened public'.[40] The press is expected to impart information and ideas concerning matters which come before the courts, very much as in other areas of public interest. In *Sunday Times* v. *UK No. 1* the public concern caused by the thalidomide disaster contributed to the Court's finding that there was no pressing social need for the restraints imposed on the applicant. This conclusion is particularly important because the respondent government sought to argue that the publications in the *Sunday Times* newspaper, while the case was *sub judice*, undermined the authority and impartiality of the judiciary. The Court held that:

> It is not sufficient that the interference involved belongs to that class of the exceptions listed in Article 10(2) which has been invoked; neither is it sufficient that the interference was imposed because its subject-matter fell within a particular category or was caught by a legal rule formulated in general or absolute terms: the Court has to be satisfied that the interference was necessary having regard to the facts and circumstances prevailing in the specific case before it.[41]

Considerable weight was attached, *inter alia*, to the fact that numerous victims of the thalidomide disaster were unaware of the legal difficulties involved in the case, and also had a vital interest in knowing all the underlying facts and the various possible solutions.

The Role of Non-Governmental Organizations (NGOs)

Non-governmental organizations (NGOs) are a central feature in the Council of Europe. This should come as no surprise especially after their long-established and continuing reputation in the field of human rights at the international level.[42] The hundreds of human rights NGOs which are registered with the Council of Europe are today recognized as a special category within which there are further specialisms, such as NGOs devoted to the advancement of specific rights – freedom of expression – (Article 19), privacy (Privacy International) the right to life, the prohibition of torture (Amnesty International) fair trial (Fair Trials Abroad, Interrights, International Commission of Jurists) and so on.

Unlike with the press, the relationship between the Council of Europe and NGOs is defined by aims of cooperation with a view to achieving an effective protection of the rights in the various European human rights initiatives. Participation in all levels of Council of Europe activities is open to NGOs, and joint actions to organize and execute programmes is not uncommon. In addition, NGOs act as watchdogs against human rights violations in countries; they also publicize the work of the Council of Europe and its institutions – especially judgments of the Court of Human Rights – throughout their membership and to the wider community. Selected high-profile NGOs, such as the International Commission of Jurists and Amnesty International, have a consultative relationship with the Committee of Ministers in the development of human rights standards.

Of considerable interest, however, is the role of NGOs in the processes of human rights litigation under the European Convention on Human Rights. NGOs, including those whose focus is the advancement of the rights under Article 10, can petition the Court of Human Rights if they allege violations against their organization.[43] This provision, however, is not one that has engaged the attention of NGOs. Instead, they have focused considerable attention on assisting the work of the Court in various ways. Most NGOs including those with specialist focus (for example, freedom of expression) provide a free legal advisory service to litigants whose complaints affect their area of speciality. This often involves an explanation of the law and possible arguments to advance before the Court. They have also been known to provide legal representation before the Court for litigants who request it. The applicants in *Lingens* v. *Austria*,[44] *Goodwin* v. *United Kingdom*[45] for example, received the assistance of London-based Article 19 and Interights. This is a particularly useful service because it provides the essential counterbalance for ensuring a level playing field in the litigation before the Court.

NGOs may also participate in the development of the scope of human rights before the ECHR as third parties. The legal basis of this responsibility is now encoded in Article 36(2) of the Convention which provides that:

The President of the Court may, in the interest of the proper administration of justice, invite any High Contracting Party which is not a party to the proceedings or any person concerned who is not the applicant to submit written comments or take part in hearings.

This provision is culled more or less verbatim from Rule 37(2) of the Rules of the former Court which provided the basis for NGO involvement in the proceedings of the Court. NGO involvement through this provision has so far been in the form of invitation to submit *amicus curiae* briefs. The practice before the Court makes it clear that in submitting such briefs, the NGOs' responsibility is to the Court and not to either litigant. The Court expects such briefs to be as objective an analysis as possible and often to answer specifically defined questions.

In the *Prager and Oberschlick* v. *Austria*[46] case, the Court requested Interights and Article 19 to provide a comparative survey of the laws and jurisprudence in member countries of the Council of Europe relating to the criticism of judges. The Court is not bound by such briefs and so, although the consensus of opinion in the NGO brief in that case was to tolerate more criticism of judges, the Court's decision was more towards the alternative bias towards the independence of the judiciary. The value of NGO briefs do not cease to be significant at the end of the cases for which they are requested: the Court may often fall back on the ideas and recommendations in subsequent cases. In this regard it can be asserted with some degree of confidence that the Court may have had to rethink its position in the matter of criticizing judges in the case of *De Haes and Gijsels* v. *Belgium*.[47] Although there was no NGO intervention in this case, the Court seemed to depart from its adherence to the importance of protecting judges from criticism and relaxed its approach in this case, tending to endorse a bias in favour of freedom of expression in line with its general case law under Article 10. One cannot help but wonder about the extent of the NGO *amicus curiae* provided by Article 19 and Interights in the *Prager and Oberschlick* case.

Conclusion

Most European countries have laws on the statute books designed to punish the criticism of public officials. Most of these laws have slowly ceased to be used as the democracy in each of those countries continues to mature. This process of maturity has no doubt been hurried by the developments within the Council of Europe and especially in the interpretation of the European Convention on Human Rights.

In its effort to respond to the dynamic nature of the Convention the Court of

Human Rights has, in the interpretation of the Convention, focused firmly on the objects and purpose of the Convention to enhance democracy through the protection of individual rights and liberties. It is therefore not particularly surprising that the Court attaches such high regard to the freedom of expression which, it has confirmed, constitutes one of the essential foundations of democratic society. In relation to public officials in this context, the Court is mindful of the other demands in democratic society for them to be accountable and transparent. As representatives of the people their actions should necessarily be open to comment and criticism. Therefore, the Court has, through its case law, built a bias in this regard in favour of para. 1 of Article 10, thus making it difficult, if not impossible, for public officials to seek protection under para. 2 of that provision.

The process of the bias in favour of Article 10(1) of the Convention takes a variety of forms in practice. It has, for example, meant a restricted margin of appreciation for governments in matters relating to the criticism of public officials. The bias has also been represented in the form of the distinction between facts and value judgements only the former of which is, according to the Court, subject to proof. The weight expected to be given to freedom of expression in the context of criticizing public officials according to the case law of the Court is clear from the potentially broad nature of value judgements.

Another factor to emerge from the Court's attitude to the criticism of public officials is the recognition it has given to the press in the development of the rights in Article 10. Seen as the key avenue through which the public may be informed and as watchdogs against potential abuse, the press have been acknowledged to be indispensable in any democratic society. In this position, their actions have received greater protection than the public officials whom they criticize. The Court's case law has been remarkably consistent in this regard.

However, any impression that the Court is unconcerned about the position of the law in Member States is wrong. On the contrary, the Court draws considerable reliance on the fact that the laws which were originally designed to punish the criticism of public officials are not obsolete, although the majority have not been used for years. The Court recognizes an emerging European standard upon which it bases its thinking. It has often taken deliberate steps to solicit research and reports on such practical matters. It regularly allows such information to be infused into its deliberations through *amicus curiae* briefs and other forms of third-party interventions. Each decision of the Court is supported by a reasoned judgment which, in practice, includes evidence of the Court's preparedness to explore all possible alternatives.

Notes

1 Convention for the Protection of Human Rights and Fundamental Freedoms (Rome 1950), as amended by Protocol No. 11.

2 Under the old Convention the supervision of contracting states' compliance with the Convention was undertaken by the European Commission of Human Rights (Articles 19–37 of the old Convention), the European Court of Human Rights (Articles 38–56 of the old Convention) and the Committee of Ministers (Articles 31, 32 and 54 of the old Convention), although in practice the Court's responsibilities were always the most important (see Article 45 of the old Convention). Under the amended Convention (text reprinted in *Human Rights Law Journal*, **15** (1994), p. 86) the Court and the Commission merged into a single Court on 1 November 1998 with the coming into force of the Protocol. On Protocol No. 11 see A. Drzemczweski and J. Meyer-Ladewig, 'Principal Characteristics of the New ECHR Control Mechanism as Established by Protocol 11, Signed on 11 May 1994', *Human Rights Law Journal*, **15** (1994), p. 81; H.G. Schermers, 'The Eleventh Protocol to the European Convention on Human Rights', *European Law Review*, **19** (1994), p. 367; A.R. Mowbray, 'A New European Court of Human Rights', *Public Law*, (1994), p. 540.

3 *Handyside* v. *United* Kingdom, Eur. Ct. HR, Series A.24 (1976); 1 EHRR, p. 737; *Sunday Times* v. *United Kingdom No. 1*, Eur. Ct. HR, Series A.30 (1979); 2 EHRR, p. 245; *Lingens* v. *Austria*, Eur. Ct. HR, Series A.103 (1986); 8 (1986) EHRR, p. 103; *Oberschlick* v. *Austria*, Eur. Ct. HR, Series A.204 (1991); 19 EHRR, p. 389.

4 Article 10 of the ECHR provides that:

> 1. Everyone has the right to freedom of expression. This right shall include freedom to hold opinions and to receive and impart information and ideas without interference by public authority and regardless of frontiers. This Article shall not prevent States from requiring the licensing of broadcasting, television or cinema enterprises.
> 2. The exercise of these freedoms, since it carries with it duties and responsibilities, may be subject to such formalities, conditions, restrictions or penalties as are prescribed by law and are necessary in a democratic society, in the interest of national security, territorial integrity or public safety, for the prevention of disorder or crime, for the protection of health or morals, for the protection of the reputation or rights of others, for preventing the disclosure of information received in confidence, or for maintaining the authority and impartiality of the judiciary.

5 See *Lingens* v. *Austria, op. cit.*; *Schwabe* v. *Austria*, Eur. Ct. HR, Series A.242-B (1993), (politicians); *Thorgeir Thorgeirson* v. *Iceland*, Eur. Ct. HR, Series A.239 (1992); 18 (1994) EHRR, p. 843 (police); *Castells* v. *Spain*, Eur. Ct. HR, Series A.236 (1992); 14 (1992) EHRR, p. 445 (government policy).

6 Article 31 of the Vienna Convention on the Law of Treaties provides, *inter alia*, that: 'A treaty shall be interpreted in good faith in accordance with the ordinary meaning to be given to the terms of the treaty in their context and in the light of its object and purpose.' For text, see, *International Legal Materials*, **8** (1969), p. 679 (1969) and I. Brownlie, *Basic Documents in International Law* (Oxford: Clarendon Press, 1995) p. 388.

7 Article 1 of the Convention provides that 'The High Contracting Parties shall secure to everyone within their jurisdiction the rights and freedoms defined in Section I of the Convention'. On the subject of subsidiarity, see Herbert Petzold, 'The Convention and the Principle of Subsidiarity', in R.St.J. Macdonald, F. Matscher and H. Petzold (eds), *The European System for the Protection of Human Rights* (London: Martinus Nijhoff, 1993), p. 41.

8   For an analysis of the principle of subsidiarity under the Convention, see ibid.
9   *Handyside* v. *United Kingdom,* Eur. Ct. HR, Series A.24 (1976); 1 EHRR, p. 737, para. 49; see also *Sunday Times* v. *United Kingdom No. 2,* (1992) Eur. Ct. HR, Series A.217; 14 (1992) EHRR, p. 229, para. 50.
10 Ibid.
11 See D. Evrigenis, 'Recent Case-law of the European Court of Human Rights on Articles 8 and 10 of the European Convention on Human Rights', *Human Rights Law Journal,* 3 (1982), pp. 121, 137.
12 Para. 65; see also *Thorgeir Thorgeirson* v. *Iceland, op. cit.,* para. 63; see also *Sunday Times* v. *United Kingdom No. 2, op. cit.,* para. 50.
13 *Handyside, op. cit.,* para. 159 and also *Sunday Times* v. *United Kingdom No. 2, op. cit.,* para. 50.
14 *Lingens* v. *Austria, op. cit.,* para. 40; *Bathold* v. *Germany,* Eur. Ct. HR, Series A.90 (1985); 7 (1985) EHRR, p. 383, para. 55 and *Sunday Times* v. *United Kingdom No. 2, op. cit.,* para. 50.
15 In tolerating harsh criticism of politicians for example, the Court has reasoned that because a politician 'inevitably and knowingly lays himself open to close scrutiny of his every word and deed by both journalists and the public at large, . . . he must consequently display a greater degree of tolerance': see *Lingens* v. *Austria, op. cit.,* para. 42; see also *Oberschlick* v. *Austria, op. cit.,* para. 59 and in relation to other public servants generally and to the police in particular, see *Thorgeir Thorgeirson* v. *Iceland, op. cit.,* para. 64. The Court has been similarly charitable with criticisms of government policy, the permissible limits of which, according to the Court are wider than they are in relation to politicians:

> . . . the actions and omissions of the government must be subject to the close scrutiny not only of the legislative and judicial authorities but also of the press and public opinion. Furthermore, the dominant position which the government occupies makes it necessary for it to display restraint in resorting to criminal proceedings, particularly where other means are available for replying to the unjustified attacks and criticisms of its adversaries or the media (See *Castells* v. *Spain, op. cit.,* para. 46.)

16 *Lingens* v. *Austria, op. cit,* para. 42; *Oberschlick* v. *Austria, op. cit.,* para. 59.
17 A similar view has been upheld by the Supreme Court of the United States in the case *of New York Times* v. *Sullivan,* 376 US 254 (1964). The Court in that case refused to permit the recovery of damages by a public official for alleged libellous statements made against him. The court endorsed the view that 'public men, are, as it were, public property and discussion cannot be denied and right, as well as the duty, of criticism must not be stifled', (ibid., p. 268). Justice Black was more unequivocal in his concurring opinion when he interpreted the First Amendment to the US Constitution as leaving 'people and the press free to criticize officials and discuss public affairs with impunity'. He argued further that, in a country like the United States which elects its officials, it follows that:

> These officials are responsible to the people for the way they perform their duties. . . . freedom to discuss public affairs and public officials is unquestionably, . . . the kind of free speech the First Amendment was primarily designed to keep within the area of free discussion. To punish the exercise of this right to discuss public affairs or to penalize it through libel judgements is to abridge or shut off discussion of the very kind most needed. (Ibid., at p. 295)

For a British endorsement of this line of reasoning see the House of Lords judgment in *Derbyshire County Council* v. *Times Newspapers Limited and Others* [1993] 1 All ER 1011.

18   *Thorgeir Thorgeirson* v. *Iceland, op. cit.* para. 64. In principle, it is arguable on this general view of the Court that that actions of private individuals of public concern or interest can be subject to public discussion or criticism.

19   The Convention leaves a margin of appreciation to contracting states to determine the nature, scope and permissibility of any interferences with individual rights and freedoms. On this subject, see *Handyside* v. *United Kingdom, op. cit.*, para. 48 and *Sunday Times* v. *United Kingdom No. 2, op. cit.*, para. 50. Used in the interpretation of the provisions of the Convention, the doctrine of margin of appreciation has had a pervasive influence on all the substantive provisions of the Convention including Article 10. The doctrine has proved particularly useful to the Court in balancing the conflicting demands imposed upon it as an international tribunal with intrusive powers of supervision which seeks to operate an independent supervisory regime based on the application of objective and autonomous standards. Such an autonomous regime can so easily be perceived as posing potential threats to the sovereignty of the contracting states unless the international tribunal has a mechanism by which this dimension of sovereignty is taken into account in its decision-making processes. The principle of margin of appreciation is also useful for redressing the imbalance created by the need to supervise compliance with the Convention on the one hand and the Court's remoteness from the factual events leading to the complaint on the other.

20   R. St J. Macdonald, 'The Margin of Appreciation', in Macdonald *et al.*, *The European System for the Protection of Human Rights, op. cit.*, p. 83

21   Ibid., p. 85.

22   Ibid., p. 84.

23   Ibid., p. 84.

24   *Lingens* v. *Austria, op. cit.*, para. 46; *Oberschlick* v. *Austria, op. cit.*, para. 63 and *Thorgeir Thorgeirson* v. *Iceland, op. cit.*, para. 65.

25   *Lingens* v. *Austria, op. cit.*, para. 46.

26   *Oberschlick* v. *Austria, op. cit.*, para. 63.

27   Ibid., para. 63.

28   *Sunday Times* v. *United Kingdom No. 2, op. cit.*, para. 50.

29   *Sunday Times* v. *United Kingdom No. 1, op. cit.* and *Observer and Guardian* v. *United Kingdom*, Eur. Ct. HR, Series A.216 (1992); 14 (1992) EHRR, p. 153.

30   Article 34 of the Convention provides, *inter alia*, that:

> The Court may receive applications from any person, non-governmental organisation, or group of individuals claiming to be the victim of a violation by one of the High Contracting Parties of the rights set forth in the Convention.

31   See, for example, *Bathold* v. *Germany, op. cit.*; *Weber* v. *Switzerland, op. cit.*; and *Thorgeir Thorgeirson* v. *Iceland, op. cit.*

32   *Lingens* v. *Austria, op. cit.*, para. 41; *Sunday Times* v. *United Kingdom No. 2, op. cit.*, para. 50.

33   *Lingens* v. *Austria, op. cit.*, paras 29 and 41.

34   *Observer and Guardian* v. *United Kingdom, op. cit.*, para. 59(b); *Thorgeir Thorgeirson* v. *Iceland, op. cit.*, para. 63; *Sunday Times* v. *United Kingdom No. 1, op. cit.*, para. 65; and *Lingens* v. *Austria, op. cit.*, para. 41.

35   *Sunday Times* v. *United Kingdom No. 1, op. cit.*, para. 42; *Oberschlick* v. *Austria, op. cit.*, para. 58.

36   *Sunday Times* v. *United Kingdom, op. cit.*, para. 41.

37   *Lingens* v. *Austria, op. cit.*, para. 42.

38   Ibid., para. 42; *Oberschlick* v. *Austria, op. cit*, para. 59.

39 *Oberschlick* v. *Austria, op. cit.*, para. 61.
40 Para. 65.
41 Para. 65.
42 For a review of the origins and work of NGOs in human rights, see Eya Nchama, 'The Role of Non-Governmental Organisations in the Promotion and Protection of Human Rights', *UN Bulletin of Human Rights*, **90** (1), p. 54. See also Davis Weissbroadt, 'The Contribution of NGOs to the Protection of Human Rights in International Law', in Theodor Meron, *Human Rights in International Law*, (Oxford: Clarendon 1985), p. 403. See also Felix Ermacora, 'Non-governmental Organisations as Promoters of Human Rights', in F. Matscher and H. Petzold, *Protecting Human Rights: The European Dimension* (Köhn: Carl Heymanns, 1988), p. 171.
43 See Article 34 of the ECHR (as amended by Protocol No. 11).
44 Eur. Ct. HR, Series A.103; (1986) 8 EHRR, 103.
45 22 (1996) EHRR, 123.
46 Eur. Ct. HR, Series A.313; 21 (1996) EHRR, 1.
47 25 (1997) EHRR, 1.

16 Article 10 of the ECHR and the Criticism of Judges

Michael K. Addo

Introduction

One of the primary aims of the supervisory system under the European Convention on Human Rights (the Convention)[1] is to provide an independent and impartial system of review without assuming the role of a Court of Appeal. Despite the limitations of this supervisory role – including having to respect principles of subsidiary and any common European standards – the Convention institutions have proved to be immensely influential in the policy-making of member states. In this regard, the views of the Convention institutions on the issues relating to the criticism of judges in a democratic society are crucial. Furthermore, the opinions of the ECHR institutions in this matter are preferable because they carry a more credible standard of objectivity than those of judges within the domestic context. The natural justice concerns in the domestic context where colleagues of a criticized judge sit in judgement over disputes arising from the criticism of another judge do not apply to the institutions of the ECHR.

Criticizing Judges

The judicial branch of government of which judges form a part undertakes services on behalf of the public, and the relationship between the work of the judicial branch and the freedom of expression had evidently been anticipated by the drafters of the Convention when they endorsed the imposition of permissible limitations on the freedom of expression in order to uphold the authority and impartiality of the judiciary.[2] On a number of occasions the Court has addressed some of the wider issues of freedom of expression in relation to the judiciary's work and, in the process, has confirmed that the general principles of interpreting Article 10 'are equally applicable to the field of the administration of justice, which serves the interest of the community at large and requires the co-operation of an enlightened public'.[3] In the *Sunday Times No. 1* case,[4] for instance, in which the issue before the Court was whether an injunction prohibiting the publication of an article dealing with a case which was then pending before the UK courts was necessary, the Court held that being a forum for the settlement of disputes did not mean 'that there can be no prior discussion of disputes elsewhere, be it in specialised journals, in the general press or amongst the public at large'.[5] In general, the Court will not tolerate the prohibition of comments on the work of the judiciary, and there could conceivably be a sense in which the interweaving of harsh comments about the general aspects of the work of courts, as well as comments about individual judges, will be acceptable as part of a general criticism of the work of the judicial branch of government. When the Court held in *Weber* v. *Switzerland*[6] that the conviction of the applicant for disclosing at a press conference that he had lodged a criminal complaint against an investigating judge alleging misuse of official authority was not necessary in a democratic society 'for maintaining the authority and impartiality of the judiciary', it had essentially endorsed all the critical comments about the Swiss cantonal system of justice which had been made by the applicant in that case.

The general and indirect criticism of the work of judges as part of a wider criticism of the judicial system is clearly permissible under the terms of Article 10 of the Convention.[7] This must, however, be distinguished from the instances of specific criticism of individual judges and their work in which the Court normally insists on a higher level of proof and endorses a much wider margin of appreciation for the respondent state. In the *Barfod* v. *Denmark*[8] case the High Court of Greenland, composed of a professional judge and two lay members, rejected an application to challenge the decision of the Greenland local government's introduction of a new tax structure for Danish nationals working on American bases in Greenland. The applicant published an article in a local magazine in which he argued that, as employees of the Greenland local government, the two lay judges were disqualified from sitting on this particular case by Article 62 of the Danish Constitution. He also questioned the lay judges' ability to decide impartially in a case brought against their employer. In the words of the applicant:

> Most of the Local Government's members could . . . afford the time to watch that the two Greenland lay judges – who are by the way employed directly by the Local Government, as director of a museum and as consultant in urban housing affairs – did their duty, and this they did. The vote was two to one in favour of the Local Government and with such a bench of judges it does not require much imagination to guess who voted how.[9]

Bias and Public Interest

The applicant in the *Barfod* case was charged and found guilty of the defamation of the character of the two lay judges by suggesting that they were biased – an accusation which was likely to lower them in public esteem. The Court reasoned, *inter alia*, that he was unable to prove justification of his assertions of bias and his plea of freedom of expression by itself was held not to provide a defence. There was little doubt that the applicant's comments were in an area of public interest. According to the Commission:

> ... even if the article in question could be interpreted as an attack on the integrity or reputation of the two lay judges, the general interest in allowing a public debate about the functioning of the judiciary weighs more heavily than the interest of the two judges in being protected against criticism of the kind expressed in the applicant's article.[10]

The High Court of Eastern Denmark agreed with this view in its judgment,[11] and so also did the respondent government before the Commission,[12] that the two judges ought 'to have considered themselves as disqualified and thus refrained from participating in the case' and that the applicant was correct in drawing attention to this fact.

The Court of Human Rights reiterated the relevant general principles of interpreting Article 10 of the Convention,[13] including its concern about the potential chilling effect of punishing expression. However, the Court did not endorse the opinion of the Commission that the applicant's statement concerned matters of public interest involving the functioning of the public administration, including the judiciary, for which the test for the necessity of interference had to be particularly strict.[14] The Court disagreed with this view of the Commission on the reasoning that the applicant's conviction for alleging that the lay judges did their duty to rule in favour of their employer was neither an interference with, nor a limitation on, the applicant's freedom of expression because 'it was quite possible to question the composition of the High Court without at the same time attacking the two lay judges personally',[15] and in addition the applicant had failed to justify his assertions. The need for justification was central in another case involving allegation of bias against a group of judges – *De Haes and Gijsels* v. *Belgium*.[16] After reiterating its view that courts, as guarantors of justice, must enjoy public confidence and must accordingly be protected from destructive attacks which are unfounded,[17] the Court of Human Rights was satisfied in this particular case that:

> The articles [which accused the judges of bias] contain a mass of detailed information about the circumstances in which the decisions of the custody of Mr X's children were taken. The information was based on thorough research into the

allegations against Mr X and on the opinions of several experts who were said to have advised the applicants to disclose them in the interest of the children. . . .

That being so, the applicants cannot be accused of having failed in their professional obligations by publishing what they had learned about the case.[18]

The conviction of the applicants in that case for publishing articles in which they accused four judges of bias in their handling of a child custody case was held not to be necessary in a democratic society.

In what may, for the time being, be seen as the general rule in this aspect of the Court's general practice to insist upon proof of the allegations of bias, the Court has often tended to exercise its discretion in the direction of a much broader than usual margin of appreciation for the respondent government. In the circumstances, this may appear to be departure from the norm established under the general case law relating to Article 10.[19] The proposition, for example, in the *Barfod* case that the applicant should have contented himself with questioning the composition of the court and not to venture an opinion about the subject was similarly surprising. The venturing of personal opinion on matters of fact – that is, value judgement – has been vigorously defended by the Court in previous cases.[20] In the *Barfod* case the Court failed to articulate any reasoned explanation for the limited scope of value judgements in relation to comments about judges. One may, however, speculate that the European Court of Human Rights saw judges as a potentially vulnerable group of public officials who are unable to answer back to criticism and, for that reason, deserve protection. Such protection cannot, however, be applied to all criticism from whatever quarter and in whatever form. A blanket ban, which will have a chilling effect on freedom of expression, is unacceptable in a democratic society. There is no evidence in the case law of the Court that a blanket ban was ever contemplated. This much is confirmed by its decision in the *De Haes and Gijsels* case where, on the facts of that case, the Court was willing to tolerate harsh criticism of the Belgian judges.

Although the *Barfod* case was the first of its kind to be decided by the Court, it is not in conflict with the other decisions of the Court on the subject of criticizing judges, especially the *De Haes and Gijsels* case. Judicial impartiality is essential to any society governed by law, as evidenced by the great lengths to which such societies will go to ensure that judges do not have any interest in the cases on which they sit. Allegations of bias can therefore touch the raw nerves of the democratic process and must be proved unequivocally; anything less will undermine public confidence in the judicial and democratic processes. This approach must be correct in a context where the integrity of both the law and the judges needs to be maintained not for any personal satisfaction on the part of the judges themselves, but for the benefit of the community as a whole. The cursory treatment of allegations of bias against judges can have the effect of interfering with the due course of justice, a consequence which cannot be argued as necessary or beneficial in a democratic society.

The *Prager and Oberschlick* v. *Austria*[21] case presented the Court with another opportunity to consolidate its reasoning on the relationship between freedom of expression and the criticism of judges. In the main, the Court justified its insistence on a stricter treatment of such criticism by distinguishing between the necessity in a democratic society of criticizing the judiciary on the one hand and other public or governmental bodies on the other. The Court declared that:

> Regard must . . . be had to the special role of the judiciary in society. As the guarantor of justice, a fundamental value in a law-governed State, it must enjoy public confidence if it is to be successful in carrying out its duties. It may therefore prove necessary to protect such confidence against destructive attacks that are essentially unfounded, especially in view of the fact that judges who have been criticised are subject to a duty of discretion that precludes them from replying.[22]

The Higher Standard of Proof

Consistent with its previous case law in this field, the Court in the *Prager and Oberschlick* case endorsed the domestic courts' insistence on full proof of the allegations and criticisms against the Austrian judges. The case involved a 13-page article entitled 'Danger! Harsh Judges!', in which Mr Prager, the first applicant, accused the judges of the Austrian criminal courts – especially those of the Vienna regional criminal court – of 'exercising absolute power "in the domain of their court", exploiting the smallest weaknesses or peculiarities in the accused', treating the accused at the outset as if they had already been convicted and of turning the courtroom into a battlefield. He alleged further that a convicted person who caused the slightest offence to the self-esteem of the judge risked, through the effect of the latter's so-called unfettered discretion to assess the evidence, an extra year of imprisonment. The article hinted at judges who acquitted only as a last resort and handed down heavier sentences than most of their colleagues.[23] In addition to these general comments, the article also gave descriptive profiles of a number of individual judges including Judge J who was described, *inter alia*, as 'rabid' and an 'arrogant bully'.[24] The article was written on the basis of evidence collected by the applicant, during a number of trials, on statements of lawyers and legal correspondents as well as from surveys carried out by university researchers.[25] The applicant was found guilty of defaming Judge J and ordered to pay heavy fines. The domestic court concluded that the applicant had failed to substantiate his allegations, *inter alia*, because the statement:

... according to which Judge J. treated every accused at the outset as if he had already been convicted, was not proved merely by the fact that the judge in question had, in a given case, asked defence counsel to be brief, as he had already made up his mind. Similarly, the three decisions of Judge J. reported by Mr Prager in support of statement no. 3 [that 'Nothing was comparable to . . . Judge J's arrogant bullying'] were not sufficient to bear out the allegation that the judge had adopted bullying tactics. . . . Lastly, the accusations made in passage no. 5 [giving legal advice without authorization] had been definitely refuted by a disciplinary decision of the Vienna Court of Appeal of 6 December 1982.[26]

The applicant's request for the production of files which, he alleged, contained information likely to support his claims was not accepted because the information contained in those files was considered unlikely to alter the court's conclusions because 'the first file contained no information on the personality of Judge J. and the second, relating to the judge's candidature for office of public prosecutor, had to remain confidential'.[27] Finally, the applicant's case was unsuccessful before the domestic courts because he was held not to have exercised appropriate level of journalistic care in the preparation of his article.[28] He had failed, in this direction, to give Judge J an opportunity to comment on the article before its publication, and also his research for the article had been conducted in a superficial manner. The applicant's admission that he had not attended any trials presided over by Judge J and that he reproduced the contents of old newspaper articles without checking their accuracy[29] was considered fatal to his plea of good faith.

It is rather ironic that the Austrian courts arrived at the conclusion that the applicant had failed to substantiate his assertions after dismissing his request to adduce evidence of proof as immaterial. According to the Vienna Court of Appeal, for instance, the criticisms had been so comprehensive and general that it would have been impossible to specify evidence capable of establishing its accuracy.[30] This irony is compounded by the fact that those courts' conclusion that the applicant failed to exercise journalistic care was based on his failure to give Judge J an opportunity to comment on the allegations. Quite clearly, on the surface at least, the courts themselves had denied the applicant what amounts essentially to the same right to a hearing which he is accused of denying to Judge J. This refusal to afford the applicant an opportunity to present his evidence, on account of the fact, in the opinion of the Austrian courts, that the evidence is unprovable, will come as a surprise and perhaps as unacceptable to a common lawyer. It is a breach of the principles of natural justice[31] and most likely a breach of the right to a fair hearing which is enshrined in Article 6(1) of the Convention. Although Article 6(1) does not prescribe any specific rules about the adducing of evidence as part of the right to a fair hearing,[32] it is compelling that an outright refusal to hear evidence which is central, or possibly decisive, in the prosecution of a criminal charge is likely to be in breach of

Article 6(1). This expression of apprehension about the compliance with Article 6(1) is made here, not unmindful of the general principle in the case law of the European Court of Human Rights, to the effect that whether or not a decision breaches Article 6(1) in this regard must be judged on the basis of the case as a whole.[33]

A Chamber of the European Court of Human Rights reiterated the pre-eminent role of the press in the dissemination of ideas and opinions in matters of public importance, including the functioning of the system of justice, but concluded by a five votes to four majority decision that the interference in this case was not unjustified. The Court held the view that, because of the seriousness of the allegations, it was not surprising that the higher level of proof was required by the Austrian court. The Court was particularly concerned by the implications which were inherent in the applicant's allegations that the judges had 'broken the law or, at the very least, [had] breached their professional obligations. He [the applicant] [had] thus not only damaged their reputation, but also undermined public confidence in the integrity of the judiciary as a whole.'[34] The European Court of Human Rights was prepared to endorse the higher standard of proof required in this particular case because of the breadth of the applicant's allegations. The Court held that:

> The reason for Mr Prager's failure to establish that his allegations were true or that his value judgements were fair comment lies not so much in the way in which the court applied the law as in their general character; indeed it is that aspect that seems to have been the origin of the penalties imposed. As the Commission pointed out, the evidence shows that the relevant decisions were not directed against the applicant's use as such of his freedom of expression in relation to the system of justice or even the fact that he had criticised certain judges whom he had identified by name, but rather the excessive breadth of the accusations, which in the absence of sufficient factual basis, appeared unnecessarily prejudicial.[35]

However, in another case, *De Haes and Gijsels* v. *Belgium*[36] in which the Court was confronted with a different set of facts and circumstances, its approach to this issue was completely the reverse. In this case, the Court concluded that the refusal to afford the applicants the opportunity to prove their case constituted a breach of Article 6(1) of the Convention.[37] Nevertheless, there is some merit in the Court's wider concern about the potential damage to the due course of the judicial process. This is, again, the appropriate context in which to perceive the Court's support for the Austrian government's submissions that the applicant in the *Prager and Oberschlick* case must not be given the benefit of a plea of journalistic good faith on account of his failure to exercise sufficient professional care in preparing and writing the article.[38] The Court was still prepared to acknowledge that subject to para. 2 of Article 10, freedom of expression is applicable to information and ideas which could be offensive and shocking; and also that journalistic freedom under Article 10 could include recourse to a degree of exaggeration or even provocation, but in the circumstances of this case the interference was 'necessary in a democratic society'.[39]

The Court of Human Rights was, no doubt, confronted with a rather difficult state of affairs, especially in seeking to adopt a contextually different approach from its established case law on the subject of journalistic freedom of expression. In its previous case law, neither the poor quality of journalistic research nor the breadth of criticism of public officials in matters which were evidently of public interest were considered as sufficient reasons for upholding government interference. However, the Court had a completely different scenario before it in which the endorsement of a wide breadth of journalistic freedom could undermine the object and purpose of the Convention as a whole. The Court's primary failing in the *Prager and Oberschlick* case, however, lay in its refusal to articulate its reasons in full for the adoption of a stricter approach to the criticism of judges.

In that case the Court also endorsed the Austrian courts' distinction between factual matters and value judgements, pointing out that such an exercise was within the margin of appreciation of the respondent state, in terms of deciding for itself how best to protect the public confidence in the judiciary. The domestic courts' claim for such a wide margin of appreciation would normally have attracted the critical attention of the European Court of Human Rights. Instead, in this case, the Court endorsed it expressly,[40] superficially at least – another clear departure from its normal practice.

The Court uses the doctrine of margin of appreciation as the 'reason' for its conclusions. This is unfortunate because, as has been forcefully argued by another author,[41] 'if the Court gives as its reason for not intervening simply that the decision is within the margin of appreciation of the national authorities, it is really providing no reason at all but merely expressing its conclusion not to intervene, leaving observers to guess the real reasons which it failed to articulate'.[42] The Convention system has surely passed the vulnerable stage of its early years where the priority was understandably given to upholding the sovereignty of states in the event of any doubts. On this issue, Judge Macdonald has argued that:

> The Convention system is sufficiently mature to be able to move beyond the margin of appreciation and grapple more openly with the question of appropriateness which the device [of margin of appreciation] obscures. The principle of accountability demands nothing less than that the Court articulate for why a particular amount of deference is considered proper. The challenge should be seen not as the search for the principles which govern the width of the margin of appreciation, but as the articulation of the factors which determine the appropriate amount of scrutiny.

The margin of appreciation should not permit the Court's evasion of its responsibility to articulate the reasons why its intervention in particular cases may or may not be appropriate. Until this responsibility is taken more seriously, the principled reasons which both justify and limit the Court's role will remain buried beneath the pragmatism of the margin of appreciation, and the emergence of a theoretical vision of its role in the European legal order will continue to be limited.[43]

Judge Macdonald is correct in his conclusions about the potential effects of the doctrine of margin of appreciation if used as the reason in itself for the Court's decisions. In practice, though, this occurrence is rare and only happens when policy has not been fully thought through by the Court or when the case involves extremely sensitive political issues. In such circumstances, caution counsels that the matter be kept open so that the Court may have another opportunity to deal fully with the subject on another occasion. In a complex legal regime which is essentially not totally out of its infancy such an approach is not unacceptable. In a majority of the cases before the Court the value of the doctrine of margin of appreciation is immense. It is an excellent term of art in the language of the Court to cover all the permissible limitations. Of course, when the Court adopts the doctrine in this sense, it is always necessary to provide additional explanation, based on the facts, as to which of the permissible limitations warrant the margin of appreciation. It is when the additional explanation is missing that one is confronted with the situation described by Judge Macdonald.

Conclusions

It is clear from the case law of the European Court of Human Rights that the Court began dealing with cases where judges are the target of critical comment by applying its principles for interpreting Article 10 rather differently – using a relatively stricter approach. Because of the wider margin of appreciation granted to the Contracting States, the scope and effect of the permissible limitations are also wider in the instances involving the criticism of judges than in the majority of instances where other public officials are the subject of critical comment. The Court's traditional bias in favour of the first paragraph of Article 10 was evidently reversed in favour of the second paragraph in cases involving the criticism of judges, prompting the question at this point whether such a reversal of approach is, in itself, an irreconcilable contradiction in the Court's policy. That there are differences in the application of principles does not necessarily amount to an irreconcilable contradiction in the Court's policy as long as the Court aims to uphold the ideals of democratic society relating to freedom of expression. It is true that these ideals may require different approaches when the facts, contexts and circumstances are different.

It is possible, for example, to distinguish the *De Haes and Gijsels* case from, say, the *Prager and Oberschlick* case because of the subject matter of the criticism and probably, to a limited extent, because of the difference that one was a state-sponsored action and the other a civil litigation. It is possible, even if difficult, to identify the impact of these differences on a consistent policy direction of the Court.

Paying attention to differences in facts and circumstances conforms with the principles of treaty interpretation set out in Article 31 of the Vienna Convention on the Law of Treaties.[44] The requirements in that provision to take account of the context; in addition, the object and purpose of treaty terms allows tribunals to arrive at different conclusions in cases which may seem to possess common elements – in this case, the scope of freedom of expression in relation to a particular kind of public official. The Court has expressly highlighted differences in the application of its principles of interpretation between the criticism of politicians on the one hand and the criticism of governments on the other, pointing out that the limits of permissible criticism are higher with regard to the latter.[45] Similar distinctions have been drawn between the criticism of public officials and private individuals in the *Lingens v. Austria* and *Thorgeir Thorgeirson v. Iceland* cases. There are conceivably other differences of general characterization, such as between political expression, commercial speech and civil expression under Article 10, which may necessitate alterations in the application of the general principles. In *Barfod v. Denmark*, the Court insisted on a higher standard of proof because, in the opinion of the Court, the criticisms were of the lay judges personally,[46] presupposing that a different, perhaps lesser, standard of proof would have been enough if the criticism related to them in their official capacity. Overall, the point is here well made that the ideals of democratic society necessitate a different approach to the criticism of judges and, in this sense, the Court has been remarkably consistent. In his strong dissenting opinion to the *Prager and Oberschlick* judgment, Judge Martens endorsed the principle of treating different forms and targets of criticisms differently as long as the scrutiny remained consistently rigorous. There is no evidence in the case law of the Court that this is not the case. Viewing the Court's decisions relating to the criticism of judges as belonging to a separate category of cases to which the general principles apply differently, it is beyond doubt that the Court's conclusions were correct.[47] However, it would have been preferable for the Court to have been much more open and precise about its reasons rather than leaving it to commentators to speculate on them.

The scope of freedom of expression is constantly changing, and the law under Article 10 of the ECHR has to change in response to this changing scope. Although all countries in Europe have an offence relating to the criticism of judges on their books, only a few continue to punish for this offence. There is an emerging common European standard which the Court must not ignore. Across Europe, judges and the systems for the administration of justice which they represent have ceased to be vulnerable. There is ample opportunity, through the press and the media, for judges to participate in public debate and, through that, be able to refute any accusations against them. The fact that judges do not readily take advantage of this may be more a reflection of their confidence in the performance of their tasks than any kind of doctrinal inhibition in the nature of their work.

It is possible to argue that the recent cases such as *De Haes and Gijsels* v. *Belgium*[48] and *Schöpfer* v. *Switzerland*[49] represent not a group of cases which are distinguishable on their facts but rather a change of perception and approach by the Court. This change of approach – if that is what it is – will reverse the standards set in earlier cases such as *Barfod* v. *Denmark*[50] and *Prager and Oberschlick* v. *Austria*.[51] The new approach will only afford a narrow margin of appreciation to states in matters involving the criticism of judges and, in the process, re-establish the balance in favour of para. 1 of Article 10 and thus bring it in line with the Court's standard of analysis in cases involving the criticism of public officials. It is unlikely that the emerging democracies of East and Central Europe will find the new standard altogether exacting. In their continuing process of reform, these countries are well able to adapt to these new standards.

Notes

1   Convention for the Protection of Human Rights and Fundamental Freedoms (Rome 1950), as amended by Protocol No. 11 to the Convention (the revised ECHR).
2   Article 10(2) of the Convention.
3   *Sunday Times* v. *United Kingdom No. 1*, Eur. Ct. HR, Series A.30 (1979); 2 EHRR, p. 245, para. 65. See also *Sunday Times* v. *United Kingdom No.2*, Eur. Ct. HR, Series A.217 (1992); 14 (199) EHRR, p. 229.
4   Eur. Ct. HR, Series A.30 (1979); 2 EHRR, p. 245.
5   Ibid., para. 65.
6   Eur. Ct. HR, Series A.177 (1990); 12 (1990) EHRR, p. 508.
7   Ibid., *Sunday Times* v. *United Kingdom, op. cit.* and *Observer and Guardian* v. *United Kingdom*, Eur. Ct. HR, Series A.216 (1992); 14 (1992) EHRR, p. 153.
8   Eur. Ct. HR, Series A.149 (1989); 13 (1991) EHRR, p. 493.
9   *Barfod* v. *Denmark, op. cit.* para. 9. The domestic courts found that the applicant had misunderstood the casting of votes in the case: it was only with regard to the reasoning that there was a dissent; with regard to the conclusion all three judges had decided in favour of the local government.
10 Para. 71 of the Commission's opinion.
11 Para. 13 of the judgement, ibid.
12 Para. 42 of the Commission's opinion, ibid.
13 See Chapter in this volume on 'Article 10 of the ECHR and the criticism of public officials'.

In the *Barfod* case, the Court reaffirmed its powers to supervise contracting states' margin of appreciation as part of which it must consider the decisions of the Danish courts in the light of the case as a whole seeking to determine whether the interference was proportionate to the legitimate aim of protecting the reputation of the lay judges. [See para. 28]. In the Court's view:

> ... proportionality implies that the pursuit of the aims mentioned in Article 10(2) has to be weighed against the value of open discussion of topics of public concern. When striking a fair balance between these interests, the Court cannot overlook ... the great importance of not discouraging members of the public, for fear of criminal or other sanctions, from voicing their opinions on issues of public concern.(See para. 59.)

14 Ibid., para. 32. On the subject of discussing matters of public interest, see *Sunday Times v. United Kingdom No. 1*, *op. cit.*, para. 65; *Thorgeir Thorgeirson v. Iceland*, Eur. Ct. HR, Series A.239 (1992); 18 EHRR, p. 843, para. 63; *Lingens v. Austria*, Eur. Ct. HR, Series A.103 (1986); 8 (1986) EHRR, p. 103, para. 42; and *Oberschlick v. Austria*, Eur. Ct. HR, Series A.204 (1991); 19 (1995) EHRR, p. 389, para. 59.
15 *Barfod v. Denmark*, *op. cit.*, para. 33 of the Court's judgment.
16 25 (1997) EHRR, 1.
17 Ibid., para 37.
18 Ibid., para. 39.
19 See *Lingens v. Austria*, *op. cit*; and *Oberschlick v. Austria*, *op. cit*. In the circumstances of the *Barfod* case, the Court's refusal to deal with two relevant issues raised by Judge Golcuklu in his dissenting opinion, which one suspects were canvassed during the Court's deliberations, is of interest to the present discussions. Judge Golcuklu argued that: (a) the case had 'political overtones in as much as it involved criticism of a specific judicial system' – namely, the composition of the Greenland judiciary, and (b) that the wide permissible limits of criticism with regard to politicians enunciated in the *Lingens* case also applied to holders of public office, although they may not be politicians in the strict sense. These issues were not addressed by the Court at all. The aim of Judge Golcuklu's reasoning was to make the Court's previous case law relating to politicians and political cases applicable to the present case; in essence, urging that all branches of government should be treated equally in this regard. On the same point, see, further, *Thorgeir Thorgeirson v. Iceland*, *op. cit.*, where the Court concluded that 'the Court observes that there is no warrant in its case-law for distinguishing, in the manner suggested by the Government, between political discussion and the discussion of other matters of public concern', para. 64. A similar view has been canvassed by Eric Barendt, *Freedom of Speech* (Oxford: Oxford University Press, 1985) at p. 222 where he argues that 'in theoretical terms criticism of the judiciary should almost certainly be treated as a form of political speech, and therefore enjoy the highest degree of legal protection'. But see a contrary interpretation in the dissenting opinion of Mr Ermacora to the opinion of the Commission in the *Barfod v. Denmark* case itself, in which he argued that:

> The punishment [of the applicant] is, in my view, justified under the second paragraph of Article 10 in that it was necessary for maintaining the authority and impartiality of the judiciary. I base my opinion on the interpretation of the judgement of the Court of Human Rights in the case of Lingens v. Austria (. . . Series A no. 103). In this case, the Court stated that politicians must sustain more criticism than others. In the present case, however, it is not the honour of politicians which was at stake but the authority and impartiality of the judiciary. In this respect, the judiciary must enjoy a protection which in my opinion needs another legal approach than in case of protection of the rights of others as set out in the Lingens case.

20 *Lingens* v. *Austria, op. cit.,* para. 46 and *Oberschlick* v. *Austria, op. cit.,* para. 63.

21 Eur. Ct. HR, Series A.313 (1995); 21 (1996) EHRR, 1.

22 *Prager and Oberschlick* v. *Austria, op. cit.,* para. 34. This requirement of a higher level of proof must be seen in the wider context of the rebuttable presumption, in the interpretation of Article 10, that open criticism of public policy and public officials will enhance democratic ideals. The presumption in favour of criticism represents the conceptual ideal which must occasionally give way to the practical reality which in relation to judges suggests that that category of public officials represents a vulnerable link in the chain of democratic policy-making. There is merit in this argument especially as the relationship between the private and public lives of judges are, on the one hand, difficult to distinguish from the process of dispensing justice on the other. For this reason, criticism of judges without proof has a greater potential for undermining the reverence and wisdom with which judges and the system of justice are associated. In this sense any criticism of judges, according to the Court, must be treated with caution but firmly, taking into account the differences in circumstances, in an effort to uphold the ideals of democracy.

23 *Prager and Oberschlick* v. *Austria, op. cit.,* para. 10.

24 Ibid., para. 11.

25 Ibid., para. 8.

26 Ibid., para. 15.

27 Ibid.

28 This contrasts with the *De Haes and Gijsels* case, in which the Court was convinced that the applicants had exercised sufficient journalistic care in the preparation of their article and also especially because they had consulted widely with independent experts on the contents of the articles before they published them.

29 Ibid.

30 Ibid., para. 16.

31 See on this point, H.W.R. Wade and C.F. Forsyth, *Administrative Law* (Oxford: Clarendon, 1994) Part IV.

32 See *Schenk* v. *Switzerland,* Eur. Ct. HR, Series A.140 (1988); 13 (1991) EHRR, 242, para. 46. See also Application No. 7450/76, *X* v. *Belgium,* DEC. 28 February 1977, *D&R* 9, p. 108 and Application No. 8876/80, *X* v. *Belgium,* DEC. 16 October 1980, *D&R*, 23, p. 233.

33 See *H.* v. *France,* Eur. Ct. HR, Series A.162 (1989); 12 (1990) EHRR, 74, para. 61 and *Delta* v. *France,* Eur. Ct. HR, Series A.191 (1990), para. 35. In relation to the Commission see Application No. 343/57, *Nielson* v. *Denmark, Yearbook of European Convention on Human Rights,* 4 (1961), p. 494, para. 52. See, generally, on this point Stephanos Stavros, *The Guarantees for Accused Persons* (Dordrecht/Boston/London: Martinus Nijhoff, 1993) p. 222 and Olivier Jacot-Guillarmod, 'Rights Related to Good Administration of Justice (Article 6)', in Macdonald *et al., The European System for the Protection of Human Rights, op. cit.,* p. 381 at p. 392.

34 *Prager and Oberschlick* v. *Austria, op. cit.,* para. 36.

35 Ibid., para. 37. This endorses the thinking of the domestic courts on this point. For instance the court of first instance argued that 'confronted with such wholesale criticism, an impartial reader had little choice but to suspect that the plaintiff [Judge J] had behaved basely and that he was of despicable character': ibid., para. 15. Similarly, the Vienna Court of Appeal upheld the decision of the lower court 'because of the way in which he [Mr Prager] had formulated his criticism. It had been so comprehensive and general that it had been impossible to specify evidence capable of establishing its accuracy': ibid., para. 16.

36 Ibid.

37 See *De Haes and Gijsels* v. *Belgium, op. cit.,* para. 58.

38   *Prager and Oberschlick* v. *Austria, op. cit.*, para. 37.
39   Ibid., para. 38.
40   Ibid., para. 36.
41   R. St J. Macdonald, 'The Margin of Appreciation', in Macdonald *et al.*, *The European System for the Protection of Human Rights, op. cit.*
42   Ibid., p. 85.
43   Ibid., p. 124.
44   Ibid.
45   *Castells, op. cit.*, para. 46.
46   *Barfod* v. *Denmark, op. cit.*, para. 33; for a contra conclusion see the dissenting opinion of Judge Golcuklu, ibid.
47   For a contrary view, see Anthony Lester, 'Freedom of Expression', in Macdonald *et al.*, *The European System for the Protection of Human Rights, op. cit.*, pp. 465, 477. The general conclusions of other writers on similar issues would seem to support Lord Lester's conclusions. See, for instance, Clive Walker, 'Scandalising in the Eighties', *Law Quarterly Review*, **101** (1985), p. 359 at p. 382 where he argues that the offence of scandalizing a court or judge (an offence that could arise from criticizing a court or judge under English law) might be contrary to Article 10(1) of the European Convention on Human Rights; also David Pannick, *Judges* (Oxford: Oxford University Press, 1987), p. 115 who argues that 'the offence of scandalising the judiciary does survive as an unjustifiable impediment to the freedom of speech about the judiciary'.
48   Ibid.
49   Judgment of the Eur. Ct. HR of 20 May 1998, *Reports of Judgements and Decisions* (1998).
50   *Op. cit.*
51   *Op. cit.*

Index